No One Is to Blame

No One Is to Blame

Is Your Challenging Child a Link?

Susana Balán

IPBOOKS.net
International Psychoanalytic Books

International Psychoanalytic Books (IPBooks)
New York • http://www.IPBooks.net

No One is To Blame
Published by IPBooks, Queens, NY
Online at: www.IPBooks.net

ISBN 978-1-956864-48-9

Contents

Acknowledgments

This book could not have been written without the help of Sandra Dunn Delgado. Sandra translated drafts of each chapter from Spanish to English, editing, reorganizing, and writing new sections as needed so that my ideas would be developed and expressed as fully as possible. Our lively discussions and collaborative writing process over the past four years helped me to clarify many of the concepts introduced in this book.

I would like to also acknowledge those who took the time to read and share their thoughts with me on parts of the manuscript and who engaged in conversation with me about the Link personality. They include Rick and Susan Bowden, who wrote the *Link and the Shooting Stars* discussion questions, which can be found at the end of this volume; Tamara Strijack, who invited me to share my ideas at the Neufeld Institute; Ruthie Chayet, who introduced me to her; and countless friends, colleagues, and family members. I am especially grateful to my patients, whose trust and courage in sharing their stories with me, many of which appear in this book, allowed me to give birth to and shape the concept of the Link personality and to better understand myself.

Note to the Reader

The Link child's personality described in *No One Is to Blame* is "linked" to that of Link the young horse, the protagonist of the children's book *Link and the Shooting Stars* by Susana Balán and Claudia Cano. The reader, however, does not need to have read the children's book to understand the concepts and examples set forth in *No One Is to Blame*. While *Link and the Shooting Stars* is intended for children to read by themselves or with their parents and can serve to help children who may be Links to recognize and understand themselves, *No One Is to Blame* is written for parents whose children pose particular kinds of parenting challenges. It is intended to help parents determine if their child is a Link child, support them in their parenting, and provide a conceptual framework that describes the Link personality as well as concrete, accessible examples and analyses of Link children's behaviors. The book is also written for adults who are struggling to find a place of ease both within themselves and in their interactions with others and who, therefore, may be Links. Many of the examples come from *Link and the Shooting Stars*, which traces Link the young horse's journey of self-discovery; many others come from the author's experience working with patients whom she has identified as Links. The two works may be read in conjunction with one another, or each may be read as a standalone book, with no loss of context or meaning.

For those interested in reading *Link and the Shooting Stars* alongside this volume, it is available at IPBooks.net (International Psychoanalytic Books), and specifically at https://ipbooks.net/product/link-and-the-shooting-stars-by-susana-balan-and-claudia-cano/

Foreword

I was reading *Link and the Shooting Stars* to my 20-year-old daughter, and we shared a few knowing glances before she quietly said, "That sounds a lot like me." I smiled and thought to myself, "Yes, I recognized you already at the beginning!" I am so thankful that I had the framework of my father's (Dr. Gordon Neufeld) attachment-based developmental model to help me in coming alongside my daughter's uniqueness from a young age. I think I may have been lost otherwise—for I hadn't yet crossed paths with Susana Balán. Susana added pieces to the puzzle for me and helped me fill in the gaps in my understanding. My daughter also was at the age of trying to make sense of herself and found some validation and comfort both in the story and in the theory that helped explain her fears, her difficulty choosing a path, and the guilt she felt because she picked up on everyone's feelings around her.

What Susana offers in her book for parents and Link adults, *No One Is to Blame*, are valuable insights from her life's work of putting the pieces together and the years of experience she has working with individuals and families. She has put forth a powerful model for understanding how the Link personality type develops that gives much hope! Once we have some insight into the dynamics, we also have the path to finding our way through. I believe this book will be a gift to all who are drawn to read it.

I would also like to say a few things in response to Susana's mention of play. In my roles as a therapist, a parent consultant, and a trainer of educators and counselors, play has been an area close to my heart and central to my work with children. I have long witnessed the power of bringing learning and therapy into the play mode—without pressure, expectation, or repercussion. For a Link child, this would be even more true.

In fact, play was the way through for my own Link daughter. Providing the kind of emotional safety that she needed to explore her world was a challenge sometimes, as she was attuned to reading my reactions and what I desired for her to do or be. Because of this, I had to work extra hard to create spaces for her to pursue her own interests, which were everchanging (and often got messy as she moved from one activity to the next, with little explosions of creativity left behind). Being in nature has been part of this play for her, and it has been a place for her to connect in meaningful ways. She continues to engage with her world full on, with gusto and talent in so many areas that at age 20, the options feel overwhelming at times. I felt that one of my "jobs" when she was younger was to keep the pressures of the world, of school, and of her family from crushing her spirit.

Play came in the form of opportunities to express herself, without worrying about repercussions or expectations; to try things out, without having to get it "right"; to bring down her alarm and give her a rest from taking the lead for a while; to be released from constantly reading the cues of those around her, so that she had a chance to figure out what she wanted, felt, or thought. Easy? Not always. But so worth it. And at the core of it all, I knew that my daughter needed to feel my unconditional acceptance and needed to feel that there was enough room for all of her.

What I wish for you, dear reader, is that you come to these pages with openness and curiosity and that you be filled with "aha" moments that translate into healing and growth—whatever your situation may be. You are in good hands with Susana—gentle, compassionate, gifted, knowledgeable, and experienced hands.

Tamara Strijack
Registered Clinical Counselor
Academic Dean of The Neufeld Institute
www.neufeldinstitute.org
Co-author of *Reclaiming our Students*
https://reclaimingourstudents.com

Tamara Strijack is a Registered Clinical Counsellor who lives and works on Vancouver Island, Canada. Tamara has worked with children and adolescents in various roles over the last 25 years. She is currently the Academic Dean of the Neufeld Institute, where she develops and delivers courses on child development for parents, teachers, and helping professionals. She is a keynote speaker, workshop facilitator, and educator of counselors and educators in training. Tamara works primarily as a parent and educational consultant, helping put adults back in the driver's seat in a way that facilitates growth and learning for the child. As Dr. Gordon Neufeld's daughter, Tamara offers a unique inside view, bringing together her own experience and insight with her father's theoretical material. Connection, relationship, and play continue to be central themes in all her roles, both personally and professionally.

Preface

Even now, amazement and disbelief run through my body as I recall my mother banging her head against the living room wall of our small apartment one day when I was 12 years old.

My mother was saying to me, "I can't take care of you, I don't know what to do with you. You're an eagle, and you go places where I can't follow because I'm a hen and you don't stay by my side."

I was crying, but I didn't know why. I felt bad, guilty, and ashamed, but I didn't understand what I had done wrong. I felt afraid, paralyzed, and, above all, confused and all mixed-up inside. Was my mother acting this way because my grandmother had been insufferable, because my father had arrived home from work angry with life, as always, or because, as she herself had told me, she was hormonal due to her period? Or was I the one who had brought her to her wit's end and caused the unbearable anguish that she was displaying in this violent way?

For years I asked myself this question, and because of my sense of guilt and responsibility and my extreme capacity for feeling another's pain as my own, I decided early on that, yes, I was the cause of these blows to the head that my mother was inflicting on herself. I was far from knowing that over the course of my life I would bang my head many times (metaphorically) against walls that I erected in front of myself, sometimes unnecessarily, sometimes because of feeling overwhelmed by the unrealistic demands that I subjected myself to, believing that they were great and worthy obstacles that I needed to overcome if I was indeed, as my mother had declared me to be, a powerful eagle.

Yes, I was a difficult daughter—difficult because of how hard it was to understand what the difficulties involved in raising me were all about. I used to say to my mother that I felt that my thoughts were galloping around in my brain like wild young horses, raising such a huge cloud of dust that I wasn't able to tell where they were headed. My mind couldn't control them. Was it a matter of breaking the spirit of those young horses or of taming them? I grew up feeling that she was trying to break those horses inside my head, to clip my eagle wings—so much larger than her own hen wings, small and impotent when it came to dealing with me. The truth was that she was neither trying to break me nor tame me, because she was incapable of doing either. She did not know how to tame the horses, which was what I really needed, or how to help me to learn to control them myself. She was also not strong enough to clip my wings or to do the opposite, which was teach me how to fly. Although she was incapable of teaching me how to soar with the wings of an eagle, she did give me permission to be the eagle that I was. This is, fundamentally, what saved me. I did not realize it at the time, but by allowing me to be my eagle self, my mother validated who I was, and she never stopped being affectionate and loving with me. This, in turn, allowed me to feel that we were alone but together in the face of this problem that was me.

I was, in short, like the young protagonist in *Link and the Shooting Stars*—disobedient, overconfident (at least on the surface), full of energy and ideas that I couldn't control, stubborn, "different," and difficult. Like Link, I suffered despair, bewilderment, and confusion due to not being able to understand what for me (and for all Links) felt like contradictory demands that my parents, my school, and society in general were bombarding me with. And like the young horse and all Links, I was a source of concern, deep frustration, and exasperation for my parents.

I recall two episodes in particular that helped me to understand the effects my challenging behaviors had on my parents. Even though in Argentina at that time (the 1940s and '50s) hitting children when they behaved badly was considered an acceptable form of teaching them respect, my parents were too sophisticated (something I intuited but also didn't understand) to want to impose their truths on me and, therefore, did not hit or spank me when I disobeyed. They wanted me to adopt their truths through my own convictions. They wanted me to be obedient through my own desire to be so—a difficult task as much for them as for me. In the end, this resulted in two unexpected and transformative episodes: a slap in the face from my father when I was 12 years old and another one from my mother when I was 15. These slaps were the consequence of my having driven them to the edge because I was defending what I believed they had taught me, whereas they believed that I was disrespecting them. Both things were true.

❖ ❖ ❖

My father was an overly critical, ill-tempered person. One of his recurring behaviors that left an indelible mark on me was his unexpected, volatile reactions, which would leave me feeling afraid because of how abruptly they would appear and because I was capable of provoking so much passion in him.

I was 12 years old, and it had been only two years since our migration to Buenos Aires from a small town in one of the poorest provinces of Argentina. I was still having a hard time adapting to school life and making friends. We lived in an apartment above the pharmacy that my father and his cousin owned. I had just arrived home from school in tears and was telling my mother about how much I was suffering because I felt like a foreigner, an outsider, and, therefore, incapable of understanding the games and jokes of my schoolmates. My mother understood my fears and, as a result of her provincial sensibleness and her vision of herself as a mom who was confident in her ability to take under her wing anyone who needed protection from the dangers of the world, she was saying at that moment that I had permission to give up my studies in order to learn manual work, such as cooking, playing the piano, and domestic activities. I would at last be able to leave school, where I was paying a high price to be, given my daily stomach problems. She herself hadn't completed elementary school, and apart from her economic dependence on my father, things hadn't gone so badly for her in life.

I was breathing a sigh of relief and was about to enjoy a snack that she was preparing for me when my father came upstairs, although he was supposed to be downstairs working in the pharmacy. My mother told him about the decision we had just made—that I would not go to school the next day and that we would look for vocational training focused on learning activities that would allow me to quickly enter the labor markets appropriate for a woman of that time. Out of nowhere, I felt the heavy sting of my father's hand slapping me hard across the face, jolting me completely out of the brief feeling of peace and relief I had been enjoying with my mother. I looked up in shock to see his angry, red face, and he shouted, "No daughter of mine is going to drop out of school!"

My father could not understand why it was so hard for me to adapt to the way of life of the capital, to become friends with classmates who saw me only as a girl from one of Argentina's poorest provinces, a girl who spoke with an accent and couldn't pronounce the letter "s" correctly, and who dressed in a manner "unworthy" of the capital. To make matters worse, the teacher really liked me and one day had made me stand in front of the class while she said to the entire grade, "You should make friends with this girl because she is a real treasure." I imagine I must have inspired immediate hatred. But my father understood nothing about how being uprooted from the province to the capital was affecting me. In the end, he got what he wanted: I stayed in school and continued on my academic track.

Over time, in my efforts to make peace with my father, I came to understand his anger with me as an expression of his own deep fear of failing in his professional life. My adolescent desire to pursue a non-academic course of study—due to how hard it was for me to adapt to school life and feel I fit in with the "city kids"—likely brought to the surface his own feelings of not being able to easily adapt to the city. For him this was connected to a feeling of professional failure. Whereas in our small town he had been a successful political leader, in the capital he was not experiencing success as a pharmacist. My father wanted to soar like an eagle and, therefore, had high professional goals for himself. This feeling of failure, bound up with resentment, led to his prolonged depression and physical deterioration—conditions that profoundly affected my childhood and adolescence.

I share this about my father to highlight the importance of the effects that parents' struggles, feelings of failure, and frustrations have on the Link child and the complex interplay of cause and effect. My father's feelings and behavior affected me, but mine also affected him. My difficulty adapting, which led me to want to abandon my studies, reminded him of his own struggle to adapt and of not being able to fulfill certain dreams. I was mirroring what he found most frustrating within himself, and he was not going to allow his daughter to repeat his failures. His explosive reactions to my decisions and behaviors, however, would have lifelong effects on me.

❖ ❖ ❖

A few years later, I didn't understand why the high school had believed it was necessary to call my parents to let them know about my behavior. All I had done was respond correctly to a teacher's question and then smile when she wasn't able to challenge me. I knew what she wanted: to catch me not paying attention, given that she asked me the question when I was talking to a bench mate, assuming that I was distracted. I always had the ability to stay connected to several places at once and to follow several conversations simultaneously.

As with other times I had been called out for my behavior, the accusation was lack of respect. Why? I asked myself. Hadn't I responded correctly to the question? What do they want, for me to be an antisocial robot, right when I'm finally belonging to the coolest group of girls in the whole grade?

Climbing the steps to the school entrance with my mother, I started to explain to her how she had to behave, how she had to respond to the principal, how she needed to talk, and what things she should say and not say. As I was dictating to her my "rules" for how she should handle this meeting, her hand suddenly came down hard across the side of my face, shocking me into silence and stillness there on the school's front steps. I couldn't believe what had just happened. How was it possible that this mother hen had lashed out with the force of an eagle? The surprise—perhaps for us both—was enormous. My mother's slap across my face left a mark that, symbolically, is there to this day. The slap was accompanied by her stating in no uncertain terms: "I am not a babysitter who takes care of your father's children. I am your mother, and I do not give you the right to treat me the way he does or to be ashamed of me."

At the time I did not understand the full import of this incident. Many years later, however, I would come to understand her slap as a gesture of protection—protecting herself against my disrespectful behavior toward her and protecting me from future difficulties in life by setting a clear limit, drawing a distinct line that was not to be crossed. I came to understand that the force of that hand was the force of a beautiful wing—powerful, enormous, enveloping, and all-encompassing, as if it emanated from the top of a mountain. I came to understand that she was doing for me what all Link children need their parents to do: set clear limits, which is a true sign of love and protection.

❖ ❖ ❖

Twenty years later, it was my turn to play the role of the parent of a difficult daughter.

At the tender age of two, my daughter Paula made clear to me how she could not trust me, her mother, to take care of her. She had just begun attending preschool in Rio de Janeiro, Brazil, where we had moved from Buenos Aires. As I was saying goodbye and trying to leave the school during the drop-off period, Paula ran out of the classroom and hid among the thick foliage in the huge schoolyard, which was more like a jungle from the perspective of a two-year-old girl raised in Buenos Aires. The teacher's attempts to make her feel safe and protected in order to coax her out of her hiding place were to no avail. Nor was I able to help and comfort her, which led me to scream at her in an act of despair as I saw her running and hiding in the schoolyard "jungle." Paula did not feel protected by the teacher or by me, her mother, and in that moment was unable to share with me something I later learned: that she felt afraid, alone, and abandoned. As she continued hiding, I tried to convince her that she could trust me because, as her mother, I knew her better than anyone, and I knew how to protect her. But she did not and would not trust me, choosing to remain alone and, in her mind, "safe" compared to how she would have felt upon returning to the classroom and being with the teacher and me.

A few years later she revealed to me that when we first moved to Brazil she knew that my Portuguese wasn't the "real" Portuguese she heard from her nanny and that she thought she understood this new language and the proper way to behave and live in this strange new land better than I did. She did not dare trust me. How could she? Nevertheless, at that moment in the schoolyard, I could not understand her lack of trust, her choice to hide and be all alone in a potentially scary place instead of seeking out my maternal protection. This distrust stayed with her well into her 30s. Many years later, I realized that she could not trust me because she observed and understood that I was not taking good care of myself, not only in relation to her father but also in my interactions with authority figures, whom I sometimes approached with too much fear and submissiveness. Furthermore, my way of loving her was by providing her the best school, the best activities, the best instruction on how to behave well; but it was not by embracing her, by being tender, by entering into her good-natured, playful way of being and loving and caring for her in the ways that *she* needed, as opposed to the ways that I thought were best.

Around her sixth birthday, Paula awoke from a nightmare, crying inconsolably. Nothing could calm her down. Her face made clear the terror she was feeling, and her eyes were darting around to different places in the room as if she were trying to figure out where the dangers that were threatening her were coming from. After a few moments that seemed to last an eternity, she was able to tell her father and me that she had two characters in her head at the same time: One was a *saci-pererê*, a one-legged Brazilian youngster who smokes a pipe and wears a disgusting-smelling, magical red cap that allows him to disappear and reappear wherever he wishes (usually in the middle of a dust devil). Considered an annoying prankster and a potentially dangerous and malicious creature, he nevertheless grants wishes to anyone who manages to trap him or steal his magic cap despite its bad smell. (See https://en.wikipedia.org/wiki/Saci_(Brazilian_folklore)) Paula told us that the *saci-pererê* was pushing her to be aggressive toward her sister and me because we were mean and we spoke Spanish instead of Portuguese. The other character was an angel, with a beatific smile, beautiful wings, and a magic wand, who was encouraging her to protect her sister and me, because we were weak among the Brazilian people, not knowing how to live or protect ourselves in this new, strange land and culture.

How was she to behave in order to feel like she was a good person? And how was she to behave in order to feel *safe*? Despite my feeling that, as her mother, I understood her, neither she nor I knew how to protect ourselves and each other against the threats her nightmare was alerting her to: Should Paula listen to the scary, strong, but "bad" *saci-pererê* or to the benevolent, "good" angel? Should we speak Portuguese or Spanish? Would we feel safer in Brazil or Argentina? She knew we had had to leave Argentina because of the dangerous political situation at that time, but Brazil was such an unknown and different place from where she was born that it seemed to her to be both the paradise promised as a salvation (from Argentine political oppression) and the frightening jungle, threatening to engulf us and in which we might lose ourselves forever. Paula's dilemma was her internal tug-of-war between contradictory forces, specifically: Which was the most magical and powerful tool—the malicious *saci-pererê* or the tender, loving angel?

In the schoolyard Paula had disobeyed her teacher and me, or behaved "badly" and been "difficult," because she did not trust that her vulnerability would be well cared for by either of us. Feeling the need to take of herself, then, she ran away to hide, which allowed her to feel more protected than she would have if she had shared her fears with her teacher or me. Feeling the vulnerability of the need for love, coupled with the loneliness of misunderstanding, makes "difficult" children feel they are in worse danger than their feelings of meanness or rage make them feel.

❖ ❖ ❖

As a Link myself, I have discovered that despite being a difficult person, one can learn, as I have, that exhausting contradictions can be transformed into enriching paradoxes.

I belong to the first generation of psychologists to graduate from the National University of Buenos Aires in the early 1960s. My years of clinical practice in Rio de Janeiro (in the 1970s) and my exposure to the thinking of anthropologists, philosophers, historians, and Brazilian psychologists—so different from that of my Argentine colleagues— obliged me to rethink my ideas about the forms of human joy and suffering. For example, dancing to samba and celebrating its sensuality is not the same thing as dancing the tango and celebrating its complexity. Similarly, *saudades*, a Brazilian concept akin to nostalgia and one full of loving, positive connotations that emphasizes the ongoing and comforting presence of the person or thing that is absent, is not the same thing as *melancolía* (melancholy), the feeling that is more pervasive in Argentine culture and that emphasizes emptiness and loss in the face of absence.

I must also credit my years in Brazil for teaching me, long before I began working in the United States in the 1990s, to think in images, to understand feelings through bodily sensations, and to pay attention to the senses—practices that are fundamental to current celebrated therapeutic techniques thanks to what neuroscience has taught us about the human brain and the connection among emotions, sensations, and thoughts.

My hope is that the ideas I set forth here—a culmination of my more than 50 years in clinical practice and over 20 years spent developing a conceptual framework about the Link personality based on my work with clients all over the world—will help parents give their Link children what they need to feel supported and loved. This book exists to let parents of Link children know that their relationship with their son or daughter is riddled with complexity, making for a dynamic that is hard to understand and hard to grasp—not only for the parents but for the child as well. Although I share my insights and, in the final chapter, some suggestions, this book does not belong to the "how-to-parent" genre. My purpose is to help parents understand the challenging situation they are living every day with their Link child by offering ways of understanding what their child is going through. I hope that, with this deeper understanding, parents will feel more empowered to discover and trust their own unique, loving ways of caring for their Link child.

I hope it will also allow adult Links who read it to discover how to create dialogues and connections among the many aspects of their multifaceted self so that they learn how not to destroy themselves. I hope it will allow them to construct their own harmonious Link identity out of their heterogeneity and complexity.

This book also exists to let me know every day as I write it at the age of 78 that, as a "difficult" daughter, I was not the one responsible for my mother's decision to bang her head against the wall when she couldn't handle the eagle child that I was. I was also not responsible for my father's emotional overreactions and angry outbursts. And, just as importantly, my parents were not responsible for the untamed galloping of my thoughts and feelings.

If there is one thing I would like the reader to take away from this book, in addition to learning how to better love and care for their "difficult" Link child, it is that neither the parent nor the child is at fault: No one is to blame.

The Making of a Link Child

Does this sound like your child?

Depending on the moment, they are **alternately**:

The most affectionate and the most aloof of children

The most confident and the most insecure of children

The most joyful and the saddest

The most talkative and the quietest

The most rebellious and the most obedient, often in strange ways

The most confrontational and the most conciliatory

The most dedicated to studying what they like and the most resistant to studying what they don't like

And regardless of the moment, they are **always**:

Curious

Unusual

Searching for "deep" answers, never satisfied with answers like "That's just the way it is" or "Because I said so"

Preoccupied with social injustices such as poverty, though they may mask the fear related to the suffering of others with denial

Denouncing unfairness, while behaving unfairly without realizing it

Wanting to do what they want without considering the risks or
preparing themselves to face dangers or inconveniences

Feeling that others don't allow them to be who they are

Doubting their own decisions, though they may not realize,
accept, or tolerate this feeling

Feeling afraid while trying not to show it or to run away from it

If any of these characteristics or behaviors are familiar to you because
you observe them in your own child, then your child might have a
Link personality. Link children are considered to be "difficult" by their
parents, but parents find it hard to know how to best take care of them
or to give them what they need because Link children are characterized
by constant contradictory behavior. In addition to the contradictory
traits in the list above, Link children might also be the calmest and the
most irritable of children, the most courageous and the most fearful, the
most independent and the most dependent, the most creative and the
most apathetic, the most indifferent and the most volatile in how they
express pain, frustration, and fear of abandonment. Most importantly,
Link children are typically the most accusatory as well as the most fearful
of being accused. They feel and behave simultaneously like the victims
and the offenders.

All of these contradictory and extreme behaviors cause parents to
feel they are at their wits' end and to even act like "bad" parents—losing
their patience and temper, and saying, doing, and feeling things they
would normally consider unthinkable and that they would not say, do,
or feel in relation to other (non-Link) children they might have.

What is a parent or caregiver to do?[1] Beyond trying to follow any and all "expert" parenting recommendations, trying both conventional and experimental therapies, or coming up with "solutions" like sending the child away to live with grandparents or, in more affluent families, shipping the child off to boarding school, what can parents or caregivers do to ensure that each of them as an individual, the couple, and the family do not end up devastated in the process of trying to raise their difficult child?

As a former Link child myself—with a Link daughter and a vast client base of adult Links who have told me their stories, in addition to the parents of many of these adults remembering aloud with me their experiences raising their children—I will share what I have learned over the many years that I have navigated the turbulent seas of the Link personality. While I have no magic solutions or cures for the pain that raising a Link child can entail, my fervent wish for you, as readers of this book—whether you are a parent struggling to understand, care for, and love your Link child in the best way possible or whether you are an adult Link—is that you take away an understanding of what elements and behaviors constitute the Link personality so that you may better understand, love, and accept yourself or your unique Link child.

---

1 Throughout this book, I generally use "parents" and "mother and father," while recognizing that Link children, like all children, may be raised by a single parent, two women, two men, grandparents, other relatives, or foster parents. "Mother and father" should be interpreted as referring to any primary caregiving configuration, regardless of an individual's biological sex or gender identity.

"Difficult" Children and the Four Circumstances that Produce a Link Child

The behaviors of any "difficult" child (not necessarily a Link child) are so easy to describe, so common, and so similar, although the family circumstances vary, that their universality allows many authors to agree on how to describe them. At the same time, what causes the behaviors of difficult children is so complex and specific to each child, regardless of the family circumstances, that this specificity results in experts' producing many different explanations of their underlying causes.

These behaviors occupy a wide spectrum: from "pitching fits," throwing tantrums, being aggressive, defying authority, disobeying the rules, making dangerous decisions, and engaging in risky behaviors to having panic attacks, crying uncontrollably, allowing themselves to be abused by others, submitting to authoritarian orders, and not being able to remove themselves from conflictive situations. All of these behaviors are detectable, observable, and recordable by parents, caregivers, and teachers. But only through precise descriptions and conceptualizations of different kinds of "difficult" children can parents recognize their child as a certain kind of difficult child, thus allowing them to take the first steps toward better understanding and loving their child, which means loving the child in the ways they need to be loved.[2] Although we all need to be cautious about rushing to "categorize" our children and defining them in ways that are limiting or prescriptive, finding the right classification or type helps to alleviate the anxiety that parents feel as a result of not knowing what is making their child behave in intolerable ways and of not being able to control their child.

---

2 Throughout this book, "he," "she," and "they" will be used interchangeably to refer to the Link child in the singular.

I am proposing the concept of the Link child in order to give parents and other caregivers a way to understand their difficult child, especially if they do not fully recognize their child in the existing classifications and categories of the professional psychological establishment. The principal categories or types of difficult children, and the psychologists responsible for describing and defining the types include, among others, the Gifted child (Alice Miller), the Indigo child (Lee Carroll and Jan Tober), the Alpha child (Gordon Neufeld), the Highly Sensitive child (Elaine Aron), the Hyperempathic child (Judith Orloff), and the Spirited child (Mary Sheedy Kurcinka).

While Links have certain characteristics and behaviors in common with some of these more well-known personality types, they also have a constellation of several elements, or conditions, that must always be present in them or their upbringing in order to be identified and understood as a Link child and, later in life, as a Link adult. In my therapeutic work with more than 250 clients whom I have identified as Links, I have found four variables that are always present in their upbringing:

1. They have an extreme capacity for empathy.
2. They are exposed to very different and often contradictory values and points of view (feelings, goals, ethics, aesthetics, thoughts, and beliefs). They appreciate and assign the same importance to each and every one of these values or points of view, and because of this, they incorporate some of each into themselves to the same high degree.
3. They know that their parents are "good people," and they also know, even if they do not *feel*, that their parents love them. But they have ambivalent feelings toward their parents because they know that their parents don't understand them and can't help them to understand themselves.

4. The circumstances of their birth or infancy were unusual, or there was some trauma or major transition in the family around the time of birth, during infancy, or in early childhood that caused them to experience, very early on, the finitude of time and space.

In this introductory chapter, I will first briefly outline each of these conditions, or circumstances, and then discuss each one in more depth. More comprehensive discussions of each circumstance and the characteristics it produces in the Link child make up the rest of this book, through a chapter-by-chapter analysis of the children's book *Link and the Shooting Stars*, the companion volume to this book. *Link and the Shooting Stars* tells the story of Link, a young horse, who exhibits all of the characteristics described in this Introduction and who is trying to understand himself, his place in the world, and his relationship to his parents and peers as he seeks the landing place of the elusive and fleeting shooting stars. While the behaviors and emotions of Link the horse serve as the starting point for discussing and understanding the Link child, each chapter of the current volume delves deeply into the analysis of the characteristics and behaviors of the Link child that so often lead to the challenging parent-child dynamics that make parents feel desperate and hopeless and that make children feel guilt-ridden and even unloved.

Why "Link"?

Before discussing the details of the four circumstances that must be present to produce a Link child, we need to consider the name "Link" itself. What does "Link" mean in this context? As the discussion that follows will make clear, Link children are born into a world characterized by uncertainty, which produces in them feelings of anguish because, as children, they do not yet know how to manage this uncertainty. This is compounded by feelings of confusion that result from not having a fixed or well-defined identity because they adapt so easily to different situations the way a chameleon changes its colors depending on its environment. While this adaptability can be positive, it is also a challenge for Link children because they do not know which "self" is their true self since they feel and act differently depending on the situation. They are constantly trying to navigate the waters of an "in-between" space—a place filled with doubt, vacillation, tensions, and intellectual and emotional tugs of war that they feel they must negotiate, which comes at a high emotional cost. Though I use the term "Link" throughout this book to describe a certain kind of child, it is important to understand that Link children are not yet able to fully claim their "Linkness." That is, they have not come into their own as Links. This is because, since they are children, they have not yet gone through the profound changes that will allow them, over time, to integrate the different aspects of their personality so that they can feel at ease with themselves and exist harmoniously with others.

When Link children become adults, as they go through what is often a prolonged process of finding themselves and discovering their purpose in the world, they begin to understand that existing in the "in-between" is manageable and that it is manageable precisely because they are Links. That is, they themselves are the key to connecting, or linking, the disparate and conflictive forces around them, to joining the opposing, contradictory elements that characterize this space of uncertainty. When Link adults finally discover who they are and find the place of inner calm that they are seeking, they at last understand that they are "links"—people who contain within them what was earlier in life the confusing, anguish-producing in-between space but who now are able to resolve the contradictions and confusions by embodying the connections between them, by finding a place of peace in the very act of linking the opposing forces. Their ability to transform confusing contradictions into interesting paradoxes makes them valuable members of families and communities because they are able to link disparate elements in any given situation in unique, atypical, and useful ways. These ideas will be explored in detail in the chapters that follow this Introduction.

The Four Circumstances that Create the "Perfect Storm"

1. Link children are born **gifted in empathy** and have a tremendous capacity for global empathy.
   - Global empathy is sometimes positive: The child truly feels what other people feel and can respond in positive ways to that in order to meet other people's needs.
   - Global empathy can also be negative:
     - It causes the child to **suffer** tremendously because she is always feeling other people's feelings and can't distinguish them from her own. She absorbs and assimilates others' feelings so that inside her there are always conflicting feelings.
     - It causes the child to **"obey"** any definitions or preconceived notions that the parents have about him derived from the character of either parent. For example, when a parent says or feels something like "He's just as bad as I was when I was a kid" or "He is so hardheaded, just like his mother," the child picks up on these "prescriptions" and then enacts the objectionable behaviors. In short, the child ends up being what the

parents (and other family members) think, fear, and project onto him. The child thinks something like, "Since they think I'm bad, I must be bad, because when I'm good, they don't even notice and so it doesn't make any difference."

▢ They do not know what they feel and, therefore, they develop the **defense mechanism of anger** or other negative reactions in order to "believe" that this is who they really are. They do this without realizing that they are actually just obeying the contradictions of the parents, making them, paradoxically, more obedient than they themselves or their parents realize.

2. Link children are exposed to **multiple perspectives** in the form of very different, sometimes even contradictory, values, points of view, feelings, ideas, goals, ethics, and/or aesthetics.

- Typically, the parents of the Link child are different from each other in ways that often cause conflict within the family (and between the parents) and that expose the child to contradictory ways of thinking, believing, behaving, etc. Link children assign the same level of importance to each and every one of those values, points of view, ideas, etc. Their capacity for empathy causes them to internalize these contradictory ways of thinking, world views, belief systems, etc., and then they feel pulled in different or contradictory directions in their desire to please their parents. They cannot please both if the demands or expectations of one parent are radically different from those of the other.

- This leads to **problems with trust and extreme self-doubt.** They are not able to put their faith in, trust, or let themselves be taken care of by their parents because they see these adults as contradictory, confused, or wrong.

3. Link children know that their parents are "good people," and they also know, even if they do not *feel*, that their parents love them. But **they have ambivalent feelings toward their parents** because they know that their parents don't understand them and can't help them to understand themselves.

    • As well as being related to problems of trust and self-doubt, this produces various kinds of **guilt**:
        ¤ Guilt about specific actions that they know have caused harm ("normal" guilt)
        ¤ Guilt about the guilt that they make their parents feel; i.e., Link children know their parents feel guilty about not giving them what they need, and they feel guilty for making their parents feel this way. They also absorb their parents' guilt through their capacity for global empathy.
        ¤ **Paranoid guilt**—Beyond specific instances of guilt, Link children constantly feel, at every moment, what is known as "paranoid guilt"; that is, they feel guilty all the time and are always afraid of being "found out" even if they haven't done anything wrong.
    • This ambivalence toward their parents also produces internal **ethical conflicts** in Link children because they love their parents and know that they are well-meaning, but they are almost constantly angry with the ways that they try to raise them and care for them. The Link child has the *feeling* that he does not love his parents (even though he does love them), but because this feeling is unbearable, he transforms

it into the opposite—that his parents don't love him, which causes the child to suffer as well as to blame his parents, projecting onto them the negative emotions. This allows the Link child to not feel like the "bad guy" and to instead transform himself into the poor, pitiful, well-intentioned victim by provoking his parents to not love him (through bad behavior).

4. **The circumstances of the Link child's birth or infancy were unusual**, or there was some trauma or major transition in the family around the time of birth, during infancy, or in early childhood that caused the child to experience very early on the finitude of time and space.

   • **Metaphysical anguish.** What is life? What is my purpose? Who am I in this world? These questions present themselves to Links from a very young age. Even if their achievements seem considerable to other people, Links question the achievements as only satisfying a part of themselves. Links feel incomplete and unsatisfied when they feel they cannot make a meaningful difference in the world.

   • **Addiction to the search.** Links seem addicted to seeking, often uncertain of what they are looking for, unable to stop in order to prove that an idea is not just a product of an irrational intuition.

These four circumstances together create the conditions for a "perfect storm"—the Link child. But if not all four circumstances are present, another kind of child will emerge—perhaps a difficult child, perhaps not—but not a Link child. For example,

- If the child is not gifted in empathy, she will not pick up from her parents their differences and their contradictory values, styles, and goals.
- If the child is gifted in empathy but the parents come from similar origins and share the same values, styles, and goals, she will receive from them a coherent map with which to navigate her own life.
- If the child does not know that his parents are good and well-intentioned people, that is, if the parents are abusive and do not show love to their child, he will grow up to be bitter and even prone to developing a psychopathic or borderline personality.
- If the child does not suffer some kind of traumatic experience very early in his life, he does not develop an extraordinary sensitivity to painful situations in life such as social injustice and the suffering of others.

1. Gifted in Empathy and Prone to Volatile Behavior

Link children share with hyperempathic and highly sensitive children the characteristic of having "thin skin," that is, of finding it impossible to not feel deeply wounded or personally attacked or insulted by criticism, even when it is offered in constructive ways. As Judith Orloff says of the hyperempathic child: "I emphasize that empathic children feel too much but don't know how to manage the sensory overload. They see more, hear more, smell more, intuit more, and experience emotions more." In a similar vein, Elaine Aron defines highly sensitive people as those "born with a tendency to notice more in their environment and deeply reflect on everything before acting…." It is understandable, then, that these children have "thin skin," existing as they do with the burden of having to constantly receive so much external information but not knowing how to process it in a way that doesn't hurt them and not knowing how to keep it at bay and shut it out.

Link children also share with highly sensitive children the awareness of being "different" from other children. As Aron says, "Despite my emphatic belief that we HSPs [Highly Sensitive People] are normal, I do like to refer to our sensitivities as quirks. This is because, as HSPs, we're all unique. Sure, there are common characteristics, as with any personality. But we each have our own flavor. Our own HSP quirks."

Link children in particular embody the dictionary definition of "empathy" in that they have an extraordinary capacity for "the action of understanding, being aware of, being sensitive to, and vicariously experiencing the feelings, thoughts, and experiences of another of either the past or present without having the feelings, thoughts, and experience fully communicated in an objectively explicit manner" (Merriam-Webster).

Doris Bischof-Köhler, building on the ideas of M.L. Hoffman, differentiates among three types of empathy: 1) *global empathy* in which people feel as their own the feelings of others; 2) *egocentric empathy* in which people feel in their bodies the emotions of others but recognize that these emotions are not their own; and 3) *social empathy* in which people can understand what others feel but without feeling the emotion themselves. When I refer to the gifted in empathy, I am talking about the children who experience global empathy: feeling others' feelings as deeply as if they were their own.

The fields of infant studies and neurobiology converge in the belief that newborns' ability to empathize leads to the possibility of an immediate and complete identification with the people around them. As Marco Iacoboni has shown, there is a neural basis for mimicry and mirroring before the infant develops the capacity to understand conceptually and put the emotions they are experiencing into words.

When a child is born gifted in logical-mathematical, spatial, musical, naturalist, linguistic, existential, bodily-kinesthetic, or intrapersonal intelligence (following Howard Gardner's approach), families can react either by ignoring these abilities and letting the child develop them on their own, or by encouraging them and giving them the tools to further develop their gift. Whichever option the parents choose, they do not typically feel threatened or overwhelmed by the child's gift.

This is not always the case when a child is born gifted in empathy. The first difficulty with this circumstance is that people tend to assume that all human beings are equally capable of empathy. Acknowledging that their child could be more empathic than they themselves are is often very difficult for parents, who can feel threatened, overwhelmed, and uncertain about how to treat the child or how to behave in the face of this skill which is so difficult to grasp and so easy to misunderstand. Parents can also feel naked, disqualified, and even invaded by their child if the child "discovers" emotions that the parents don't want to share or don't even admit to having.

The parents' inevitable reaction, then, is one of fight or flight, of becoming angry or distancing themselves from their child because they feel threatened by this subversion of the expected hierarchy, prompting the thought, "How dare this child know better than I do what I am feeling?" This discomfort and vulnerability vis-à-vis their child creates a vicious cycle of mutual anger (rooted in fear) that looks something like this: When parents deny what the child is able to feel through empathy and either scold or otherwise distance themselves from the child, he feels confused and alone and feels that he is "bad" or even crazy. He begins to develop a tendency to think for himself and to not try to determine if what he thinks about any aspect of the world around him is the truth or if it is just his own emotions that he is feeling. This, in turn, makes the parents even angrier and causes them to accuse the child of lying about what he says he feels, which angers the child because they don't believe him, giving birth to a vicious cycle between parent and child.

Likewise, children who are gifted in empathy find themselves trapped in a vicious cycle: Their greatest talent (their ability to feel others' feelings and needs as their own) is also their greatest danger (not being able to identify their own feelings and needs); their greatest ability (to understand others so brilliantly as to be able to do what others want and win their love) is also their greatest limitation (if they stop doing what others want, they fear they will arouse feelings of hatred). If they use their talent in the service of others, they will be loved by them and will feel less fear about being judged as "bad," but they could feel resentful because they are not seeing their own needs and because they are not taking care of themselves. They risk feeling stupid and weak. If they use their gift in the service of their own desires, they risk being punished by others and by themselves. They are afraid of being accused of being bad, manipulative, and selfish; and they risk feeling guilt and fear that their gift is a tool of evil.

The consequence for Link children of their gift of empathy is their volatile feelings and, by default, their unpredictable behaviors.

2. Exposed to Multiple Perspectives that Lead to Problems with Trust

The parents of Link children chose to be with someone who was different from them; that is, they chose difference over similarity.[3] This is the crux of the internal conflicts that Link children experience because from very early on they identify with the strongest values (implicit or explicit) of each of their parents. Just as global empathy gives Link children an innate capacity to "grasp" the feelings of their parents from the time they are born, because they are raised in an environment that exposes them to very different, and even opposite, beliefs and/or value systems, they also "grasp" that there is no one single truth. The changeable, unstable nature of life is a premature presence in the lives of these children.

For the Link child, the already complex scenario of having been born with such a taken-for-granted, yet unique, gift becomes even more tangled because the child is exposed at the same time, with the same intensity, and with the same importance for their survival to different, contradictory, and conflicting points of view and world views. This causes the child to develop a very versatile and definition-defying subjectivity that is hard to pin down. At the same time, precisely because of the parents' difference from each other, one of the values that parents and child share is respect for diversity, different ideas and opinions, and humanistic values related to equality and the rejection of authoritarianism. In most of the families that produce Link children, however, these

---

3 Links in single-parent families grapple with multiple, contradictory perspectives as well because they, like all Links, must deal with the differences between the values systems they are exposed to within their family and those they encounter outside of their household. This produces yet another powerful tension that Links deal with constantly: that of inside (messages they receive at home) vs. outside (messages they receive from authority figures outside their home). In a single-parent family, a Link may also be exposed to a worldview in conflict with that of the parent through a relative who has substantial influence over the child.

positive values become a detriment when parents try to exercise the necessary authority to offer the child a sense of security and protection and of being prepared to confront life's challenges.

Children who are gifted in empathy perceive that each point of view holds some unquestionable truth. Therefore, they internalize the concept of relativity, of allowing for multiple and simultaneous perspectives from the very beginning of the development of their own point of view. On the surface this way of seeing the world might appear to be desirable in that it suggests open-mindedness, flexibility, and acceptance and appreciation of differing points of view—all positive traits. The deeper underside, however, is that these children feel that no point of view and no manner of being cared for by their parents or other family members is solid or comprehensive enough to give them the certainty needed to create an unbreakable trust. Nothing is definite. If there is more than one unquestionable truth, this means that no truth is completely unquestionable; that is, nothing is completely closed, fixed, or reliable. So, whom can they trust? Better to take care of oneself—a classic behavior of a Link child.

While Link children do not trust those around them, the pain that they feel when they themselves are treated as untrustworthy, unreliable, and irresponsible is enormous because deep in their hearts they are looking for something else, for their own truth. They want to be completely loyal to their own truth in order to be able to give those around them their most profound—and trustworthy—loyalty. If they seem not to be committed, it is not because they are disloyal but because they are trying to understand the best way to be able to commit in spite of their doubts, ambivalences, or confusion about their own contradictory desires—all of which cause these children tremendous anguish, though they are not able to express it as such.

Sometimes, when parents transmit too much information and knowledge or expose their children to too much diversity and different environments, this can leave these children with feelings of profound emptiness, heightened anxiety, loss, and solitude. They feel ill-at-ease in the aspects of their lives where they grasped from infancy or early childhood contradictory but equally important and relevant messages for them.

These children are contradictory beings in search of a certain kind of love, or metaphorically, what I call a *precise embrace*—one that is spacious enough to contain their internal conflicts and contradictions, open enough to give them the freedom to live, to know they can leave and still be loved. They long for a fixed, stable place to inhabit, to grow up and develop in, but one with a removable platform that allows them to depart at any time—and then come back. They long for an embrace that they can always return to and that always receives them with love. They long for an embrace that allows them to discover and create an integrated identity for themselves, an identity that itself can embrace and embody in a harmonic way the diversity they inherited from their upbringing.

The consequence of being born gifted in empathy and of being raised in an environment full of contradictory points of view is the development of a subjectivity marred by inner conflicts among the contradictory feelings, desires, and parts of themselves that Link children suffer without under-standing why. This is not only because they want the approval of all the different people they were raised by but because they truly appreciate the specific value of the points of view of each of these people. All of this leads to their not trusting their parents or the adults around them enough to feel that they can rely on them.

3. Love Their Parents but Feel Guilty and Grapple with Ethical Problems

Another behavior inextricably related to the difficulties with trusting their parents due to the exposure to multiple and contradictory perspectives described above is that Link children, upon detecting their parents' difficulty in exercising authority, appropriate authority for themselves in ways that are anarchic or dictatorial. This is because they are assuming responsibilities for which they are not prepared (because they are children), although they feel as if they are more powerful or prepared than their parents to take care of themselves.

Link children share with Alpha children the characteristic of needing to be in control, either by taking care of others or by being bossy. As Gordon Neufeld says: "The purpose of the alpha instincts is to take care of, and to provide. The purpose of the dependency instincts is to render receptive to be taken care of, and to seek. One set of instincts is supposed to be the answer to the other.... When we simultaneously interact out of our alpha instincts with each other, we compete rather than complement each other. Alpha children are not receptive to being taken care of." This is also the case with Link children.

This feeling that Link children have that they must take care of themselves, in addition to being bound up with difficulty trusting their parents, is tied to other complicated feelings toward them. Do they love their parents or not? Do their parents love them or not? Do their parents understand them? And if they do understand them, why don't they feel understood or taken care of by their parents? Link children continually straddle these fences, either as overt questions they pose to themselves or as profound, inexpressible feelings. These questions plague them constantly, whether they are able to fully articulate them or not, resulting in deep feelings of anguish that they cannot always identify the source of and that play out in negative behaviors.

This situation is also the origin of the ethical problem that Link children grapple with: They love their parents and, when they are mature enough, may admire them for their "humanism," but at the same time they feel they do not love them because they feel unprotected and misunderstood by them. Furthermore, in relation to their own behaviors and thoughts, Link children *feel* themselves to be bad, although they *know* they are good. In fact they feel the need to be good, but when they are good, they feel weak or powerless. The complex flip side of the coin is that they only feel strong when they feel themselves to be bad, that is, when they behave in opposition to something, going against the desires and expectations of others, which is easier to do if they "decide" that their parents do not love them (even though deep down they know their parents do love them). Finally, these tortured feelings and behaviors produce tremendous feelings of guilt, the most complex and serious kind of guilt being *paranoid guilt*.

A telling example of the kind of behavior (in this case benign, at least on the surface) that can exemplify the pervasiveness of paranoid guilt is from an adult Link, Deborah, sharing an experience she had as a child that was a turning point for her in terms of her relationship to the adults in her life: "I was six or seven years old, and I received a small white Chihuahua as a gift from a former neighbor. I remember opening the box and my mother was beside me. I had seen something moving inside the box before opening it, but I thought that she would be pleased if I acted surprised. So, with my best Oscar- winning face, I opened the box, turned to her and said: 'It is alive!' with a big smile.... Bingo! That was the talk of the family for a week. I laughed inside because I had just learned to manipulate my family! Little did I know that this early exhilaration would become a guilty feeling afterwards."

Why the guilt? Because Link children always feel that if things go well for them it is because they are "lying," that is, because they "perform" to make their parents, teachers, and others happy. But they never feel completely trustworthy to themselves or to others if they themselves, on the inside, are not fully aligned with or do not fully feel the "act" they are performing. They feel like imposters: If they are not performing or living what they feel to be their *whole* truth, then they feel like they are lying. Any presentation of themselves they engage in is lived by them as if it were a representation of "some" truth, a partial truth. The question that plagues them is, Is this truth true? Is it the real truth? They live constantly with the fear of being caught in a lie, in a betrayal.

Another example is when my daughter's therapist told her early in her adolescence that she would be "cured" when she was able to wear the dress that she liked, in spite of my also liking it, because, in order to not manipulate me (as Deborah manipulated her parents with the Chihuahua so that her parents would love her), she negotiated the situation by not doing what she knew I would like, in spite of her also liking it. That is, she, like all Link children, vacillated between her need to be loved and her fear of not deserving that love, between giving someone else exactly what they wanted due to her tremendous capacity for empathy and the doubt about if that was exactly what she wanted. The issue of authenticity, the demand for the "real truth" along with the awareness from a very young age that there are many real truths, make these children exaggerate their "badness," display seemingly unabashedly the "wrong" feelings, and sabotage themselves at the moment that they are "winning." These are all ways of guaranteeing that they are not "lying" and that they are loved if and only if they are "true," and not because they are being manipulated by a parent's or another's wishes and expectations.

A third example also illustrates the permanent feeling of guilt that Link children experience. Cristina, age three, and her extended family are on vacation in a coastal town. Her grandparents, who are also there with her, decide to visit a nearby city for a couple of days. When they return, just as they are pulling into the driveway, Cristina sees them, makes a terrible face, and takes off running as she begins to cry inconsolably. She later reveals to her mother that she was afraid that her grandmother would no longer love her because Cristina, having spent the two days with her parents, a beloved aunt, and her cousin, had not even realized that her grandmother was not in the house. She had completely forgotten about her, and this "truth" felt like torture to her because she had done what she wanted, not what she imagined that the grandmother wanted, which was for Cristina to miss the grandmother so much that it would be impossible to feel happy. But because Cristina felt happy while her grandparents were away, she felt tremendous paranoid guilt, thinking that her grandmother would not want her to feel happy in her absence. Cristina, of course, has done nothing wrong, and the grandmother, of course, would not want her grandchild to feel unhappy in her absence. But as a Link child, Cristina feels guilty. She also feels afraid of her own ability to forget someone so dear to her. When she sees her grandmother, she projects onto her what she (Cristina) would feel if someone forgot about her or did not notice her absence for two days.

The feeling of guilt for Link children is continuous. They feel guilty if they "win," that is, if they are loved, because they are afraid of having manipulated others or lied in order to receive that love. They feel guilty if they "lose," that is, if they make themselves be hated, because they feel their parents' pain caused by not being able to love them in the way they need to be loved (the *precise embrace*), and then they feel unlovable. Since the child feels guilty and afraid of being scolded or punished without understanding why, she ends up doing something wrong or harmful or adopting a defiant or otherwise difficult attitude, all of which confirms for the parents that she is bad. This is the fundamental drama of Link children and, later, Link adults: They do not know how to distinguish between what they are accused of and what they are actually responsible for doing. That is, are they being falsely or justly accused of some wrongdoing? Did they do something wrong or not? They then either act out the guilt in objectionable behaviors and are punished, or they punish themselves through self-sabotage, ensuring that things will not go well for them in life.

The consequence of the complicated feelings toward their parents, along with their feelings of doubt and paranoid guilt, is the sensation of not fitting in anywhere, of constantly feeling uncomfortable and ill at ease. A key issue for Link children is how to live life without feeling and behaving in opposition to everyone in order to have the freedom they need and, simultaneously, without having to renounce the feeling of belonging. In other words, how to be at the same time "for me" (as an individual) and "for others" (as a member of a family and a community).

4. Unusual or Traumatic Event during Childhood and Metaphysical Anguish

Trauma is most simply defined as something that happens or impacts someone too soon, too intensely, or too quickly. A fetus can experience trauma in utero through the mother's transmission of a trauma she has experienced during pregnancy, just as newborns can experience their own trauma during the birth process. Traumatic events such as a death in the family, a major upheaval like moving to a different place or going through a divorce, and other sudden or dramatically life-changing events all affect the fetus, newborn, infant, or young child.

23

For Link children, their extreme capacity for global empathy ensures that any trauma that takes place around them, affecting them, their mother, or other loved ones, will leave a profound and indelible mark on them. From a very early age, then, sometimes from before they are born, Link children experience a deep connection with finiteness, loss, and death—with what is irreversible. This connection produces in these children two well-defined characteristics: an ever-present, underlying feeling of anguish and the need to keep searching—for answers, for meaning—which for Links easily becomes an addiction.

In spite of Link children's capacity for joy and for taking pleasure in life and enriching their peer and family groups with hope, creativity, and projects that stimulate curiosity and imagination, their feeling of anguish (also common in artists of all kinds) has to do with the certainty of life—as well as the certainty of death. That is, in addition to being acutely conscious of the limits and finitude of space and time, Link children also continually experience in their daily lives the unusual awareness that comes from their global empathy and the awareness of their many different selves—all of which causes them to constantly experience the intensity and fullness of life. Underlying all this, however, is a persistent, pervasive feeling of anguish.

The need to keep searching for answers and meaning may show up in Link children through their heightened curiosity and need to question everything—from why certain things in the world are the way they are (questions about nature, for example) to why they have to obey their parents (questions about bedtime, food, brushing teeth, etc.). When Link children do not get the answers they need, or any answer at all, they are left feeling unsatisfied and frustrated at best, or lost and abandoned at worst. They express these feelings through anger, melancholy, unruliness, and other challenging behaviors because, as children, they do not yet have the ability to articulate what is really going on inside them.

Their search, as children and adults, is typically accompanied or propelled by an addiction to adrenaline, often manifesting as the need to participate in challenging projects, high-adrenaline sports, or risky, even dangerous, pursuits. Links, however, also tend to procrastinate and feel that nothing is worth the effort, often switching from one project or pursuit to another and, as adults, moving from one career to another, exhibiting what can appear to be a cavalier attitude about their personal and professional lives. They eschew the idea of preventing or avoiding danger, only reacting with fear when danger or death is imminent. Their reactions in those situations are the usual reactions of any human being faced with fear: fight, flight, or freeze, which keeps them moving from one project to another, one career to another, one person to another.

Fundamentally, Link children have an almost innate awareness that to be born is to begin to die. In order to be alive and insert oneself into the human race, one must leave the uterus and be exposed to the feeling of un-protection, which is essentially loneliness. Link children grapple constantly with the paradoxes, differences, and contradictions not only between parents but also between family and society, personal and community traditions, being an individual and belonging to the collective, and being a unique person and being a member of a family. In short, they feel connected to—even if they cannot articulate it—time and space, and life and death, in all of their complexities.

While it is true that all human beings are inscribed into the inevitable dualities of the universe—self/other, individual/species, nature/culture, life/death, feeling/thinking, freedom/security, etc.—Link children suffer the painful consequences of these dichotomies much more intensely and deeply than the average child or person.

The consequence of experiencing a trauma early in life is having a premature awareness of the finitude of space (we each occupy a distinct, separate body

25

in this world and because of this individuation are in fact moving through life alone) and time (we all die) that results in metaphysical anguish, exacerbated by Link children's extreme capacity for global empathy. The trauma is so powerful that their parents, in large part because of their conflictive worldviews and resulting inability to agree on the "right" answers to give their children, are not able to help them escape the suffering that will be a part of their lives.

In order to give Link children what they need, parents need to understand the "perfect storm" that produces a Link child: 1) being born gifted in global empathy and, therefore, "feeling everything," 2) being raised in a contradictory, conflictive parental or family situation, 3) having unusually ambivalent feelings toward their parents, and 4) experiencing from a very young age or in utero a traumatic event. Parents also need to understand that their children will be "difficult" children until they learn not to feel burned up inside by the sparks of the many paradoxes that they perceive and feel from the moment they open their eyes to the world.

How Parents of Link Children Feel

The people who care for a Link child, whether they be parents, other family members, teachers, therapists, professionals, or peers, generally feel that they are dealing with someone who is out of control and unmanageable, a wild horse who resists being tamed, who does not surrender, and with whom they feel powerless and frustrated. They admire but also fear the child, which creates a feeling of simultaneous closeness and distance, of idealization and rejection. The child, in turn, incorporates (through both imitation and contagion) the same contradictory ways of idealizing and rejecting, defending and abandoning, loving and hating their parents and themselves.

A Link child acts in ways that are intolerable to parents because, as already described, the child is suffering, living in emotional pain and anguish, and feeling constantly guilty. Parents generally choose, consciously or not, one of two principal ways of viewing these children who make them feel powerless, afraid, and controlled rather than authoritative, confident, and in control. One way is to idealize their children, considering them to be "different" and somehow superior; the other is to see them as an aberration, a negative and unwanted presence in their lives that they did not ask for and do not deserve.

The first approach, idealizing the child, is understandable as a way to be able to love their child in spite of the extraordinary challenges of raising them. In this scenario, parents may believe that their child possesses special, unusual, and even supernatural or paranormal traits or abilities, even viewing the child as existing in the next stage in human evolution (in line with the theory of the Indigo Child developed by Lee Carroll and Jan Tober). Parents see their child as having an uncanny ability to understand reality, beyond that of the average human being. This kind of idealization, however, has the consequence of leaving the child at the mercy of her own decisions and causing her to become an autodidact. This can be positive for the child if she is very bright or gifted in emotional intelligence in addition to empathy. But it can also be painful for the child if she does not learn to be disciplined, to trust the various opportunities for learning that she will encounter in her life, or to fully belong to family and school structures where she can learn, in addition to how to be humble, the "rules of the game" for how to coexist with others.

The second approach, also an understandable way of dealing with the feelings of guilt, frustration, and impotence that taking care of these children produces in their parents, is to consider their children to be tremendously problematic, in spite of trying to resist these negative feelings and in spite of truly loving their children. That is, parents may view their children as abnormal or defective in some way, as something they "didn't sign up for" and do not want to have to deal with. This attitude also leaves the child feeling rejected and like an outsider, someone who is not worthy of belonging to the family (or any other) unit, someone to be feared and ostracized rather than celebrated.

Whether they take the form of idealization or of rejection, these extreme, but typical, parental attitudes leave Link children feeling that they have permission, even a mandate, to take care of themselves and to do whatever they want. This is the origin of the strong will of these children. This feeling comes with attendant risks and possibilities: Because of their strong will, they have the possibility of creating their own system of ethics, which can be positive. The risks, however, involve Link children becoming addicted to freedom as adults and/or becoming people who "take the law into their own hands." Fortunately, Link children *know* that their parents are well-meaning and love them, although they do not always *feel* that. They know that their parents are desperate to understand them and not abandon them. This causes Link children to always be trying to find a way to exist between being, on the one hand, the way they need to be and, on the other, the way they have to be in order to not mistreat their parents and other people in general.

In this situation in which parents and children alike feel guilty, as well as powerless and incapable of making decisions, it is imperative that parents resist any temptation to assign blame for the challenging situation they find themselves in with their Link children. No one is to blame for the existence of Link children. Parents of Link children are not narcissists, deserters, tyrants, or psychopaths. Link children themselves are not bad, selfish, ungrateful, or impossible to satisfy.

THE MAKING OF A LINK CHILD

In short, the parents are not to blame. The children are not to blame.

In order to be able to care for a Link child in the way that will best serve the child, parents need to develop tremendous patience so that they can detect and help the child to work with the singularity of each decision in each moment of her development, until the child succeeds in identifying or creating an internal roadmap—one that is completely unique and based on her own ethics—that allows her to feel she can be good without also being weak or a "loser," that allows her to feel strong without having to behave badly or violently, to feel capable of being nice without feeling she is giving in to something or being submissive, and being authentic or true to herself without hurting others. This map or guide must allow the child to feel worthy of being loved, capable of loving others without losing himself, and capable of distinguishing himself from others without feeling he must abandon them.

In addition to a great deal of patience, parents of Link children must develop confidence in their own capacity to love and to feel compassion. They must feel and show a great deal of compassion for their children, who suffer because they are the way they are, and for themselves, who suffer because they cannot prevent or ease the suffering of their children—children who see at the same time and with the same intensity the ugliness and cruelty of life as well as its beauty and goodness.

The dilemmas that parents of Link children and Link children themselves live with are many and complex, requiring subtle explanations to allow parents to understand how this deeply painful situation is produced and how they can try to resolve it. Fundamentally, the situation is caused by mutual misunderstandings: Link children do not feel understood by their parents, whom they love, and parents of Links feel they do not understand their children, whom they love.

❖ ❖ ❖

The purpose of this book is to help parents (and other primary care-givers) to better understand and care for their Link child, for it is only through understanding that parents can be more aware of their own behaviors and hold themselves as well as their child accountable in the process of improving the relationship. In short, it is only through under-standing and awareness that parents can love their child in the best way possible *for the child*, providing their child with the longed-for *precise embrace.*

Finally, my most important message to parents of Link children bears repeating: The challenging situation that you are living daily with your Link child is not your fault. And it is not your child's fault. *It is nobody's fault.* Only through accepting this truth, which I hope this book will allow you to do, can you move forward on the path toward a calmer, healthier, and more loving relationship with your Link child.

Chapter 1

The Link Child: A Blessing Disguised as a Challenge

If you are the parent of a Link child, you may already be recognizing yourself and your child as you ponder the Link characteristics outlined in the Introduction. Parenting this particular kind of "difficult" child is fraught with daily challenges that both in the moment and over time can feel unbearable. Like all good parents, parents of a Link child constantly strive to meet the child's emotional needs, but because their child is a Link, nothing they do seems to be good enough. All parents have this feeling from time to time, but parents of Link children experience it almost continuously and are increasingly exhausted and mystified as to how to appease, satisfy, and calm their child when the child's main behavioral mode is defiance and disobedience accompanied by a constant questioning, including an unreasonable and disrespectful (for the parents) questioning of their authority.

Link children, however, also have innumerable positive, beneficial, and unique traits and behaviors, endearing them to many, if not to all, and causing their parents and loved ones to appreciate them as talented, original, interesting, and loving beings. In *Link and the Shooting Stars* the young horse Link exhibits many key characteristics of Link children. In the opening scene, despite the late hour and his friends' sleepiness as they munch on a bedtime snack of grass, Link's playful, energetic, imaginative, and determined way of being convinces them to join him for more hours of play and one final game that he invents for all to enjoy—the game of connecting the stars.

Like this spirited horse who feels himself to be different from the others (and whom others throughout his childhood will categorize as different or even "weird"), children with Link personality traits are naturally playful, energetic, imaginative, charismatic, determined, over-confident, excited, excitable, and curious. They are what we might call "free spirits" because of their unflagging belief in and commitment to exploring the possibilities that life holds. Life for them is full of magic, and Link children are propelled by the power of their desires. They are so eager to embrace the world in its enormity that they are always ready to run to another adventure, and another, and another . . . as if they feel they don't have time to waste just passively existing or settling for the life that others try to hand them. Instead, they have an urgent need to create, discover, and invent new ways of being alive.

These wonderful characteristics in and of themselves, however, are at the core of the extremely irritating and sometimes dramatic confrontations between Link children and their parents and peers alike. While these children may be free spirits, they also experience extreme and almost constant distress due to an ever-present impulse to question absolutely everything (much more than other children) and the resulting disappointment of receiving unsatisfying answers or dismissiveness from those around them. These questions can range from the seemingly mundane and quotidian to the most profound questions related to the meaning of life and one's place in the universe. They can range from "Why do I need to brush my teeth?" or "Why do I have to go to bed now?" to "Why is the sky so big but I'm so small?" or "Why are the stars so far away and out of reach?" This despair at constantly having questions they feel compelled to ask—sometimes accompanied by the frustration of not being able to formulate them clearly for themselves or for others—and then not receiving satisfactory answers or any answers at all, creates a profound emptiness in Link children.

The despair also stems from a disconnect between the Link child's fundamental question about life and that of his parents. While parents are usually preoccupied with the question of what living life involves, that is, the business of organizing their lives and what to do in life, the Link child's most profound and abiding question is about the nature and meaning of life itself, that is, "*What is life?*"

In contrast to how most people seem to see the world, which one might characterize as through a unidimensional lens or a frame that only allows for viewing one aspect or facet of life at a time, Link children have minds that see and think in 360 degrees, like a periscope. This was my own feeling as a Link child when I told my mother that my thoughts were like hundreds of horses galloping around in my head without any possibility of controlling them. It was as if all of my thoughts and all of my ability to focus were headed in the same direction but with a speed that made me feel tremendous anxiety and made my heart pound uncomfortably fast in my chest.

When Link invents and proposes that he and his friends play his Connect-the-Stars game, he is acting on his impulse to create, to discover something new in the world that will allow him to feel valued, appreciated, calm, and secure. The need to suggest and urge others to play a new game, rather than one that everyone already knows, is rooted in his deep curiosity, another defining trait of Link children.

Neuroscience has allowed us to understand that the human brain treats curiosity much like pleasurable activities such as eating. When we actively pursue new information through our curiosity, we are rewarded with a flood of the chemical dopamine, a neurotransmitter in the brain that is responsible for, among other things, feelings of pleasure and calm. Seeking out new games, new activities, and new experiences, then, triggers the calming effect of dopamine. Hand in hand with this constant need to experience something new is a desire to go deeper, to feel the confidence (and accompanying calm) of mastering a new field of knowledge, of reaching a level of expertise in something.

In addition to satisfying a deep and continually present curiosity, the Connect-the-Stars game also allows Link to experience a meaningful connection with nature—in this case, a night sky that is vast, distant, and out of reach. Why does Link have this impulse to connect with the unknowable, with what is mysterious and beyond one's grasp? Link children (and adults) feel from very early on in their childhood a division between **life** and **world**. Another way to understand this division is the classical philosophical distinction between **essence** and **existence,** or between **nature** and **nurture.** These well-known ways of trying to understand our place in the world and how we come to be who we are relate to questions of personality: Who am I deep down, who am I *truly*? vs. Who am I when I am behaving as society expects me to behave?

The first time it seemed that I had an inkling about what might be happening to these children with respect to this feeling of being ill at ease in the world was 25 years ago while listening to Kaito, a 35-year-old patient who was sharing with me a childhood memory. In this scene he was six years old and had emigrated with his family from Japan to New York two years earlier.

As Kaito was lying in bed he looked out the window and saw a breathtaking star-filled sky. He began to think about how far away the stars were, how many there might be, about the immensity of this huge, inaccessible space. But what began as a feeling of fascination suddenly turned into a panic attack that caused him to cry out, burst into tears, and run around all over the house. He was not able to explain to his parents, who were trying without success to calm him

34

down, what was happening to him or what had provoked so much anguish in him.

In that moment he did not have access to the right words, as he did years later with me, to explain to his parents what he was feeling: desperation at being confronted with the certainty of being alone, enclosed in his own body, in his own time. The universe promised him a world so big into which he would be able to fit his entire life—this life that was so rich and full of possibilities and intriguing mysteries. But the immensity of the universe also made him feel so small and defenseless when faced with the mysteries of life and the fascinating challenges of the world that he could not find, in that moment, answers that would make him feel at peace. He did not know how to insert his *life* into the actual *world*.

Kaito's feeling of being overwhelmed by the night sky, which caused his extreme reaction of feeling frightened, alone, and defenseless, was exacerbated by the ongoing tension between his parents' different ideas about how he should make his way in the world. The solution to finding his place in the world that was offered—and demanded—by his father was to win as many sports competitions as possible. He encouraged Kaito in his tremendous physical abilities and assured him that in this way he would be guaranteed admission to the best universities of this new idyllic country. The solution presented by his mother was emotional sensitivity. She would show him affectionate devotion when Kaito would achieve prodigious new heights in his study of the violin, his favorite instrument at that time.

Where could he find refuge? Where could he find relief from his loneliness? Where could he feel loved beyond the limits of time and space—in the physical, masculine, powerful world where his body felt the satisfaction of muscular tension and precision or in the sensitive, feminine, loving world where his body felt the satisfaction of calm, sensual wonder and imagination?

When Kaito shared this childhood memory with me, he also described his sense of feeling extraordinarily capable of helping his friends in their different activities, but of not knowing what his own true area of interest was. He felt exactly like a small line, a hyphen that only had meaning when it was connecting dots, which gave him a feeling of serendipity. He had also recently discovered that he felt useful, like he was *somebody*, when his linking abilities allowed him to connect an artistic idea with a business endeavor. He eventually realized that being a "link" could also be a legitimate, valuable way of being in the world.

The aforementioned tension between the questions "Who am I deep down, who am I *truly*?" and "Who am I when I am behaving as society expects me to behave?" is illustrated perfectly on the back of a postcard that was part of a multimedia exhibit by Cameroonian artist Barthélémy Toguo. The artist had posed the question, "Where do you fit in American society?" to different groups of people in the community where the exhibit took place, and community members wrote their responses on postcards, which Toguo collected and displayed. The response from a young member of the Shinnecock Nation reveals this fundamental tension that Link children experience: "[I fit in] everywhere, until I tell them the truth. Then only with my friends and in the arms of another girl who doesn't fit in."

The question of authenticity, of knowing and behaving as one's true self rather than the "self" that others expect, is a deep preoccupation for Link children. My daughter Paula experienced this concern as unbearable pain, saying to me at around age 12, "I want to be my pure me, my true me. I don't want to disguise myself as a woman or a mother, or as a professional or even a dancer. I don't want to be just one part of me, because people might think that I am only one of my many different me's, and that would be a lie."

Nature is the place in the world where Link children (and Link adults) feel they are not lying. As human beings, they are part of nature. And what is the most awesome manifestation of nature that can include all the possibilities of being, if not the sky or the sea? Yet, as Kaito's childhood experience of the vastness of the universe indicates, nature also provokes anguish and despair because it serves as an overwhelming reminder that we are small, insignificant, alone, and mortal.

Returning to the story of Link the young horse, we can interpret his desire and attempts to connect the dots among the stars as an attempt to connect himself to the universe—as Link children need to do, without understanding why or how—and to others. It is a desire, born of an inexplicable and unarticulated impulse, to connect to being alive as a whole "self," to find peace in this delimited and restrictive world in which he, and all of us, must exist.

Connecting the Dots and Empathy

From the time they are born, Link children display a capacity for empathy that is far above normal. Doris Bischof-Köhler calls this kind of empathy "global empathy"—the empathy that makes someone feel others' emotions as their own, without being aware that they come from the outside. She uses "egocentric empathy" to refer to empathy that allows someone to feel others' emotions while knowing that they belong to another "I"—hence the reference to "ego." She uses "social empathy" to describe empathy that provides the necessary distance to understand others' emotions only from a cognitive point of view.

As soon as they enter the world, Link children feel the emotions of those who surround them so powerfully and internally that they feel those emotions to be their own. They begin to develop a personality that should be rooted in their own emotions but that is actually formed on the basis of the emotions of others. They see themselves in the eyes of those who look at them and believe that they are seeing themselves as they are "feeling" the doubts, insecurities, contradictions, and vulnerabilities of the environment that receives them. This is an environment that is laden with what Leon Festinger calls *cognitive dissonance*: the tension and lack of harmony that people feel when incompatible ideas and emotions coexist within them. Coexisting in these children are not only the contradictory messages transmitted by the different people who care for them and try to educate them (Kaito's parents, for example, with their different ideas about what life path he should pursue) but also the contradictory ideas and emotions that inhabit each and every one of these different people.

Link children are born with an extraordinary ability to connect dots—any kind of dots related to any aspect of the world, from their own emotions, others' emotions, their own perception and experience of reality, and other people's observations about the same reality. They connect dots, however, indiscriminately—without a rigorous or logical way to do so, without a deliberate selection or editing process regarding how many, in which directions, or which criteria their mind uses to trace the links.

These thought processes and patterns trigger behaviors in Link children that are difficult for others to understand—including and especially their parents—and for the children themselves to understand. Whereas the children suffer, in part, because they lack both sufficient intellectual information and the capacity to regulate their emotions, the parents suffer because their Link child is continuously connecting dots in ways that are unknown and unfathomable to the parents. A parent, for example, might tell a child to do something in a way that seems clear and straightforward, but the child will interpret the parent in a completely different and unpredictable way and then act on that interpretation. The parent, in turn, reads the child's action as defiance or lack of obedience, while the child is left confused and bewildered about what she did wrong.

The extreme ease with which Link children connect cognitive and emotional dots is not something they can control or avoid. Their high level of global empathy, in effect, forces upon them and *into* them—their psyches, their entire beings—the emotions of others, including the confusing and tortured internal contradictions of others. While the parent of a Link child is experiencing anguish and desperation related to the child's difficult behaviors and helplessness at not being able to figure out what the child needs, the child is experiencing tremendous inner turmoil related to the "galloping" thoughts and feelings of everyone else that he is internalizing.

Link children and adults crave inner peace, a profound need to feel that all the different impulses, desires, thoughts, and emotions that race around at a high speed in their brains are not in conflict with each other. It is impossible for them to behave in a normal or conventional way or to follow a clear and organized path in the search for a "home" where they can feel at ease. To complicate matters, the more conventional people in their lives—often their parents or other caregivers—do not understand how these children think, feel, and behave.

Links "On the Outside"

For better *and* for worse Link children are different from their peers. Their innate and tremendous capacity for empathy—at the core of their uncontrollable impulse and ability to continually connect the dots, to see the links among things that others cannot see—is so overwhelming for them and their parents that they develop extravagant, eccentric, defiant, and unique ways of coping with all the contradictory emotions that they feel are constantly invading them. These behaviors inevitably affect Link children's relationships with their peers as well as their parents.

Link the horse's insistence that his friends play one more game—a game of his invention that relies on the vastness and mysteriousness of nature, in this case the night sky—has to do not just with his impulse to create a game but also with his need to create one that is more elaborate and original than any that the other children might come up with. While of course every child is unique and different from every other, the particular "brand" or "flavor" of uniqueness that a Link child exhibits almost always strikes others as extreme, exaggerated, strange, too complicated, or weird.

The characters of Gray and Pink illustrate nearly opposite reactions that Link children can provoke in their peers. Link's cousin Gray feels a kind of attraction to playing the game because of the repulsion he feels toward the apparent confidence and arrogance that Link exhibits when he presents his ideas. Gray competes with him and wants to disqualify him in front of the others, especially in front of Pink. Pink, on the other hand, idealizes Link. She never doubts his ideas and goes along with them, even when she suspects she might be putting herself into danger as in later in the story. As is the case with peers of Link children, neither Gray nor Pink are aware of Link's insecurity and constant doubts and fears underlying his apparent confidence.

Link children can also produce other reactions in those around them. Although not all possible reactions appear in the story, other responses to Link's insistence that his friends play Connect-the-Stars with him might include some friends preferring not to interact with him because he comes across as too demanding, too complex, or too difficult to please. Others might just remain indifferent to Link, not even noticing his originality and creativity as these traits manifest themselves in the uniqueness of the game. Still others might dismiss Link, not as Gray does when he categorizes him as an overly cocky "know-it-all," but because they perceive that he does not act anything like an innovator or creator and that he is not introducing anything new when he presents his ideas. They think that if Link cannot show any evidence demonstrating his expertise in a field, then they should not take him as seriously as he wants to be taken.

In addition to Link's relationship with his parents and peers, from the beginning of the story it is clear that another adult has tremendous importance for him—Grandma Violet. Unlike others in his life, including some of the characters he will meet later in the book once his journey of self-exploration begins, his grandmother knows who Link is. She recognizes and understands his strengths, weaknesses, confusions, and unique traits. She is confident that sooner or later Link will find equilibrium within himself and integration of the different ideas and emotions that pull him down a different path. She understands why the "normal" and familiar landscapes push him away, compelling him to search for the integrated identity he can create around his own truth, once he discovers and understands it.

An apt and beautiful metaphor says that you first have to recognize the seed that you are in a tree that you find in the world and that you then have to be recognized by an authority in the relevant field as the seed of the tree you want to become. For Link, his grandmother is the legitimizing authority who tells him that yes, he will become the tree he wants to be. When the horses are returning back to the ranch at bedtime, Link's brief conversation with his grandmother is crucial to his developing understanding of himself in the world and to his expression of the specific dream of growing up and making it his mission to find where the shooting stars land. Rather than criticizing or dismissing his dream as unrealistic, Grandma Violet validates it by acknowledging the challenge and by subtly and wisely shifting the emphasis from the destination (where the shooting stars land) toward the journey and the importance of all that Link will learn on whichever path he chooses. Grandma's loving and supportive voice inspires positive, joyful feelings in Link, connecting with and valuing who he is in all his originality.

Links "On the Inside"

Link's grandmother's validation of who he is stands in stark contrast to the scene that immediately follows when Link's parents approach him, having overheard the conversation between him and his grandmother. Instead of connecting with Link's imagination, curiosity, and big ideas, his mother and father immediately begin imposing on him their own hopes and dreams for him, leaving completely to the side his own dream for himself. Link responds with enthusiasm to their saying he should be a riding horse (his mother's dream for him) and a racehorse (his father's dream for him). Link would like to be both, not yet able to understand that these two paths are not necessarily compatible and that, therefore, his parents are presenting him with conflicting ideas that are rooted in their own respective desires and that, as such, reflect a conflict between them.

Link children are born and raised in environments where they are exposed to contradictory demands, both of equal and utmost importance and of equal emotional value to them. At the very end of the conversation about his parents' dreams for him, his mother and father exchange a serious look with each other. Link perceives in this look a certain uneasiness or lack of connection that he feels but can't put into words. This cognitive dissonance that Link children grow up with produces three kinds of feelings that characterize their world view:

1. **Fear**—Due to the constantly shifting realities that accompany the constantly shifting messages that they receive, Link children often feel overwhelming fear. Thanks to their tremendous capacity to detect and read signs that are imperceptible to others, these children register these signs, messages, and, other "hidden" elements of their reality generally without understanding their true meaning. The look that Link's parents exchange, for example, is for the young horse an important sign of *something*, but he is not clear about exactly what. It throws him into confusion, self-doubt, and inner turmoil, at the root of which lies an inexpressible fear—of not knowing things he needs to know, of getting something wrong, of not understanding what the world is about, and of being alone because he feels he cannot trust his parents.

2. **Difficulty making decisions**—For Link children the contradictory messages have the same emotional weight, and they are not able to discriminate between them, set priorities, or harmonize within themselves the contradictions. This is related to their ability to perceive many things at once—the "periscope" character of their mind mentioned earlier. This ability does not indicate the presence of Attention Deficit Disorder in a child but rather something I call Decision Deficit Disorder (DDD), which causes Link children to have tremendous difficulty editing their desires; that is, leaving to one side or abandoning their interests, even if only for a little while. The example of a young Link girl named Anita illustrates the condition of DDD. When faced one day with having to choose between watching a movie by herself on her laptop or watching a movie with her grandparents who were visiting from out of town, Anita felt such self-doubt, confusion, and anxiety that she burst into tears, unable to decide. Should she be a good granddaughter and satisfy her

grandparents' wishes, which would also give her the satisfaction of feeling like a good girl? Or should she be good to herself and satisfy her own desires? What for another child might have been either a bit uncomfortable or entirely unproblematic was for Anita extremely upsetting and anxiety-producing.

3. **Guilt**—Guilt is a constant in the interior lives of Link children. They feel guilty about not being able to please both parents at once due to what they perceive to be contradictory demands from the parents. Not being able to please both parents simultaneously leads them to feel that they are "less than" or "not good enough," which then makes them feel guilty for being "bad" instead of "good." In the majority of Link children guilt is manifested as tantrums or angry outbursts, which then causes a vicious cycle: The children behave badly due to feeling guilty, but when they behave badly they feel more guilt, which then causes them to keep behaving badly. In order to defend themselves from this terrible feeling of always being at fault, of never being as good as they believe a truly good child would be, they need to find someone other than themselves to blame. The parents, then, become an easy target, creating a vicious cycle between parent and child. Due to their large capacity for empathy, Link children live continuously with paranoid guilt—the feeling that they are to blame for pain and suffering they see around them but did not cause. They fear being accused of being bad and of not being able to defend themselves against this accusation. Any suggestion, correction, or admonishment from the parents—no matter how benign or mild—lands on Link children as a crushing accusation, causing them to lash out.

❖ ❖ ❖

Link children's subjectivity cannot *not* be difficult. Understanding them, helping them to understand themselves also cannot *not* be extremely difficult. It is inevitable, then, that these children doubt themselves and doubt others—those who love them and try their best to care for them in spite of their challenging and defiant behaviors. They doubt life. They doubt the world. Because of their profound doubts and because they don't trust those around them, they need desperately to be believed. They need their thoughts, desires, and feelings to be validated by someone else.

For Link the horse, as we have seen, his grandmother is this legitimizing figure. She validates his desire to find where the shooting stars land, appreciating it as ambitious and different, but not as crazy or bad. At the same time, his most important need and desire is to find an embrace in which he can let himself go, that will allow him to let go of fear and doubt and feel at ease, at home, that will allow him to feel safe enough to be who he is. Link does not yet know where or what this place is or how he will get there because he is still too young to know who he is. His grandmother, however, assures Link—with love, understanding, and acceptance of his difference—that it is okay to search for answers, to search for something stable that is not constantly shifting, for something concrete to hold onto, for the much-needed and longed-for *precise embrace* that will allow him to accept and fully be who he is—a "Link."

Chapter 2

Dangerous Crossings: The Struggle to Place Limits on the Link Child

In *Link and the Shooting Stars* (*Link*), the young horse Link feels happy, with great enthusiasm for new adventures, an amazing desire to embrace the world, and an inner confidence that makes him feel that he can do whatever he wants and that he will succeed at whatever he sets out to do. Link children feel these things as well. But this exuberance is the delightful flip side of—and exists in a complex relationship to—the "unhappy" behaviors that make the parent-child relationship so difficult—the willful, unbridled, sometimes dangerous behaviors that create conflict and frustration for both parent and child. Link children's "difference" is mirrored back to them by family members and peers. In Link's case, for example, he is continually observing and absorbing his mother's worries, his father's anger, his grandmother's expectations, his uncle's joy, his cousin Gray's rage, and his cousin Pink's admiration.

Is Link a defiant horse-child? Is Link a disobedient, disrespectful horse-child? He behaves as if he is. But in my decades of experience working with adults who began their life feeling like children who did not fit in with their families, communities, and peer groups, I have learned that Link children are exactly the opposite: They are too obedient and too empathic, actually caring about others' feelings—including those of their parents—too deeply. They also feel overwhelmed by the responsibility of handling all of these different emotions, which they feel to be their own, because they are not equipped with the tools to fulfill or manage the contradictory desires, requests, teachings, and values they are exposed to. Their profound empathy is a beautiful quality that can lead to tragic results.

Because I insist that the challenges parents and children face related to the behavior of a "difficult" child is nobody's fault, I want to focus as much as possible on the parent-child relationship. Actions and reactions (a chicken and egg problem) between parent and child create vicious cycles that end with everyone feeling sad, frustrated, desperate, and even enraged. In "Curious Link Explores His Limits" (Chapter 2 of *Link*), this occurs when Link plunges fearlessly into the river, disobeying his mother and putting himself in great danger. The other key player in this scene is Uncle Indigo, someone who also has tremendous influence on Link. While the influence of a close relative or friend may be subtle, it can have a huge impact on the subjectivity of Link children and their ideas about how the world works and what the meaning of life is. Not only is Indigo his mother's brother, he is also Grandma Violet's son, and therefore occupies a legitimate and meaningful place in Link's life even though he is not a constant, daily presence for Link.

While the story does not reveal the details of the relationship between Link's father, Onyx, and Uncle Indigo, it is useful to surmise what the family dynamics might be in order to understand how family dynamics affect and influence highly empathic Link children. For example, it is possible that Link's father dislikes his brother-in-law's independent, free-spirited lifestyle, which often takes him away from the extended family constellation. It is possible that Onyx also dislikes that his wife Amber continues to love her brother although she did not choose to marry someone like him, choosing instead a strict, structured, responsible mate with a deep sense of duty. Slowly but surely Link takes in these conflictive and contradictory ways of appreciating people, life-styles, values, and norms—just as Link children do in their own families. Assimilating so many different and contradictory values and points of view, however, creates constant doubt within Link children about which "system" to subscribe to, which path to follow, so they inevitably end up following their own instincts and impulses, creating their own path, in order to be true to themselves and to discover fully what their "truth" actually is.

This "instinctive" or impulsive behavior typical of Link children is evident in Link the horse in the scene at the river. Why is Link compelled to cross the river against his mother's orders? Link and Link children are very complex, with many layers of pulsating forces at work inside them, sometimes in contradictory ways. Three main factors are in play in the river scene that can help despairing parents understand some of the challenging behaviors of their children: a deep and continuous curiosity and fascination with novelty, a chameleonic impulse to imitate others, and a strong will and self-confidence.

1. **Fascination with novelty** stimulates activities in the brain cortex and produces feelings of connection and attachment to others. It also requires the use of imagination, language, creativity, and empathy. For Link children, the world's beauty is there to enjoy, to embrace, and to be embraced by. Excitement about overcoming fear and resolving life's mysteries triggers curiosity and the desire to seek out pleasant experiences, bringing with it an adrenaline rush inherent to the adventure. This occurs, however, without the child's being conscience of the perils that the passion for spontaneous adventures without careful prior preparation can bring. The child can become addicted to "imagining," wandering, and seeking out new

adventures instead of observing and learning from others' experience and knowledge.

2. **A chameleonic impulse and ability to imitate others' actions**—the result of Link's (and Link children's) extraordinary empathy—makes him think that he already "knows" how to do what he observes others doing. Because he incorporates the experiences of learning almost directly into his body through his experiences of observing, he really "feels" that he can do exactly the same thing that his mother and Uncle Indigo are doing. For him, his diving into the sparkling water is an uncontrollable impulse, prompted not only by the need to imitate the adults he loves but also by the beauty of the sun's reflection and the freedom and pleasure that he imagines, or *knows*, that crossing the river to a distant and mysterious shore will bring. It is possible he is thinking that by crossing the river he will perhaps even find where the shooting stars land. He does not realize that, through empathy, he feels in his body the happy emotions that swimmers feel and, subsequently, the happy emotion of being a swimmer himself. He feels this, but without realizing that he does not know how to swim. Again, the deep capacity for empathy is an extraordinary skill that can put him—and Link children—in danger, if not well implemented.

3. **Strong will and confidence** are other important Link personality characteristics. From the earliest moments in their lives, Link children feel to a large degree that they exist by themselves and, therefore, are alone in the world; that they exist as individuals more than as members of a family; and that others perceive them as being "different." For some people who interact with Link children, this means different in a good way; for others, it means different in a bad or dangerous way. Link has ideas about

50

anything and everything. Most of the time he can apply his ideas to the external world, so he invents interesting games or goes on adventures with successful endings. These good outcomes, then, in a way increase his certainty about "knowing"—they feed his confidence—but without his realizing that he is far from mastering the task he feels compelled to perform. He may have good intuitions, which are helpful in many situations in life, but in almost any activity or decision intuitions alone are not sufficient to produce the best outcomes.

When Link crosses the river without listening to his mother, he obeys both the spirit of adventure that his mother and uncle share and the command to be strong and brave that he has learned from his father. At the same time, he disobeys the recommendations to be careful and the fearful apprehensions of his mother as well as the instructions to only apply strength and bravery to activities that will be compensated in transcendent social ways, not solely for the immanent individual pleasure of engaging in adventurous activities like crossing the river.

Another cause of Link's uncontrollable impulse to plunge into the river without paying attention to, much less obeying, his mother's order includes the desperation he feels about being left alone, abandoned, or excluded by the circle of people who make him feel good, loved, and worthy of being loved. This fear is typical of a Link child, who sometimes does not even realize he is afraid, and at other times, more often than not, realizes it but without understanding that the fear is not justified and without being able to fully articulate it to anyone, including himself. Precisely because a Link child feels himself to be an autonomous individual more than a member of the family, he is always afraid that the family unit will cast him aside in anger because he imagines that the family members perceive that he is rejecting them as a unit—even though there may be no evidence at all that the family feels this way.

Young Link does not realize (consciously) that he is afraid of his mother's leaving him, yet his gift of empathy allows him to intuit that often she feels nostalgic for her previous freedom and the adventures she used to enjoy with her brother, beyond the confines of the ranch and the family. Impulsively, then, he jumps into the river's embrace. He trusts and needs to believe that something will support him, that he will find his home, the place where the shooting stars land, and the feeling of wholeness, of being one with everything that he longs for so deeply. When his mother scolds him and he reacts with frustration and anger, he no longer feels that he is "nice" or worthy of being loved because he is caught up in a strong feeling of rejection: He both feels rejected by his mother and rejects his mother, not understanding her, not understanding himself, not understanding the situation. In these moments he does not love himself or anyone else, though he does not understand his feelings in this way. He only knows that he is angry at them for thinking he is a bad horse instead of a horse who just wants to have fun.

The Vicious Cycle

The case of Giorgio provides another example of the contradictory, confusing, and upsetting feelings that Link children experience in many different kinds of situations, causing them to act out in ways that trigger conflict with their parents. Giorgio is a child of divorced parents who speaks English and Italian, living some of the time with his father in New York and some of the time with his mother in Rome. At age six Giorgio tells his father in a defiant tone, while refusing to do something that he had earlier agreed to do: "I told you that I'm not afraid of anything or anybody. I told you so, right?" His father responds angrily, scolding him. Giorgio retorts by reminding him that he didn't keep his promise of not scolding him so violently, and he gives his father a hateful look. Immediately afterward, Giorgio says (of himself) that he is a stupid idiot who hurts people, who hates his life (despite their having spent an excellent day together during which his father had given him everything he wanted), and he asks his father to lie down beside him and sleep with him. Only then, in his father's arms, is he able to calm down.

On a different occasion, during a camping trip with family friends, Giorgio retreats to a corner and accompanies himself on the guitar as he sings this song, composed as his father watches him intently: "I have a friend, and I don't have anyone to help me. I don't have anyone to hug me. I am a little boy who doesn't know anything. I know a word, and this word is my name. My name is Billy. I don't have anyone to... help me do my math...."

Which is it, then—I'm not afraid of anything or anybody, or I don't have anyone to help me? I can take care of myself, or I need a hug?

Giorgio's song is complicated. If he truly did not trust his father to be able to help him, he would not have sung the song in front of him. And if he truly did not have anyone, he would not be asking for help with his math. Given that at that moment, there was no math homework or assignment that he needed help with, "math" can be interpreted as a substitute for anything in life that a child typically needs help with, while understanding that a Link child vacillates constantly between declaring that he can take care of himself and desperately needing to be taken care of. In the song Giorgio asserts that he doesn't know "anything," but he knows enough to know that he doesn't know certain things, at least—expressed here as "math"—and that he might need help with those things. More importantly, he knows "a word, and this word is my name." Yet he undermines this assertion by saying that his name is Billy when his name is actually Giorgio. We can assume that, without knowing it, he is bringing up his need for help so that he can understand if he has or does not have someone he can count on to help him. Equally importantly, he is trying to understand if he "has" himself. In other words, he is exploring in this seemingly simple, but complexly layered, song his own identity and situation, asking what he has and does not have, whom he can count on and not count on (including himself), and who he is or is not. In short, is he Giorgio, or is he Billy?

Link children, then, grapple with the following internal conflicts and confusions:

- feeling themselves to be more autonomous than other children their age, acting as if they were independent and did not need help, and negating their needs for care and instruction;
- being bold and not assessing the danger in denying their need for protection, but having nightmares and feeling irrational fears that they do not know how to calm by themselves;
- obeying one of the received messages (from a parent, for example) through disobeying one or more other received messages that are just as strong and as internalized as the one that they obey.

These factors are at the root of the most serious misunderstandings between these children and their parents. Children like Giorgio risk generating a vicious cycle: By not surrendering to others with complete trust, with enough faith to accept guidance and nurturing from their family, they aggravate the feelings of impotence, rejection, and not being "good enough" in the very people who are trying to do an excellent job as caretakers in circumstances that are extremely challenging. Because the parent-child relationship is such a personal and intimate one, it is hard for a parent not to interpret the child's behaviors as personal aggressions, pronouncements of inadequacy, and even mini-betrayals of their attempts to create a satisfactory and necessary symbiosis with their child that is rooted in sincerity and the best intentions.

More concretely, the vicious cycle can look like this: The child desperately needs to be hugged, but since she is afraid that accepting this hug will make her feel trapped, unable to be herself, and like she is "giving in," she refuses to surrender to it. She masks her fear by acting as if she does not need this from her parents or by asking for it in the wrong ways (through rebellious behaviors, tantrums, etc.). The parents try to give her the hug, but because of the child's behavior, they feel rejected, which can make them feel angry and cause them to not give her the hug that she needed in the first place. In the end the child confirms for herself that her parents are incapable of giving it to her, do not want to give it to her, and do not know how to give it to her—even though it was her own behavior that drove the parents away.

Parents of children like Giorgio typically believe that what they must try to correct or control is the rebellious, negative, or defiant reaction, not understanding that this behavior masks the extremely high level of fear and the desperate need for a hug that these children feel on a deep level. A large part of the difficulty of the vicious cycle is that the children are not consciously aware of this need, and their skepticism and wariness lead them to not trust those who most want to meet their needs and to care for them in the best ways possible. Given, however, that they also want and need to believe that they *can* trust others and that they *can* have their needs fulfilled, they carry within them a perpetual longing for the *precise embrace* that will make them feel they are getting what they need. The downside of this longing is that it can cause them to naively trust and surrender to everyone, that is, people who are not their parents or primary caregivers and people who might not have their best interests at heart. This, in turn, causes great despair for the parents, who do not know how to become deserving of this "giving over" or surrender, of this trust that the child grants to those who, much of the time, do not deserve it and who, undoubtedly, do not love or worry about the child the way they do as parents.

One of the keys to gaining the child's trust is trying to understand, in each and every moment of their inappropriate or rash behavior, what the fear is that is overwhelming them to such an extent that they themselves are unable to identify why they are afraid. Parents need to take the time to understand what persecuting thoughts their child is defending themselves against, at every moment, through their reactions of rebelliousness, tantrums, or other objectionable behaviors. The Link child's persecuting thoughts typically involve fears of being labeled as "bad" or accusations they feel others are hurling at them. The parents' focus, then, needs to be on the child's internal struggle at that moment, not on the child's external manifestation of that struggle.

Link children are born free, spontaneous, curious, and active. They observe everything and absorb everything. But it is not easy for them to create a clear, linear map when they want to—and feel that they must—obey simultaneously all of the teachings they internalize and follow to the letter all the contradictory instructions they receive, whether they are given as suggestions and proposals or as orders and demands from the adults responsible for raising and caring for them. Since their high degree of empathy causes them to not know if what they are thinking or feeling is their own feeling or someone else's, they exaggerate the feeling or thought that is the one contrary to authority and they decide that this, the opposite route, is the position they should defend to be fully themselves. The conflict between self and other, the absence of limits, the confusion between their own feelings and those of others, and the tendency to be easily influenced and doubt their own criteria for decision-making are conditions that loom so large for them that the way out that they choose is aggressive confrontation. They believe they are supporting their own truth by completely opposing someone else's idea, without realizing that it is in this interaction with the other that their own idea is produced.

This is precisely the problem of the Link child: They recognize and condemn the incongruences, contradictions, unkept promises, frustrated projects, and feelings of dissatisfaction that the parents have with their own lives, both as individuals and as a couple. But this condemnation comes from a child who still does not know who they are or which "I" is their true self, since a Link child is the product of multiple complex and heterogeneous circumstances, in contrast to people who were raised in homogeneous environments and who were exposed to teachings and values that were not in conflict with each other. And although Link children "know" how to detect what their parents do not know, or do not know well, being children they still do not know how to handle themselves in life. Yet they do not realize or want to believe and trust that the same parents who do not know what they (the children) would like them to know, *do* know many other things that they (the children) do not think are necessary to learn but that are actually necessary to positively coexist, to have a life together rooted in mutual respect.

Self-imposed Timeouts

The deep anguish and suffering that Link children feel due to the constant internal battle among the many contradictory influences that others have over them, often leads them to isolate themselves in order to find some calm and solace. Do you recognize the phrases "I don't want to talk now" or "I need to be alone" or simply the look on a child's face of tuning you out, covering up her ears, running to hide in her room, or disappearing into a closet? Or an action such as what I did at age seven, hiding under the sewing machine, watching my family look for me and seeing how long it would take them to notice my absence? Or my daughter Paula's behavior when she wanted to punish her sister and succeeded in remaining still, as if she were unconscious or dead, for 40 minutes when she was only five years old?

The need to be alone appears many times in the story of Link the horse, the first time being after he experiences the dangerous, scary river adventure, when he walks away from his uncle before he can even respond to Link's plea for understanding. Link does this because it is the only way he knows of to not come face to face with his own contradictions. When he is listening to his mother scold him or pleading with his uncle, he may feel forced to acknowledge that his mother was right, but he does not want to give in and accept that he is not as self-sufficient as he thinks he is. Contradictory emotions shake him up inside: fear as a result of having confronted death; anger and humiliation because he was saved by his uncle, exposing in him a lack of power and lack of ability to survive challenges by himself; and embarrassment at having embarked on something that was such a failure, "proving" to him that Gray's criticism of his ideas and his parents' attempts at teaching him things are completely justified. When he is surrounded by the voices and perspectives of others, in this case his mother and his uncle, he is also forced to grapple with the awareness that his rejection of others' ideas stems from his misunderstood pride, his sought-after but premature feeling of autonomy, and a disconnect between his ideas (intuited and generated by his fertile imagination) and the things he actually knows, which should be acquired through practice, experience, and the learning process. As we have seen, Link thinks and feels in his body that he knows how to swim and can cross the river just as his mother and uncle have done. He has not yet learned that what he "knows" in his imagination is not always enough. He does not yet understand that swimming is a skill that he must learn and practice in order to truly have the autonomy that he erroneously feels he already has.

Link's self-imposed timeout after the river adventure, then, stems from a profound and urgent need to silence the voices of others, which feel like torture because of the confusion and worry they create in him. Yet the timeout is not initially a place of peace. It is also the space where he tries to rid himself of the anxiety he feels—an anxiety that produces a ruminating, circular, and exhausting thought process: "What should I have done?" "Why can't I do what I want?" "Do I know or not know how to swim?" "What happened?" "Did I do something wrong, or is it my mom's fault for scaring me with her shouting?" Not only do the voices of others torture Link children, making them feel they must escape to a place of solitude and silence, but they are also tortured by their own multiple voices, multiple desires, needs, motivations, longings, fears, and hopes that never get organized into a thought system that is comprehensible, coherent, and easily communicated to others. So while a Link child's self-imposed timeout is a kind of necessary refuge, it is not always a place of peace, unless the child has the tools to calm himself down and allow the incessant questioning and self-doubt to dissipate. Nevertheless, this place of solitude is preferable to being subjected to the scrutiny, admonishment, judgement, and differing opinions of others, all of which Links internalize because of their capacity for empathy.

In Link's moments of solitude at the end of this chapter of the story, although he is consciously feeling and expressing anger, he is probably feeling on a deeper, unconscious level that he very much needs his mother and uncle as well as other members of his family and community, whom he wants to be loved and needed by. He is probably beginning to understand, although he cannot yet put it into words, that what he was looking for when he crossed the river and what he is looking for when he wants to find the place where the shooting stars land is a time and space where he can be simultaneously himself for himself *and* himself for others. A time and space where his different "I's" can be harmoniously integrated into one self that contains the essential elements of his most important "I's," those that *he* feels are the most important and self-defining. A time and space where he can be, at the same time and in the same place, both a unique, autonomous individual *and* a member of his family, community, and species, just like everyone else.

Little do Link children know that this elusive time and space that they seek lies within them. Little do they know that only through understanding that the contradictions and multiple perspectives they are constantly absorbing from others, in addition to their own internal conflicting emotions, are the raw materials that will enrich their lives and allow them to be their most authentic selves. Little do they know that the solution lies in learning to be, precisely, the links they are meant to be.

Chapter 3

To Disobey Is to Obey: The Effects of Contradictory Messages on the Link Child

The complex makeup of a Link child's disobedience produces confusion, frustration, and even rage in both parent and child. As we have seen, at their most benign, Link children may hide or run out of the room in order not to feel bombarded by the words and emotions of others; and at their most exasperating and terrible, they may throw tantrums, hurl accusations, or behave badly in other ways. Meanwhile, parents of Link children, who love them and are trying to be good parents, cannot understand why their children continually behave in these challenging and unpredictable ways. Because of their empathy, Link children know from very early on that their parents are good people and want the best for them. Therefore, they do not hate their parents, and assuming they are not being raised in a violent home environment, they are not at risk of becoming unusually manipulative people, thanks to their capacity for feeling guilt and regret. But also because of their tremendous and fearsome capacity to "know" what other people are feeling, even before others notice their own emotions, they can read the pain, resentment, dissatisfaction, envy, rage, and rivalry that reside in the private inner world of each parent and/or between the parents. They also read and feel their parents' fragility, vulnerability, and doubts. Finally, and perhaps most importantly, Link children read and internalize each

61

parent's values, goals, worldview, and culture, which, because they are in conflict with each other, create an upbringing characterized by contradictory messages that Links internalize as their own and that they must continually grapple with.

Link the horse's experience of the contradictions between his parents, which he first notices at the end of "The Shooting Stars" (Chapter 1 *Link*) in the conflictive, troubled (and therefore troubling) look that his parents exchange, is clear in his thoughts at the end of that chapter: "I wish I could make them both happy, but it's so hard to do two things that are the complete opposite of each other. I'm realizing that the world is much more complex than I thought." Link's struggle with contradictory messages from his parents plays out fully in Chapter 3, "Racehorse or Riding Horse?" Link is now an older, stronger horse—a strapping adolescent who is approaching young manhood. Link's father, Onyx, notices his son's skills as a racehorse very early in his childhood. He also notices Link's determination and desire to excel in any activity he undertakes and that if he cannot master something very quickly, his impatience with himself causes him to abandon it. His father thinks that to become a racehorse could be the best of Link's options as a profession and as an identity. He even uses language that will appeal to Link to push him to follow this path, inviting him to "play a game.... [Y]ou will be one of those shooting stars that you love so much and run as fast as you can." This way of enticing Link to run fast in front of the ranch owner increases Link's interest in his father's suggestion.

Link's mother, Amber, on the other hand, lets him know from the time he is very young that she is intent on his becoming a riding horse like her, a horse who is reliably gentle and approachable and who poses no threat to people, especially children. Link also responds to this suggestion enthusiastically, thinking he is pleasing both parents by wanting to be what they each want him to be.

Link's global empathy makes him feel, internalize, and embrace his father's desire for him to be the fastest horse and win races. For Onyx, Link's success as a racehorse would be a vicarious way of becoming a successful racehorse himself. But Onyx also wants this for Link because he genuinely desires the best for his son and wants him to feel proud as much as he himself wants to be a proud father. Link also feels, internalizes, and embraces his mother's desire for him to be a riding horse, as well as her potential happiness at knowing that she was a good mother who raised a good son, one who is caring, considerate, and gentle. That is, Link's parents want these things for him because he gives them signs that he can and sometimes wants to be both things. He incorporates the contradiction and does not want to commit to either option, which would make him feel forced into being a prisoner of just one identity.

The global empathy that Link cannot avoid feeling, then, results in two things: 1) It causes him to embrace the idea that he *is* a racehorse and that he will be successful, thereby making his father happy by satisfying the longing for recognition that he has felt since his youth; and 2) it compels him to embrace the idea that he *is* a riding horse and that he will be of service to the community, thereby feeling the positive feelings that his mother feels each time she helps someone or behaves selflessly in relation to others.

Link's behavior in the big race is key to understanding the catastrophe that conflicting demands cause for Link children. His father's desires and expectations have "programmed" Link to want to run fast and win. His mother's desires and expectations, however, have "programmed" him to want to be of service and help others. Sadly, these two different trainings, correct in and of themselves, were not intertwined with each other in a conflict-free setting. This is why, even though he is winning the race, in the moment that he sees Blue fall he turns around and runs to help him without hesitation, without pausing to think how this will affect his performance in the race. In the same impulsive way that he runs as fast as he can in the race because he enjoys the freedom the wind makes him feel when it caresses his body in motion, he suddenly and surprisingly stops to enjoy the sense of belonging and connection to another through the feeling of compassion that Blue's pain awakens in him. Two kinds of impulses are in play here: Link's own simultaneous need to feel free and independent and to feel connected to others *in addition to* his need to please both parents by embodying their conflicting desires.

When Link disappoints his father, the ranch owner, and everyone in the crowd who placed their trust in him and bet on him at the race, he is disobeying the rules of competition but obeying the rules of caring and compassion. He follows the rules of belonging to the community by exhibiting empathy and compassion for a fallen horse, but he does so in a situation in which he is supposed to follow the rules of being an individual who separates himself from the community by being competitive rather than empathetic and by using his unique skills to be "the best." Compassion is appropriate in a horse giving rides to children in a field—not in a horse trying to win a race at a racetrack.

Not only does Link disappoint his father and the spectators during the race when he stops to help Blue, he also later disappoints the young children and their parents by running too fast and scaring them, though he is just expressing his excitement at seeing so many children at the ranch. In this scene, the opposite occurs from what happens at the racetrack: He does not follow the rule of prioritizing others' needs over his desire to run fast. Instead, he obeys his deeper need for freedom to do what he feels his body wants to do by expressing his joy and excitement through running fast. This behavior is of course appropriate in a race, but it is not appropriate in a horse giving rides to children in a field, a situation in which his behavior must be in service of taking the best care of the children.

Link the horse, then, like all Link children, disobeys because he is too obedient. This paradox is precisely what confuses parents of Link children as well as the children themselves. In their erratic, changeable, contradictory, incomprehensible, challenging, and yes, *loving* behaviors, these children demonstrate their allegiance to the contradictory messages that they are exposed to. Link wants to be, can be, and knows he is an excellent racehorse. Link also wants to be, can be, and knows he is an excellent riding horse. But he does not understand "the rules of the game" of different situations so does not know that he is supposed to behave one way in one situation and a different, even opposite, way in another situation.

These two scenes in the story highlight two of the four key variables that help us understand how the complex and difficult relationship between parents and their Link children is created: 1) The children are born gifted in empathy, and 2) the messages (emotions, values, needs) that the children receive and internalize from the parents are very different and most of the time contradictory. Neither all children born with the gift of global empathy nor all children whose parents' ideas are in conflict with each other exhibit Link personality traits. It is the combination of both conditions that causes this particular style of vicious circle interaction between Link children and their parents.

Although Link children behave in ways that are difficult, inappropriate, exasperating, and even infuriating to parents and others around them, they are actually too obedient, too empathetic, and too sensitive—all of which causes them tremendous internal distress and suffering. They suffer for several reasons: 1) because they are feeling others' emotions of suffering and distress, 2) because they do not know they are feeling others' emotions due to not being able to distinguish between which emotions belong to them and which belong to others, and 3) because others perceive them as disobedient or "bad," although what they feel inside is a deep sadness that comes from feeling confused, feeling they have disappointed others, and feeling they have not behaved like they are supposed to. This last reason is clearly evident in the effects on Link of the reactions to his sudden, unexpected behaviors by the race spectators and, later, the parents and children who want a ride at the ranch. Link feels sad because he feels rejected, although he does not know what he has done wrong. Link children try to rid themselves of the feelings of sadness or anger that continually and, for them, inexplicably invade them due to the deep connection they have with the people around them, especially the ones they love, need, admire, and respect. They also want to make sense of the contradictory messages they receive from these loved ones.

It is helpful to think of the child's emotions as feeling to them like excess air that they must release, and sometimes they literally release "air" as they are struggling with the inner turmoil that they feel. The mother of a Link child asked me why her daughter, once again, was having trouble sleeping: "For several nights she's been sighing and sighing, exhibiting a profound distress, like an anguish that disrupts her breathing, but she isn't able to tell me what's going on inside her." I recalled my own mother, when I was an adolescent, raising my arms up high to help me breathe. I also recalled being in a private yoga class as an adult and feeling that I was suffocating because I could not get enough air into my lungs. When in desperation I asked the instructor to help me alleviate that feeling, he said sarcastically, "You're not going to suffocate, you're not going to die because you feel that you can't breathe." This made me angry, but I realized in that moment that the solution was not to "take in" more air but to "take out" air (anger) that I didn't know how to release, which I did by letting out a huge, noisy groan. This forceful expulsion of air allowed me to unblock and unleash the anger I was feeling, providing me with instant relief from the emotion that was suffocating me.

Often the only way Link children have of releasing the excess air they feel is inside them as a result of feeling the deep "negative" emotions of sadness, anger, frustration, and fear is through their shouting, anger, tantrums, and impassioned speeches about unfairness. Although disguised and hard to decipher, these are ways of externalizing their feelings of anguish, which are inscrutable even to them. As one Link child, Kara, told me, "I feel too much. What can I do to not suffer? How can I become less sensitive?" And my answer was, "Well, you try very hard to push everybody away from you.... With your rage and your constant complaining you are trying to suffer less. Is it working?" Her answer left me feeling stunned: "Rage is bad, but sadness is worse."

Link children, then, cannot avoid being disobedient. They do not disobey because they want to or merely to be rebellious, but because they construct their identities by knitting together their feelings, thoughts, behaviors, doubts, belief systems, and faith with all of the substance they absorb as a result of their global empathy skills.

What makes these children hard to care for and to accompany in their development? Their contradictions. The difficulty of knowing (deeply) who they are, what they want, what they need, how and when they need our presence, when and why they trust us, and when and why they reject us. They are the most generous and affectionate of children and at the same time the ones who feel themselves to be the least loving toward their parents when they are reacting rebelliously to what they perceive to be their parents' infringement upon their freedom. They are the most independent and adventurous and at the same time the most emotionally dependent and the most afraid, although this fear might appear disguised as picking a fight or throwing a tantrum. They are children who understand us down to the core of our being, but they are also children who condemn us for our deepest contradictions and incongruences.

The Case of Michelle

Perhaps the most dramatic situation that I have encountered profession-ally is the tremendous and desperate indecision of Michelle, a woman who feels bad but guilty when she "wins" and feels good but angry when she "loses."

Michelle grew up admiring her grandfather's strength, financial power, and ability to make people do what he wanted. At the same time, she admired her father's goodness, emotional sensitivity, and ability to make everyone around him feel good. But these were contradictory qualities, and because Michelle was so gifted with global empathy, they marked her way of being in the world as an infinite sum of unresolvable conflicts: Either she acted strong and felt bad and guilty, or she was good and felt weak and angry.

At the same time that she believed that all people are potentially dangerous and that she needed to be "bad" because bad people are the ones who run the world and know how to take care of themselves, she suffered because this way of thinking led her to feel that there was no place in the world for good people. There was no place in the world for her own generous, loving, sensitive, and caring "I," an essential part of her personality.

She would move from anger to guilt, then from guilt to pain, then pain to anger, then anger to success, then success to guilt, repeating the vicious circle she learned during childhood and with which she identified.

Parents of Links and Complementarity

As in the case of Michelle, the relationships and contradictory and confusing family dynamics and polar opposite roles of key family members, going back two generations or more, not only have an impact on Link children but are also *essential ingredients* in the formation of a Link child. Some people seek out life partners because of their similar values, cultures, languages, and interests. Others, including parents of Link children, look for difference and complementarity. People who are in committed relationships or marriages based on the pleasure of difference and the search for completion or wholeness through complementarity in the couple are also people who enjoy being exposed to constant change. They choose professions that require that they travel, change their place of residence, and move through different cultures; and the pleasure they receive comes from describing, experiencing, and improving their tremendous capacity for adaptation, flexibility, quickly learning the new rules of the game, and knowing how to play it like the "locals." But after the honeymoon period in the new place or new job or new relationship, what is different in the known, familiar, and habitual now takes on its own relevance and shows up as unexpected, undesirable, and uncontrollable inconveniences. Thus begins the period of anger, sadness, regret, and accusations: "This isn't what I thought it would be" or "This isn't what I was promised" or "I want to move back home."

The parents of Link children choose each other because they are different from each other and because they dazzle each other with mystery, newness, creativity, exoticism, and a seemingly desirable way of life. They seek complementarity, the richness of diversity, the thrill of the foreign and unknown, and new possibilities. The problem begins when controversies start to arise, when the differences no longer feel enriching but irritating, when the diversity confuses instead of helping to reveal the mysteries of life, and when the alternative values begin to be conflictive and threatening for the selfhood of each person in the couple.

The children born to this kind of couple grow up receiving each and every one of these diverse and contradictory messages from their parents. Not only are these messages too much information for them to organize in any coherent way in their developing brains, but they are also often delivered in the form of contradictory orders: "Don't pay attention to your dad because he's very out of touch" along with "Don't believe anything your mom says because she watches too much reality TV." Or "You must attend Mass every Sunday" at the same time as "Spirituality can be practiced privately, at home." Or "Mind your manners, and don't put your fingers in your mouth" alongside "It doesn't matter how you eat. Every culture has a different way of eating."

With the passage of time, the couple's irritation resulting from the misunderstandings takes up more space than the joy resulting from their previous harmonious relationship. The constant need to explain, justify, accuse, and apologize produces more aggressions, fights, negotiations, bad moods, and resentments that explode at the wrong time and in the wrong place. The experience of life as suffering then instills itself in the Link child, the parents, and often even the other children in the family. Only the Link children, however, incorporate so much information into their head. Only the Link children are porous sponges, organisms with no skin, stretching out all of their little dendrites, arms, looks, and desires to these parents whom they, in the first place, adore, and in the second place, dismiss. While they love their parents, they also reject them because they feel (even if they cannot articulate the feeling) that they cannot trust anything that the parents say: If there are so many truths, then no truth can be the absolute truth. This is because the ideas, teachings, and expectations that the parents impart to the children are born of a place of conflict and turmoil between the parents. To complicate matters further, Link children internalize their parents' conflict with each other, creating even more confusion and doubt about their own truths. Link children also internalize their parents' contradictory points of view, which causes distress for these porous, empathetic souls who are only trying to find a place where they can feel at peace.

Links' Connection to Their Parents

One of the most interesting exercises that I presented to my patients was asking them to imagine that they could feel their parents when they (the patients) were conceived. The responses of Link adults (as opposed to those patients who did not have the sparks of opposite flames as their origin) demonstrated, in the majority of cases, a double-sided narrative: a passionate, emotional encounter that was at the same time an important intellectual disconnect due to the love of one's own truth that people who hold opposite points of view cling to.

What always struck me in these patients was the strong presence of the emotional bond that they maintained with their parents, that is, the importance that their families of origin had in their daily lives, not necessarily the degree of satisfaction or wellbeing that this presence provided them. Even in individuals who were completely economically independent, lived at a considerable geographical distance, and had decided to break off ties with their family, the internal debate with these figures persisted: *I know you don't agree with me; I should have listened to you; thank goodness I didn't listen to you; I don't care what you think; why should your opinion matter to me; don't butt into my life....* These are the interior dialogues that are constantly hammering away inside the minds of Link adults.

Why this lingering parental influence? The answers to this were also consistent: *Their intentions were good. They couldn't have done anything else. They didn't know better. They also suffered a lot as children. I'm sure that they loved me. I was very difficult. I always behaved very well until I would explode when I felt that they had done something to me that was unfair.*

Inside this knot is precisely where we find one of the fundamental strands of the Link personality. They are obedient children—as much to the passion they feel toward their own truth as to the attraction they feel for what is different, mysterious, and unique. They also have a profound sense of loyalty to those who tried to take care of them. But because they are obedient, they are continually grappling with a conflict of loyalties related to trust. This creates yet another paradox: Because they partially trust both parents, they cannot fully trust either of them. And, as we have seen, if they obey one order, they disobey another. This predicament leads them to continually ask themselves, *Who am I most like? Who do I want to be like? How do I get out of this mess and figure out who I am?*

Chapter 4

"Nobody Gets Me": The Link Child's (Mis)Understanding of Self and World

Link children's tremendous creativity and curiosity are in part what impels them to move freely through their environments. They take uncalculated risks both by trying new things (to the point of transgressing boundaries imposed by others, as when Link the horse crosses the river without knowing how to swim) and by plunging into new friendships without adequately judging if these new relationships are good for them or not, if the "friends" will treat them well or not. Repeatedly experiencing painful, difficult situations that leave them feeling confused and distressed, Link children develop strategies—which often appear in the form of objectionable or difficult behaviors—for dealing with their feeling that they understand everyone (thanks to their global empathy), but that no one understands them.

A common strategy Link children employ to deal with this feeling of being misunderstood—and therefore often marginalized or shunned by peers—is to behave rebelliously and defiantly, opposing any advice or counsel from others, even though deep down inside they feel insecure, alone, and afraid. Link the horse exhibits this behavior repeatedly, including in "Toward the High Summit" and "Over the Mountain" (Chapters 4 and 5 of *Link and the Shooting Stars*). Before even trying to understand someone else's argument, he opposes it. For example, when Link, Pink, and Gray are outside playing and see a shooting star, Link shares with them his excitement. But as soon as Gray challenges his ideas, Link reacts with arrogance, insisting that he knows where the shooting stars land. He takes action by leaving the ranch and going to the mountain, rather than carefully deliberating the wisdom of this impulse. Link is so afraid of ending up doing what someone else wants that he ends up not even doing what he himself would like to do and what he *could* do if he were able to stop and think about the risks without his exaggerated anger masking the distressing doubts that are always with him.

Why do Link children react with such defiance, taking an oppositional stance (even at their own peril) rather than taking into consideration what the other person is saying? Why are they so afraid to do what others want them to do? Link children fear that if they are not "for" themselves, that is, if they are not pursuing what they want and defending their views or actions at all costs, then no one will be "for" them. They wonder who will take care of them and defend them. At the same time, they understand on some level that if they are *only* for themselves, then it says something negative about them, and they ask themselves, *What does that make me?* They also feel that if they are for themselves, others do not understand them the way they understand themselves; that is, others' perceptions of them do not correspond to who Links feel themselves to be, people whose selfhood is fraught with self-doubt, insecurity, and fear. This disconnect between who they feel they are on the inside and who others perceive them to be shows up in specific ways, depending on the family and the child. The particular relationship between the innate characteristics of the child and the characteristics of the family produces the different strategies for resolving this dissonance between existing for oneself and existing for others.

Rebelliousness is one principal strategy that Link children adopt and is the one that Link the horse exemplifies most often.

Gray is not only the voice of those peers who do not understand the Link child; he is also the voice of a judgmental community (like the spectators at the race in Chapter 3 of *Link*) and the representation of the cultural prejudices against what is unknown, different, novel, and bold—what is difficult to grasp through the accepted forms of knowledge. Because of Link's difference from what those who are more "mainstream" can comfortably accept, Gray can only understand Link as crazy, dangerous, and "bad."

Gray's attitude may aggravate Link's temperamental reactions, but Pink's idealization of Link is equally unhelpful. Pink is the voice of supportive, loving friends, though she is cautious when faced with Link's boldness. She wants to support him and not criticize him, but she is understandably afraid of his willful ways, his need to have his way (always a "different" way), and the captivating sway he has over her and others. Link is fully aware, though he does not want to acknowledge it, of his mistakes and his difficult ways, and he has to deal with the self-accusations arising from this awareness as well as being misunderstood, criticized, and rejected by others. Link children need feedback about what they are genuinely good at because their inner voice of self-criticism is so strong and they place very high demands on themselves. Pink's idealization of him in one way bolsters his confidence and in another way serves to incrementally increase his self-doubt and the feeling that he wins because he lies. This is because he knows that Pink is too credulous and naïve. So her idealizing him and telling him that everything he does is great does not actually help him.

At this point in the story, when Link and his cousins are discussing pursuing the shooting stars, Link begins to wonder about himself: "Can it be that I'm crazy? Maybe that's my problem: I don't know if I know things or if I simply imagine them." Until now, he had certain suspicions about being considered by his parents to be a difficult child. He was worried that he had indeed caused them pain—his father for having lost the race and his mother for having scared the children by running fast and for having put himself in danger by disobeying her order to not cross the river. Link felt guilty, but the sadness at not being understood (masked and acted out as defiance) was greater than any impulse he might have had to stop and reflect in order to try to comprehend the misunderstandings between him and others. Link exemplifies the difficulty Link children experience when trying to make themselves understood when they do not understand themselves, when they are not able to explain themselves or what is happening to them, what they are longing for, what is worrying them, or what they need to be able to calm down or feel at peace. This moment of self-questioning is important because Link begins to realize that the other person is not always to blame.

Equally important is that he also realizes that he is not always to blame. After all, he feels he *needs* to find where the shooting stars land. He *needs* to know if his search will have a happy ending. He *needs* to understand what he must have in order to satisfy his longing. Link believes that each shooting star will lead him to his destination, to a place where he can "land," stay put, feel at home, and feel at peace; where he can feel understood by others and by himself; where he can feel loved and lovable; and where he can love others and love himself. This is a place where he can give the best of himself, be seen as good, and feel himself to be good—as opposed to bad, which is how he has always felt—as a result of his actions and ideas. In short, he can exist for himself and for others at the same time—the ultimate place of feeling at ease in life.

Fundamentally, the shooting stars are a metaphor for the various activities that Link children and adults alike believe will transport them to the "landing place" of their identities. For Link children, these activities include inventing games and seeking out new adventures. For Link adults, these activities take the form of jobs, professions, responsibilities, places of residence, and social, professional, and intimate relationships. Links believe that when they "land," they will finally know who they are.

But when Gray questions the certainty with which Link affirms that he "knows" where the shooting stars land, it provokes doubt in Link about if following the path of the shooting stars will indeed lead to their landing place. The anguish that this questioning provokes in Link has to do with strong feelings he has lived with from a very young age related to an early awareness of finitude, death, loneliness, and futility (using Gordon Neufeld's terminology). Link has these feelings related to these notions without understanding them in words, without being able to "contain" them as concepts. In this search, Link observes, values, and is profoundly impacted by details that his cousins either do not notice or consider trivial, absurd, or bizarre. Link connects elements that belong to completely different realms, and often he does not know if what he thinks is just a figment of his imagination or if it is a brilliant observation that is not yet known to others. This uncertainty also extends to thinking that it could be either an extraordinary observation (or thought) or a dangerous one. Link the horse, like Link children, is not able to distinguish between the two. He also cannot explain how he reaches his conclusions.

Links and Evidential Thinking

Carlo Ginzburg's theory of the Evidential Paradigm can help us understand how Link the horse and Link children work to try to reach conclusions and understand reality. Evidential thinking is rooted in guessing the meaning of facts by putting together information that is gathered through reading signs. Ginzburg asserts that we can read and perceive reality not only through the sense of sight but also through the senses of smell, hearing, touch, and taste as well as kinesthetically. This way of perceiving reality guides us to what is less evident. We can learn to recognize the smallest signs, just as the hunter learned "to reconstruct the shapes and movements of his invisible prey from tracks on the ground, broken branches, excrement, tufts of hair, entangled feathers, stagnating odors. He learned to sniff out, record, interpret, and classify such infinitesimal traces as trails of spittle. He learned how to execute complex mental operations with lightning speed, in the depth of a forest or in a prairie with its hidden dangers."

Physicians use this methodology when they interpret the tiniest signs in the smell, color, posture, or any aspect of a patient in order to try to determine what kind of illness he or she is suffering from. Lawyers, detectives, and journalists also employ this way of thinking to try to solve a crime by putting signs or clues together to develop a plausible idea about who committed it, how, where, when, etc.

We can rely on the Evidential Paradigm as a way to think when and only when we accumulate enough information through multiple individual experiences, which allows us to create a pattern or patterns from the issue or the field in which these experiences are accumulated. This way of perceiving the world consists of establishing an existential experience, a kind of coincidence in just one point in which what the object is showing catches the attention of the subject that is observing it, thereby establishing a connection. We all have opportunities to use evidential thinking in our lives, though people in fields such as medicine, police investigation, and investigative journalism rely on it heavily in their work to organize what they observe into a pattern, creating a system that allows them to understand a particular reality.

Links, on the other hand, from the very beginning of their child-hood—before language, before acquiring a conceptual understanding about what they are exposed to—develop a kind of habit of knowing without thinking, learning without studying, grasping any situation without paying conscious attention to the details or "clues" of the situation. For example, they may plunge into an activity like a new sport, thinking that they understand it because they see other children running around a field and believe that they also know how to play the sport because they know how to run fast. They are, therefore, intuiting that they know the sport based on the signs they see, but their reading of the clues, or signs, is faulty because they are not paying attention to other crucial signs like the way some players are running in a certain direction and others are running in another; or that all the players on the field have particular, strategic relationships to each other; or that there is a goal beyond that of just running fast.

In short, Link children fail in their use of evidential thinking because they act based on the signs they see without verifying their reading of them or organizing the information into a map or system of patterns based on their experiences of trial and error. Therefore, they do not accumulate the necessary information to know when they should or should not follow a sign or intuition. Yet they behave as if they are good at evidential thinking because they "feel" or "know" that they can do something.

Additionally, they gather other information they use through global empathy, their extraordinary ability to notice and interpret signs that are imperceptible to the majority of children—signs that include emotions that belong to those around them but that Links experience as their own (the defining characteristic of global empathy). Because this way of processing reality is highly intuitive and "fast" rather than systematic and "slow," Link children find it difficult to take the time that is needed to fully understand a game, task, assignment, or social situation. The ability to use evidential thinking well is the skill that, once it is acquired, will allow Link children to order the chaos that results from having multiple desires and multiple and sometimes contradictory role models; and it will eventually allow them to master a field of knowledge. Learning how to use evidential thinking skillfully will also allow them to discover or create their own subjectivity, or selfhood, in a harmonious way.

If they do not learn how to use this skill well, however, they will not be able to understand their own subjectivity. The fear of not being able to demonstrate that their guess could be a good explanation about a fact or situation and the need to feel some certainty push them toward impatience and lack of rigor. Sometimes they try to convince themselves that they have thoroughly checked the information that comes from the signs and the conclusions that they have reached, even though in the back of their mind, they know that the doubts they have are more related to the lack of rigor in their research processes than to the unavoidable insecurities that come from evidential thinking.

The only thing that will give their ideas and beliefs credibility is the rigorous systematization of the constant and repetitive appearance of effects resulting from specific phenomena; in other words, learning to use evidential thinking well. So it is very important for Link children to take the time and make the effort to tolerate their doubts, which are unavoidable in this paradigm of thought. They have to determine whether or not these doubts are due to a lack of rigorous systematization, that is, whether they are making reasonable conjectures or imagining improbable realities. With this way of perceiving and thinking it is almost impossible not to feel fear until "reality," or what actually takes place in the external world, proves that their guesses were correct, making them feel that they were not crazy or liars.

A corollary to the feeling of fear is the feeling of guilt: If someone does not understand them immediately, Links feel it is their fault, that they have done or said something wrong. They feel at a loss to clearly and convincingly explain their ideas and understandings of things because, more often than not, they are the results of intuitive processes rather than the results of evidential or logical thinking. When Links make mistakes, they feel they lack the tools or ability to validate their intuitions and nonlinear ways of thinking. Their attempts to compensate for this lack can often manifest as rage, vehemence, manipulation, exaggeration, and other challenging behaviors.

Asking for Help and the Need for Reality Checks

One of the most difficult things that Link children must live with is the inability to ask for help, to acknowledge their fears, to accept being taken care of, to recognize their limitations, and to face their vulnerabilities. To make matters worse, sometimes the parents themselves do not know that they know what to do to calm their children, because they are so frustrated or uncertain about how to treat the tantrums or the chaos or the oppositional behavior, that they cannot connect with their own inner wisdom and trust themselves to be trustworthy for their children. If parents are confident in themselves as parents as well as in their children, and if they have faith, first, that they will indeed learn to understand what their children are asking for and what they need and, second, that they are going to learn to make themselves understood by their children, they can help their Link children by doing what Ms. Firefly does with Link the horse: reassuring them that they are really good while also encouraging them to improve their skills. They must not, however, point

NO ONE IS TO BLAME

out what they are bad at because the anguish these children feel about what is imperfect or incomplete in them is unbearable for them. Parents will of course not always be able to give their children exactly what they are asking for, but through their own learning process as parents, they will come to know how to give their children what they *need* to feel calmer and more at peace. In other words, what the Link child asks for is not always what they need, and not giving the child what they ask for is not the same thing as not giving them what they need.

Ms. Firefly, although she appears just briefly in the story, provides a useful, positive example of how parents can give their Link child what they need in a particular moment. She also provides an important counterpoint to the reactions of both Gray and Pink to being lost in the forest as they make their way to the mountain. Gray and Pink, expressing a combination of fear, support, and skepticism in their different ways, only serve to spur Link on in his reckless pursuit of his goal. Ms. Firefly, however, provides a more meaningful and trustworthy reality check for Link, delivered in one of the young horse's most important moments of disillusion: When she informs Link in her straightforward, no-nonsense way that he cannot fly because he is a horse, Link actually believes her, and he understands that the certainty he felt his entire life about being able to fly was a product of his powerful imagination. Because she is, by definition, a creature who flies, her knowledge, wisdom, and perspective resonate with Link. He, like Link children, can hear this kind of truth if the adult who says it really knows what she is talking about. The danger he put himself in when he crossed the river, for example, might have been avoided if it had been his Uncle Indigo rather than his mother admonishing him to not cross. This is because Link recognizes his uncle as an expert in adventures and, therefore, someone who would know whether or not it would be a good idea for inexperienced Link to try to swim across. Because he does not think of his mother as this kind of expert, however, he feels he does not need to heed her warnings, seeming to dismiss them as unnecessary, bothersome, and overly cautious, thus giving himself license (even unconsciously) to ignore them.

While Ms. Firefly is the voice of realism and disillusion for Link, she also provides a crucial double confirmation for him. First, his conversation with her proves to skeptical Gray that he really can understand other languages. Link's multilingual ability in the story symbolizes the powerful connections and understandings that Link children naturally feel that allow them to easily grasp and even assimilate different kinds of emotions, systems, values, structures, games, and tasks. Second, their conversation helps Link to begin to understand that he is not each and every one of these emotions, systems, etc. Just as Link the horse now accepts that, while he can run very fast, he does not, in fact, know how to fly because he does not have the kind of body that would allow him to do that, Link children need to face that being good at understanding something is not the same as "owning" or "being" this knowledge. Many musicians, for example, confess that their ease with playing a melody by ear prevents them from learning how to read and write music, which limits their growth potential in their chosen field. Likewise, Link children feel they understand, connect with, and intuit many different things, but their lack of *knowledge* about these things—how they work, what they are made of, what the rules are—lead time and time again to disappointment, guilt, and, in the most extreme cases, danger. The only possible way to have the freedom to create new rules is by knowing when, how, and why to break the existing rules, which you can only do if you understand these rules in the first place. If not, you will become a prisoner of your own freedom.

Ms. Firefly, then, as many other beings whom Link will meet along his journey to find where the shooting stars land, is an important influence during his brief interaction with her, and their conversation is a crucial stepping stone in his search for his own truth. It is helpful to summarize the steps he has taken so far in this search:

First, Link really believes that the shooting stars land on the other side of the mountain and wants to impose this belief on everyone around him. This irritates Gray, just as this kind of insistent, obstinate behavior irritates the parents and peers of Link children. The need to find safety, peace, and belonging is so powerful that in order to hide the doubts that they have about themselves and life in general, Links develop a counterproductive stubbornness to avoid being contaminated by the doubts that others have about them.

Second, when Link realizes that he is lost in the forest, he asks for advice. Link's being lost represents those moments when Link children realize that they do not know how to get out of a very complicated situation into which they have put themselves in defiance of the suggestions, recommendations, and even direct orders from their parents. Asking Ms. Firefly for help indicates Link's progress on the road to being able to more consistently trust adults to help him. This is a beautiful and necessary ability because not only do Links need to learn how to determine whom they can ask for help, they also need to have conversations with adults who do not judge or label them in order to learn to trust adults and accept themselves. The more of these honest but nonjudgmental conversations that Link children have with adults, the more skill they develop in choosing appropriate mentors and knowing whom to trust and whom not to trust. These conversations also lead them to a place where they can accept their failures without accusing themselves of being the worst children in the world.

Third, after the information Link receives from Ms. Firefly, he recuperates some of his confidence because he finds himself, once again, using his multiple internal resources and abilities to confront problems and solve mysteries. His heretofore hidden, unexpressed fear and doubt are now mixed with renewed enthusiasm. However, he still refuses to acknowledge in front of Gray that he was lost, and he is not yet ready or able to determine when, where, and in what situations he is actually more creative, capable, or powerful than his peers and when he is not.

Throughout the story, Link has been accumulating failures: while attempting to cross the river, while running the race, while serving as a riding horse, and now, his latest failure, getting lost on the way to the mountain. So, because he is not able to distinguish between what he really knows as opposed to what he only guesses at or, worse, imagines, he does not feel secure enough to share in the decision-making process concerning the best path to take with Gray and Pink. Instead, he assumes the authoritarian position, appointing himself the sole decision-maker so that he will be the only one responsible for the results of his action. He needs to win, to triumph, to show his cousins, his family, and the world that he is not crazy. For Link the horse, as well as for Link children, things have to be their way or no way. Link even recognizes this in a moment of self-reflection at the end of the chapter, saying to himself, "Oh, you are so stubborn, why don't you learn? You know this is a risky decision, but as usual, it has to be your way!"

The need to have things be their way begs the following question, however, which is part of the many dilemmas that Link children face: How can they become an authority in some fields without behaving like an authoritarian in all fields?

Chapter 5

Complex Choreographies: The Link Child's Dance between Desire and Guilt

Link's overly-confident insistence at the end of "Toward the High Summit" (Chapter 4) that he and his cousins take the "most exciting" path to the top of the mountain leads to yet another failure—the dangerous rockslide that physically injures Gray, emotionally injures Pink, and terrifies all of them. Gray, embodying the voice of the admonishing, judgmental, fearful, angry parent, tries to dissuade Link from what is clearly a bad idea—taking the steep, quicker path rather than the safe, slower path. And, like parents sometimes do, both Pink and Gray give in to Link's desire and insistence on taking the steep path because they are emotionally exhausted. Once the rockslide disaster occurs, they call Link a "bad horse."

As in the adventure of the dangerous river crossing, when Link did not heed his mother's warnings, here Link is once again proven wrong. His way was *not* the best way—far from it. He has again put himself in the position of being accused of being the crazy, weird, and bad horse, which is precisely the position or identity he is trying to avoid. The distressing inner conflict between too much confidence and too many insecurities, however, keeps him locked inside a pattern of behaving boldly and projecting great confidence, while privately feeling the anguish of deep insecurity and self-doubt. Not being able to openly share his doubts makes his learning process and correcting his course difficult.

Turning Points Rooted in Suffering, Guilt, and Empathy

The rockslide is a turning point in Link's life because for the first time he must directly confront the suffering that he has caused others, even though it was unintentional. Link children also experience these kinds of turning points, when their capacity for empathy allows them to feel another's suffering and, as in the case of the rockslide and Gray's injury, when they cannot deny the evidence of the suffering they have caused another person.

When Link experiences dangerous or uncomfortable situations (crossing the river, losing the race, being rejected by the children when he is trying to give them rides) he shows that these painful experiences and encounters bother him by expressing anger and being confrontational or by refusing to talk and walking away in order to try to understand the frustration, confusion, and distress he feels when others accuse him of having done something wrong. Link children may exhibit these emotions and behaviors—often through more exaggerated reactions—but they may just as easily behave outwardly as if these things don't bother them, although deep-down the opinion of others affects them profoundly. In fact, "I don't care" is very frequent in the speech of Link children. They care so much about their relationships with others, the impact that they can make in the world, and the meaning of their life, that in order to avoid pain when they don't achieve the perfection or sense of wholeness and completeness that they are looking for, they master the defense mechanism of indifference, ennui, or boredom. This protects them from suffering but also paralyzes them and shuts down the process of doing what it takes to realize their desires.

The many and varied interests of Link children also allow them to move easily away from experiences of frustration and suffering because they always operate under the illusion that the next adventure will bring "happiness." Recalling the well-known fable "The Fox and the Grapes," we can think of the fox as exhibiting the typical Link child behavior of making an "expert" decision about something that is really a dismissal and a refusal to hold oneself accountable for things that go wrong. In the fox's case, he decides to stop trying to reach the grapes, not because they are too high but because they "aren't worth the effort," being, according to him, sour and unripe. Rather than admit defeat, the fox rejects them altogether, criticizing, or "blaming," the grapes. Similarly, Link children move on from challenging or disappointing situations or "failures" by dismissing them as unimportant, distancing themselves from the unhappy consequences, and even blaming others for what goes wrong. What they feel deep inside, however, is self-doubt, insecurity, and guilt.

Link children can only discover how much suffering they themselves experience with this protective (and restrictive) defense mechanism, akin to that of a jailor-protector, when those they love suffer because of something they do or fail to do. Then they react by trying desperately to remain calm in order to ease their own pain and suffering when they feel in their own body (through their extreme capacity for global empathy) another's suffering.

Before the rockslide seriously injures Gray, Link cannot understand why others would think of him as a dangerous, crazy, troublemaking horse. When the rockslide occurs, however, resulting in extreme fear and bodily harm to his cousin, it confirms for him his worst suspicions: that he is, indeed, a bad and dangerous horse because he is capable of making other beings suffer. He suffers, then, not only because he deeply empathizes but also because the suffering he causes is unintentional and, in fact, is the result of what he feels to be his *good* intentions—his innocent need and desire to explore, discover, and understand who he really is, to seek out and find his own truth. He does not intend to be mean or to hurt others while fulfilling his own needs.

Link fully understands and accepts that his decision resulted in his peers being involved in an accident. Holding himself responsible, he feels compelled to get them out of there, making sure to find a solution in the form of a rescue. When Link meets Blue for the first time during the race, Link can exhibit his good and compassionate instincts in an extreme manifestation of global empathy in a situation in which he has not only caused no harm but has tried to help at the expense of his own success. Meeting up with Blue and his owner again after the dangerous rockslide reminds Link that his generous behavior with Blue during the race was good and right. This also allows him to feel that he can make up for his mistake by rescuing Pink and Gray. Link understands that he is not just a troublemaker but that he can also be a problem solver.

Nevertheless, emotionally he is still a mess. How to reconcile these two very different parts of himself, the one that brings pain and the one that brings joy? How to use his courage and curiosity and creativity to promote life rather than to cause destruction? These questions are precisely what propels Link to decide to take charge of his life and assume responsibility for his actions, which he feels he can only do by removing himself from his community. Link's decision to take the steep, less traveled path up the mountain is a metaphor for his life's journey: It will not be an easy or tame journey, but one full of risk, hard decisions, responsibility, doubt, and challenging negotiations.

Responding to Risky Behaviors

Although the risky, defiant decisions to leave the confines of the ranch and choose the steepest, most difficult path up the mountain occur in the absence of Link's parents or any adult, Link's ultimate reaction to the resulting tragedy of the rockslide—deciding to leave the safety of his family and community—points to a complex dynamic between Link children and their parents. The head-butting that Link engages in with Gray revives a fear that he has, just as Link children do, that his parents will not allow him to do what he wants. For Link children, this relates to their thinking and feeling that their parents do not understand their musings, desires, and, by extension, them. This feeling that their parents do not understand or "get" them causes them to decide (perhaps unconsciously) that they cannot trust their parents. So they act on their own desires without heeding the advice of others. This impulsiveness and lack of trust is a defense mechanism that allows them to disregard and repress their own concerns, doubts, and insecurities.

Furthermore, Link children "sniff out" the concerns, doubts, and insecurities of their parents. This makes the parents feel that they are not capable of helping their children calm their own doubts and insecurities. Although it is the children who are not taking care of themselves, they accuse their parents of not taking care of them well. Parents then react with fear at not knowing how to handle or take care of their uncontrollable, risk-taking children, and at times with rage due to both the frustration of not knowing how to deal with the accusations hurled at them and the sadness of seeing their child suffer and feeling themselves powerless to help them. This dynamic escalates easily into shouting matches between parent and child that serve only to throw gasoline on the fire. Kara's feeling that "Rage is bad, but sadness is worse" aptly captures the feelings of parents of Link children as well as those of Links themselves.

One result of this complex and fraught parent-child dynamic is that instead of feeling themselves to be the proud parents of a unique child, they end up being the ashamed parents of a difficult-different-untamable-uncivilized child. Again, this is nobody's fault—neither the child's nor the parents'. No one is to blame.

Donald Winnicott, the extraordinary pediatrician and psychoanalyst, asserts that to be good parents or good therapists we not only depend on ourselves but also on the children or patients that help us to be so. This is not to unburden ourselves of our responsibilities as caretakers but to allow us to be more patient and compassionate with ourselves and to allow ourselves more creativity in our attempts to be "good-enough" parents of "difficult" children. In this way we can teach them to be more patient and tolerant with themselves and their own frustrations during their learning processes.

We need to let Link children know from a very young age that their tremendous capacity for empathy allows them to anticipate and understand very quickly what other people need. We need to also let them know that they might not understand what they themselves need. Parents can help their Link child to distinguish between what her empathy allows her to understand about what another person wants or needs and what she is and is not capable of doing to satisfy the other's wants and needs. They can help her understand her own desires (making others happy, helping others satisfy their wants and needs) without transforming these legitimate, loving desires into obligations or enormous responsibilities beyond what she is actually capable of doing for others.

The case of Thomas illustrates this internal conflict. After an argument with his father rooted in wanting to do something that his father does not want him to do, Thomas looks deeply into his father's eyes and says, "Daddy, your peace is my peace." The father responds by saying, "Your peace is my peace." This is precisely the Holy Grail for Link children: how to be what their contradictory parents want them to be, or in other words, how to resolve the cognitive dissonance that has inhabited their emotions and beliefs since birth due to the circumstances they were born into (being exposed to different and oftentimes opposing values and worldviews) and the condition of being global empaths.

Artists, discoverers, pioneers, and scientists imagine a work of art, a cure for an illness, a faraway continent, or a solution to an unresolved problem. They dedicate much work, practice, and tolerance of failure and frustration in their various processes or searches. Link children, these little seekers of their own truths, also imagine a final result, a happy ending to their ideas—finally being good and lovable for themselves and for others at the same time. But they cannot tolerate the frustration and work that this process entails. Parents can help them believe in themselves and their feelings of goodness so that they can learn to tolerate the inevitable mistakes along the way. They can provide them with the knowledge, tools, and space to experiment without risk so that they can make their ideas concrete or develop new, more feasible or appropriate ideas that might arise in their "investigations."

"What an interesting idea! Let's try it out and see what happens." This is a key response to gaining the respect and trust of Link children. Legitimizing their intuitions and transforming them into controllable experiments takes them out of risky or dangerous situations and allows them to get excited by the pleasure of discovery and learning. Of course, as with Link the horse, parents are not physically present in every situation, especially as children get older, more independent, and more influenced by their peers. It is important, therefore, for parents to help their Link children understand that though they may feel that what they want to do is their own desire and that they are making a certain decision because they want to, they are nevertheless influenced by many external factors. Whether this influence manifests as overt peer pressure, worry about what others will think of them, the desire to belong, or the need for attention, Link children benefit from parents continually working with them to help them understand how and why they make the decisions they make, helping them balance their need for excitement, novelty, and adventure with their need—often less evident but no less profound—for calm, routine, and protection. With this consistent, patient work, Link children over time will be able to take calculated risks, approaching situations with more forethought and caution instead of acting on impulse and immediate desire and gratification alone.

"Badness" and Paranoid Guilt

Why does the issue of badness or guilt appear in such a pronounced way in the life of Link children? Because the innate emotions that we are born with can be boiled down to two: pleasure and displeasure. (See Antonio Damasio.) Babies feel pleasure when their basic needs are taken care of and displeasure when they are not. They seek out pleasure and try to avoid displeasure. Displeasure sets off the sensation of feeling attacked and the attendant inherent defenses: fight, flight, or freeze.

Babies born with a superior capacity for empathy feel attacked when they feel as their own and in their own bodies the displeasure that their caregivers might be feeling as they take care of them. This causes these highly sensitive children to react dramatically, openly displaying the feeling of lack of protection, of displeasure in the face of the tiniest error or mistake that their parents make. The parents, then, react with equally dramatic feelings of displeasure, fear, and the need to protect themselves as they grapple with the sensations of fight (*Why do I have a child who is so hard to calm down?*), flight (*I can't do this. I'm useless. I'm not good enough.*), or freeze (*I'm paralyzed. I have no idea what to do.*).

The issue of "badness" takes hold very early, too early, in the sponge-like brains of these children who are able to feel the anger of another person as if it were their own. Upon feeling bad because they feel invaded by the other's emotion of anger, rage, or displeasure, they feel they are bad people. And if they feel themselves to be bad, they "read" and feel the situation to be a threatening and dangerous one, which causes them to feel fear, though they do not know exactly what they are afraid of: Who is the enemy? Where is the danger? How can I know how to take care of myself and what to protect myself from?

This feeling is what León Grinberg calls *paranoid guilt*. He describes it as a diffuse fear, a feeling of being accused, of holding oneself responsible for accusations, without being able or knowing how to detect exactly what the mistake or harm was that was inflicted. It necessitates being on "high alert," having to decide, upon being attacked or accused, whether one should accuse someone else of being worse or choose among fight, flight, or freeze. Unfortunately, this feeling creates a state of permanent stress, with the attendant physical complications due to the constant exposure to the hormones (primarily cortisol) that are required to be able to confront danger.

After the rockslide, for the first time in the story Link manages to get himself out of the vicious cycle of strong will – failure – guilt – fear – self-incrimination. Though it is not caused by Link, the rockslide accident, concrete and real, is sufficiently dramatic to make him stop and think about what the cost to others has been for being the way he is and for being who he wants to be; that is, not what others want him to be in order to love him but who and how he needs to be in order to love himself. In this critical moment of reflection, he is able to put aside the anger he feels about not being able to do what he believes is best for himself as well as the fear of being accused of being bad for always wanting to do the things he wants to do, in the way he wants to do them.

Letting go of the impulse to fight, however, in order to grapple instead with the sadness and anguish that come during these intense and difficult moments of reflection is not easy for Link children.

Link, then, while battling with the fear, uncertainty, and sadness about the failure of this adventure, decides he must leave his family and his community. Even Pink's affectionate and supportive words cannot change his mind. This solitude is different from the one he sought after the near-drowning incident with his mother and uncle, when he needed to separate himself from them in order to not continue fighting once he realized his mother was right, though he was still not willing or able to acknowledge his error. By contrast, after the rockslide, admitting, or "owning," his error calms him down. He takes responsibility for the undesired and unintended consequences of his actions and chooses to suffer alone the inevitable frustrations that his faulty method of trial and error, or of evidential thinking, has brought to his life. He does this, significantly, without blaming anyone, without fighting with anyone, and without punishing himself by becoming paralyzed or giving up his search.

Links' Need to Find Their Truth

The sadness, the sense of futility, emptiness, and meaninglessness that Link (just like Link children) feels when, once again, he does not find what he is seeking—the place where the shooting stars land—is devastating. Link knows that his mother would not be able to handle seeing him suffer so much and that she would offer him words of consolation. She would say to him, "It wasn't your fault. It was an accident. See, it's better to stay home and play the games the others are playing. Don't worry, I still love you." But her words would not help him because he does not love himself. He knows what his role in the accident was, and he knows that his stubbornness about not wanting to consider or adopt Gray's opinion about which path to take to the top of the mountain put him in a position of being, although not directly responsible for Gray's injury, open to accusation by others (and by himself), given that he was the protagonist in this scenario and, like always, the troublemaker. He also knows that his mother's advice to stay home and play the games that the others play is not possible for him to follow. He knows himself well enough to know that he will not be able to play the games that the others play for long without feeling the need to invent his own game.

To be a Link child is very difficult for the child—as much as having a Link child is for the parents. Link children signify a rupture: They are the product of a unique and creative encounter of two people who chose each other because of their differences, their complementarity. But as children they do not know how to harmonize those differences into a successful whole, into a being who feels at ease in the world. Like Link the horse, Link children must strive to find and become the shooting star that they feel they are meant to be, the one that does not burn up in the atmosphere of reality but that lands on earth successfully, like a meteorite—intact and fully itself.

Link begins to tolerate his existential loneliness: He begins to accept that he is not and will never be a full-fledged racehorse like his father or a full-fledged riding horse like his mother. He accepts that he can count on the loving gaze of his grandmother but that he does not have her by his side in his daily life; that while Pink loves him a lot, she cannot help him make decisions because she lacks the necessary information to do so, thus obliging him to take charge of his own destiny.

It is only then, in spite of fear, sadness, anguish, uncertainty, and loneliness, that he feels cleansed. Now it is just he and his destiny. Now it is just he and his search for where the shooting stars land, where he believes that he will find the place and the life where who he wants to be is also who others want him to be, where he will not have to debate within himself between being bad for only caring about himself and satisfying his own desires and feeling that he is a victim for only caring about and satisfying the desires of others.

He *needs* to believe that this place exists because if he cannot lose himself in a project or a goal—something that will create meaning in his life—he falls into depression and despair: Why live? Who am I? What is the meaning of life? Where do I fit in? Where can I feel a sense of belonging that makes me feel that others see me as I am?

This fervent belief does not come without doubts, but they are not doubts that arise from an agnostic, atheistic, or nihilistic way of thinking. They are the doubts of someone who really wants to believe in a truth that he feels is *the* truth—a truth that is infinite and immutable, a truth that is capable of grounding and supporting him and others without making him feel crazy, weird, or like he does not belong to his own family or community.

He has to find this place, this truth. Not being completely for himself and not being completely for others is to live in limbo. He must get to the place where he finds the bonds of reciprocity—where taking care of himself, taking care of others, and allowing himself to be taken care of by others are mutually beneficial and enriching.

Kara again provides a helpful real-life example of the longing that Link children have for self-understanding. In a moment when she was able to set aside a "fight" response, she wrote this song:

"In the autumn when the oak leaves turn,
I will set foot in the unknown.
In the autumn when the oak leaves turn,
I will throw the wood that is fit to burn.

In the autumn when the oak leaves turn,
I will learn and yearn.
In the autumn when the oak leaves turn,
I will play all day."

Link, Kara, Thomas, and all Link children know that they must continue playing in order to understand themselves, that they need to explore the unknown inside themselves, carefully choosing the fire where they will burn the leaves of the stages they will pass through in their moments of evolving, in order to not burn themselves or others in their search for who they are, their truth, and a sense of belonging.

In the case of Link, as with so many Link children when they become young adults, it is clear to him that he must leave. After the devastating mountain adventure, he says to himself: "You will find a place where you can be who you are and where your goodness will shine through and you don't hurt anybody. Just be brave, be patient! You are a seeker! And now it's time to continue your journey."

So that is precisely what he does—alone, uncertain, afraid, but determined.

Chapter 6

"Who Am I?": The Link Child's Search for Meaning and Belonging

But still I venture, stars, to learn,
If only for some peace of mind,
Discounting my dark birth, what kind
Of crime could warrant in return
A punishment as fierce and stern
As this I live, a living hell?
Weren't all the others born as well?
If all came in the world this way,
What sort of privilege had they
I'll never savor in this cell?

Spanish playwright and poet Pedro Calderón de la Barca wrote these words for his character Segismundo in 1635 in the most famous Spanish play of the seventeenth century, *Life Is a Dream*, a philosophical allegory about the human condition and the mystery of life.

Almost four centuries later, in *Link and the Shooting Stars*, Link the horse begins to ask himself what he is looking for, what makes him different from his cousins. Why is he is unable to feel calm and at peace where he is? Why does he continually experience an unrelenting anguish, which he feels as an emotional and physical weight that will not let go, that compels him to begin to seek and to keep on seeking?

Ruth, a ten-year-old Link child, is in distress because for several nights she is unable to sleep, sighing and feeling an anguish that interferes with her breathing. She cries out to her mother for help, but she does not know and cannot explain what is wrong.

Of course, neither Ruth nor Link have read Calderón. Yet they are asking themselves the same question as Segismundo: Why can't they live and be like everybody else, without asking themselves so many questions, without having so many convictions they feel they must obey, and without having to deal with so many doubts? Part of the answer is that Ruth, Link, and Segismundo are not like everyone else. They and others like them are incapable of *not* wondering about the meaning of life, the meaning of their own lives, and about life itself. Why was I born, and not others? What if I was *not* meant to be born, but others were? Who am I, among all the people that I think I am? Who am I, among all the people that others believe me to be? Am I me, or am I a dream, just the product of the desire of those who engendered me? Am I able to live just for myself, or do I need to fulfill a mission? Yes, that's it: I was born because I have a mission. I need to know what that is. I need to run away and look for it. I need to find it.

In his wonderful book *Learning to Live: A User's Manual*, Luc Ferry discusses the two great models that human beings use to overcome the fear of death that the awareness of the finite nature of time and space gives us. The first is religion and the practice of faith, that is, believing in a superior being that protects us, takes care of us, punishes us, and consoles us. The second is philosophy, which frees us from submitting to a truth that is dictated from the outside, though it leaves us alone as we struggle with doubts, questioning, and the responsibility for finding and living with our own answers.

Both religion and philosophy are based on the premise that all human beings feel fear when confronted with the unknown, the certainty of death, the possibility of nothingness. Links, however, feel deeply from a very early age the finiteness of life, a lack or emptiness, paradoxically even when they are experiencing joy, those moments when they feel most alive and "happy." This prevents them from fully enjoying the present moment because it is always tinged with the specter of death, emptiness, nothingness.

Some people, in spite of being different from each other in terms of age, social class, family circumstance, cultural and linguistic inheritance, and/or place of birth, share in common an inescapable, urgent, and overwhelming need to question the meaning of life and the meaning of their own lives in the world. They also have in common that they do not find the longed-for answer in believing or trusting in the benevolence of a superior being or in the "diabolical" philosophical skepticism that Ferry describes that incites a solitary arrogance on the path of those who are always, systematically and as a matter of course, doubting and questioning. These people, then, opt for neither religion nor philosophy, but the complete opposite. That is, they do not believe, although they want to believe—but only in their own truths, in truths that they trust they will reach as long as they keep looking.

For Link adults, questions about the meaning of life, the inevitability of death, immanence, and transcendence in their daily lives can take hold of them with disturbing intensity, especially in old age. Other adults, regardless of their age, do not wonder about these things at all. For Link children, these questions reside in their bodies as physical sensations and in emotions that they cannot describe in words. Adult Links who do not find relief for the metaphysical anguish that both provokes and is provoked by the awareness of the presence of death in life and of the limits of time and space in human relationships end up experiencing this anguish as an ever-present anxiety. Anxiety is easier to understand than metaphysical anguish and can often be resolved with medication and/or different kinds of therapy. That is not necessarily the case, however, for the underlying metaphysical anguish.

As outlined in the Introduction, in my clinical experience I discovered four common circumstances in the lived experience of adult Links:

1. They have an extreme capacity for empathy.
2. They are exposed to very different and often contradictory values and points of view (feelings, goals, ethics, aesthetics, thoughts, and beliefs).
3. They know that their parents are "good people," and they also know, even if they do not *feel*, that their parents love them.
4. The circumstances of their birth or infancy were unusual, or there was some trauma or major transition in the family around the time of birth, during infancy, or in early childhood that caused them to experience, very early on, the finitude of time and space.

Many times, parents and other adult caregivers do not recognize these early traumas or unusual circumstances as relevant to the emotional development of their children. Yet these experiences can invade the emotional spectrum of the infant or young child, provoking a sense of danger that is incomprehensible, indescribable, and intangible. Therefore, in addition to going through the inevitable trauma of birth, an experience that is shared by all human beings upon being forced to leave the uterine paradise, Link individuals experience the entry into this world as even more dangerous. A rupture, such as an event involving illness, death, loss, or threat, inserts itself in the supposed family paradise (which the child finds in the protective embrace of his parents), exacerbating what is already in and of itself a difficult entry process into life and, at the same time, death.

A mother who is in a state of mourning the death of a loved one while she is pregnant, a father who has lost his job and finds himself having to confront the fear of not being able to adequately provide for his family, the process of relocating to another state or country, experiencing for the first time new and different languages, cultures, and previously unknown geographies—these are all examples of rupture, of irreversible and irreparable changes in circumstances that profoundly affect the Link child. Rupture signifies entry into a place of hopelessness, lack of faith, and diffuse fear that does not have a clearly identifiable threatening object as its cause, as well as bodily sensations that are the manifestation of the feelings of others that the infant absorbs without even her own parents or family members realizing that this is happening. Because of this experience of rupture, the feeling of alienation becomes an integral part of the child's subjectivity. The experience of Adam and Eve is repeated: they are expelled from their Eden paradise and abandoned to their own free will. Again, a key necessary condition for Link children to feel so affected by situations and experiences that are rooted in rupture is their capacity for global empathy.

Links as Seekers

In addition to causing metaphysical anguish in Links, rupture also provokes an incessant, almost compulsive need to seek relief—to find what will fill the sensation of emptiness, of the black hole, of existential loneliness. In short, Links are compelled to search for the meaning of life.

Daniel Boorstin describes the history of humanity using the following categories:

1. **The Discoverers**—These are people who opened up new horizons at the limits of knowledge, motivated by the desire to know, by curiosity accompanied by courage that pushes them to venture forth into unknown territories, into *terra incognita* in different realms of knowledge.
2. **The Creators**—These people are those who made the world more beautiful and life more rich by continually and systematically using their imagination, by adorning the world with experiences and objects (like literary and artistic creations and inventions in many different fields) that do not exist until the moment of their creation or invention.
3. **The Seekers**—These are people who decided to dedicate their life to the search for meaning—the meaning of their own lives, the meaning of the world, of existence—in short, the attempt to understand the purpose of each individual and the purpose of humankind.

Link children fall squarely into the category of Seeker, even though they might also share characteristics and behaviors described in Boorstin's other two categories. The point is not to try to rigidly categorize Link children but to acknowledge that these children have a profound need to feel a sense of belonging, something that is typically hard-won in their daily lives with their family members and peers.

Link's encounter with Mr. Tree in "Link and the Wise Tree" (Chapter 6) illustrates well the need that Link children have to find a place where they feel they belong, where they can be, as Link expresses it "totally myself and be accepted for who I am," where they can feel at ease rather than continually beset with metaphysical anguish and self-doubt. Link lands on the label of "explorer" for himself once he resolves to leave the life and people he has always known to continue his journey to find where the shooting stars land. When Mr. Tree begins speaking to him, however, he quickly disabuses Link of the notion that he is an explorer (similarly to how Ms. Firefly declares in no uncertain terms that Link cannot fly). After a thoughtful, nonjudgmental conversation with Link— one in which Mr. Tree both shares his observations with Link about how he might define himself *and* listens respectfully to Link as he tries to define himself—Mr. Tree declares him to be a seeker. This comes as a relief to Link because for the first time in his life he feels he belongs to a group: He is a seeker, and there are others like him. He begins to understand that his "difference" from others does not necessarily mean that he must walk through life alone.

The conversation with the wise tree is critical in Link's development because understanding himself as a seeker will allow him to transform his life and to begin the journey that will shepherd him toward moments of temporary relief (which, as he gets older, will eventually become more permanent) and away from the feeling of emptiness, of the meaninglessness of life, the black hole, the clutch in the pit of the stomach, the heart, the throat—sensations that he, and all Link children, have been seeking to calm ever since they realized that they are not "like everyone else."

The Walkabout and Songlines

The Australian tradition of the walkabout illustrates well the need to set forth and seek one's purpose, to leave in order to "find oneself," and it prepares children from the peoples who practice this tradition for their journey. The walkabout is a rite of passage in which adolescent Aboriginal Australians undertake a journey that will help transform them into adults. The journey is usually made between the ages of 10 and 16. During this journey, which can last for up to six months, the individual is required to live and survive all alone in the wilderness.

This is not an easy thing to do, especially for teenagers. That is why only those who have proven themselves mentally and physically ready are allowed to proceed with the walkabout. Only the elders of the group decide whether or not it is time for a child to undertake this journey; and during the years preceding the walkabout, the elders prepare the children, instructing them and giving them advice about the ceremony and adult life in general. The children, then, have been given the "secrets" of the tribe, the knowledge about their world.

Besides the obvious goal of the walkabout—to walk and survive—the initiate (traditionally always male) also has to devote his time to thinking and discovering himself. The teenager needs to understand the concept of bravery and to connect with his spiritual guides. While moving across the land, the initiate sings "songlines"—ancestral songs that serve as "spoken maps" that help him find his way. In the absence of modern instruments such as a compass or radio, it is believed that the young person is guided by a spiritual power.

The walkabout is an excellent metaphor for the journey of self-evaluation and reflection. One can say that the songline guides the person experiencing the walkabout to live his or her own creative and unique life in a shared and already defined world.

The "tribe" that Link was born into and the "tribes" that most Link children are born into, which do not have the walkabout tradition, do not prepare their members for going out into the world to look for the meaning of their lives, although, to complicate this process further, they sow the desire to find it—without doing so explicitly—in the curious minds of these children.

It seems obvious that Link's father, Onyx, and his mother, Amber, were born and raised in different tribes. Still, they live at the same ranch and share many activities and interests, each one bringing different customs from the tribes that they come from. Link might wonder, however: "Why didn't Mom marry someone more like Uncle Indigo, who is adventurous and always trying new things? Maybe it's because Uncle Indigo wouldn't have known how to take care of my mom, wouldn't have given her such a respectable status on our ranch, because he always seems to need to be away from the family and doing his own thing." Link might also wonder: "Why didn't Dad marry someone more like his sister, my cousin Gray's mom, who is much tougher than my mom, much more demanding and more certain about what she wants? Maybe it's because he didn't want to be with someone who was so bossy."

It is inevitable that Link children, born as they are into similar contexts as Link the horse, feel building inside themselves, along with their curiosity, the longing for something new, different, and true. It is inevitable that they feel a restlessness that demands that they look for what is essential and what is their own, including their own tribe, if it exists, in which they can harmoniously combine the best customs of the different tribes that they inhabited and that now inhabit their ways of being.

The difficulties for Links, as opposed to Aboriginal Australian adolescents, reside in that even in the case of family members who have tried to pass down their own experiences, the forms of their search have not been sufficiently legitimized or considered to be solid and successful so as to be transformed into a viable and trusted family tradition that deserves to be followed and handed down from generation to generation.

In families that value the spirit of individual seeking and the respect for and pride in the conquests of those who have gone there before in different areas of knowledge, the Link child learns to celebrate with the same measure of curiosity and gratitude the frustrations, failures, and errors as much as the discoveries, original findings, and personal creativities. The Link child also learns to respect and tolerate sadness when they do not find what they are seeking and to celebrate the joy they feel when they have "arrived" at a desired place.

By contrast, in families that deny or reject their own spirit of seeking because they feel it to be dangerous, as much for the person who embodies this spirit as for the entire family group, the Link child, just as in the case of Link the horse, will begin their walkabout with fear and guilt, and without the awareness of the resources and knowledge that the family, even unintentionally, transmitted to them through stories, customs, and traditions.

The character of Mr. Tree, upon saying to Link, "You're a seeker," gives a name to his song, one that has up until this moment only been hummed. Mr. Tree names him as a member of a "tribe," saying that he is not the only one who is like this, that there are others like him. And that his song is a kind of music, corresponding to a musical genre that is complex, dispersed around the world, and not well-known, but recognizable by those who have gone through this, who are in the know. Therefore, Link is not alone. He does not have to reinvent the wheel or start from scratch. There may not be any written maps, but there are songlines. There may not be obvious footprints along the path, but there are signs, or traces, left by seekers who have come before.

Mr. Tree offers hope to Link, saying he has seen seekers return home after their sojourns with a sense of "joy and peace" and with the knowledge that "home can really be anywhere for them." From this moment of being recognized and "named," from this moment of beginning to think of himself as a seeker rather than as someone who is crazy, bad, dangerous, incomprehensible, and misunderstood, Link is able to recall the beginnings of his own songlines—internal sounds and melodies that up until now appeared only as bothersome noises or unintelligible whispers. He is now able to understand them as suggestions, advice, orientations, possible directions, descriptions of hidden beauty, whispers from other lands, and fascinating mysteries to be deciphered. Expressed more concretely, Link is able to draw on information he observed or heard growing up rather than having this information exist only as vague or indecipherable messages. For example, he can now hear more clearly and receive more openly things his parents or others in the family shared with him, such as an appreciation of beauty, whether expressed through artistic creation or nature; the desire to understand and learn new things; ways to understand and talk about the behaviors of friends and family members in order to better understand them and himself in relation to them; and myriad other "teachings" that have been transmitted through simply sharing daily life with the family unit. It may not have been made explicit, but those who surrounded him his whole life were indeed transmitting guidance, which he was subconsciously absorbing in order to finally be able to form his own spoken map.

True to his name, "Link," he begins to connect the dots . . . and a songline slowly begins to take shape. Although Link still has no idea where his search will lead him, because he lacks clearly marked paths, the shooting stars are signposts that take away his fear of being completely lost, because he understands all too well that in the known world, where he must live, he never seems to know the rules of the game. That is, he does not know how to behave in a world where he cannot figure out his place, where he belongs, or how to fit in—a place where he feels lost and bewildered by what goes on around him as well as by the very sensation and state of feeling lost. The shooting stars, then, while they are his destination, the place where he imagines he will find *Home*, are also important parts of the songline that he is discovering and composing as he makes his way in his search.

Decision Deficit Disorder

The Decision Deficit Disorder (DDD) that characterizes Link children is evident in Link's interactions with Mr. Tree and, later in the chapter, with the purple bird. His conversation with Mr. Tree allows him to understand, for the first time, that the shooting stars land in a different place every time. In this moment, Link exhibits developing maturity, coming to terms with a kind of disillusion when he realizes that he should not be searching for a single magic landing place for the shooting stars because that one place does not exist. This step in his development leads him to decide to turn back home, as he seems to understand that the deeper Home that he is seeking can be anywhere, so he might as well return to the ranch, the physical home he was raised in and where his family and friends are waiting for him. When he unexpectedly encounters the bird on his way back, however, he is taken in by her enticing description of the ocean—a realm of mystery and paradox in which Link recognizes himself. Like him, the ocean is both constant and continually changing and in flux; it is simultaneously calm and wild, dark and bright. Like the shimmering light on the river in Chapter 2, the image of the ocean that the bird paints for Link pulls him away from his resolve to return home and once again sets him firmly on the path of seeker.

The chapter closes with Link's returning to his belief that the shooting stars land where the ocean meets the sky, which can be anywhere. DDD is typical of Link children: They are convinced that if they attain their object of desire in any given moment, they will be forever satisfied. When suddenly their object of desire changes, they have the same conviction that this new desire will be the one that gives them the satisfaction they long for. They do not recognize the incongruence in their search as they make their way along their life path. Link children may feel in the moment that their decisions are steadfast and solid, in spite of inner doubts, fears, and guilt; and when they bounce from decision to decision, they project conviction and excitement about each one. The chapter ends with Link rushing excitedly and impulsively toward the water, with as much conviction about the correctness of this new path as he had only moments before about the need to return home.

❖ ❖ ❖

Link's songline, then, makes itself known to him as a slowly emerging spoken map. Just as for Link children, the lyrics do not appear all at once because they have never been uttered by a single voice or been shared with others or been collectively legitimized. Nevertheless, they do form a fundamental part of family legend, sometimes in the form of secrets that everyone knows but never speaks about, a mixture of both admirable and deplorable acts. Unlike for a child from Aboriginal peoples, the songline lyrics for a Link child are latent and hidden, emerging during the journey as unexpected signposts that seem to come out of nowhere (though they have been "placed" in the Link child in subtle and subconscious ways their whole life) instead of existing as part of an overt ancestral tradition that is deliberately passed down through the generations, as in Aboriginal culture.

It is clear that Link the horse, Ruth the ten-year-old, Spanish playwright Calderón de la Barca, the character of Segismundo who speaks the words of *Life Is a Dream* that open this chapter, and countless others like them belong in a long line of seekers, as described by Boorstin. Seekers do not have compasses or written maps. They have songlines. Some have the good fortune to have begun hearing their songlines from a very early age from people whom they trusted. Others, like Link, must search their memory in order to recover and interweave the small musical phrases that, little by little, begin to take hold as loving, wise, and trustworthy companions in their search. When Mr. Tree names Link a seeker, then, it offers comfort, security, and the beginnings of a desperately yearned-for sense of belonging, giving Link the strength and hope he needs to continue in his search for understanding, purpose, and Home, where he can fully be who he is, both for himself and for others.

Chapter 7

Caught between Wind and Gravity: The Link Child's Quest to Find the "Good" Place

Link the horse wants to discover where the shooting stars land because he imagines that this will be the place where he will find himself. But, precisely because he doesn't know who he is, he doesn't know how to look for this place. So far, he knows that he is neither a racehorse nor a riding horse. When interacting with his father he enjoys feeling strong and assertive, but when interacting with his mother he enjoys feeling tender and cooperative. He doesn't know if he is good (like his grandmother makes him feel) or bad (like his cousin Gray accuses him of being). What kind of horse will he find if, in the place where the shooting stars land, it is possible to be a harmonious combination of the many opposites that Link is tangled up in—racehorse and riding horse, strong horse and tender horse, assertive horse and cooperative horse, and even good horse and bad horse? This place of inner harmony and ease is what all Link children seek, although they may not yet know it or be able to articulate it.

Link's conversation with Mr. Tree reveals to him that Home could be any place and that the shooting stars can land anywhere, causing Link to question what exactly he is looking for. While he himself does not yet fully know, many adult readers will understand that he is looking for himself, trying to figure out if he is a good horse or a bad one, if his ideas are only ever problematic and disappointing or if they might also be helpful to the community or the "tribe" to which he feels he belongs.

This moment is a turning point for Link, a moment when snippets of songlines (discussed in the previous chapter) that he has received from his grandmother and the firefly, for example, blend harmoniously with the wisdom of the tree—all of them telling him that if he manages to identify what he needs to feel at peace, he will find the Home he is seeking, that moment of the encounter with the gaze of another who recognizes him and makes him feel normal, understandable, and understood as well as huggable, lovable, and loved. I call this moment the *abrazo preciso*, or the "precise embrace," the gesture of love that envelops a Link child and makes them feel they are good (not bad or guilty) and makes them feel at ease (rather than anxiety-ridden or anguished). It is the gesture that allows the child to "feel felt," that takes care of the child in the exact place where they feel hurt or wounded. The precise embrace lets the child know that they are seen and understood and, more specifically, that the person offering this metaphorical embrace understands their pain. The precise embrace also signifies that elusive peace, or Home, that Links, more intensely and urgently than most, will typically spend much of their lives searching for.

Link's journey must continue because returning home at this point in his development will not bring him the peace he is seeking. He may not be able to articulate it in this way, but he *is* able to follow his DDD-influenced "nature" by reacting immediately and impulsively to the purple bird's suggestion that he find his way to the vast, mysterious ocean.

A Lesson for Links from the Albatross

Link is something like an albatross who does not know how to fly but, paradoxically, can be in the air longer than any other bird. As Carl Safina describes this phenomenon in *Eye of the Albatross*, thanks to the albatross's capacity for "exerting no propelling power of its own over long distances, it is driven by the tension between the two greatest forces on our planet: gravity and the solar-powered wind" (Prelude).[4] Link children do not know what they want because their extreme capacity for empathy causes them to internalize others' desires as their own. But because of their curiosity and their desire and ability to learn (without studying), they can reach more goals than the average person, thanks to their ability to glide within and among many different ways of life and to see life from many points of view. They then experience the joy that comes with achieving goals but also the fear of not knowing if they will be able to repeat these achievements because they do not know what it is they actually know or how they know it. This can lead to Link children, as adults, developing the Impostor Syndrome, because they are always afraid of being "found out" or "denounced" as liars or people who only know how to improvise. This causes them to refrain from trying things that they would be capable of doing if they would take the step of distinguishing between what they know through mimicry, intuition, and evidential thinking and what they do not know how to systematize because they do not know how to think deductively.

The problem with Links when they have not yet realized that they must define what they are looking for is that, unlike the albatross, they do not actually know how to work with "wind and gravity." Even though they can read the winds swirling around them (others' desires) they do

---

4 Parenthetical references denote sections in the Kindle edition of Safina's book.

not know what or where their inner center or "gravity" is. They do not know how far they must extend their wings (their movements, steps) in order not to be shaken and taken by others' desires to horizons where they do not want to go. This lack of connection with and reliance on their own intuition—which should arise from their gut feelings, from cenes-thesia, from knowing how to "read" their own gravitational, grounding force—may put them in danger or, even worse, turn them into an instru-ment with which others can reach their own peaks, places that could be completely sinister for the Link person's own ethics and worldview.

Albatrosses not only know their bodies perfectly well, they also have a clear idea about what their travels are about: to obtain food for their chicks. "She was not wandering aimlessly; she was investing" (Letting Go). Albatrosses mate and nest for life, always returning to the same place. Their mission is to look after their chicks until these are strong enough to begin their own flight, and then once again to look after their new chicks when they arrive.

This is "what an albatross is all about: traveling to the limits of any sea. No ocean stretches far enough to outdistance an albatross. They seem to bend the laws of physics; in this magic realm space collapses and single birds command whole ocean basins, and time's arrow becomes elliptic. . ." (Moving On). But the further albatrosses go in search of food, the more they feel their chicks pulling them back to the nest. They can feel the new chicks "like a rubber band, like a downy bungee cord" (Letting Go).

This is what Link individuals need to learn in order to find them-selves: 1) to recognize the signals that come from their gut—their inner feelings of being well or badly nurtured, of being comfortable or uncom-fortable, of being at ease or ill at ease with themselves or with others—and 2) to understand that these signals, which come from their reading of the information from their experience of cenesthesia, or the feelings they feel in their bodies, are the good and correct ones, the ones that they can trust.

Links must learn from the albatross that it is possible to live life in between the gravitational pull of their nests (their core sense of self) and the continually shifting winds that always surround them. That is, Links must learn how to distinguish between the information about who the "I" is that is really them, which comes from cenesthesia (symbolized by the chicks) and the information that comes from the desires of others, the ways of life that they were or are exposed to as children, and the values that they have been taught and that are those of the culture they are raised in (symbolized by the winds). Just as the chicks are for the albatross the motivating force behind their impulse to return to the nest, cenesthesia for Links is what awakens the sensation of having something special that another person needs and helping them to feel worthy and that life is worth living. The challenge for Links is that for them the nest can feel claustrophobic. Choosing and limiting oneself to just one nest (self) feels too narrow for somebody who is able to perceive and grasp the immensity of the oceans. But the only way to not get lost in the winds of others' desires, which Links usually mistake as their own, is to have a clearly defined Home, a definition of themselves, even if this definition might be seen by others (or sometimes by themselves) as not good enough. In short, Links must have the nest, even as they must have the possibility of flying above and across the ocean.

Links must learn from the albatross that in spite of the restrictions and limitations that landing (in the form of returning to solid ground, or the nest, and staying put for a while) might impose, it is nevertheless a necessity. For albatrosses, "Perhaps the idea of committing themselves to firm ground after months or years at sea seems so unfamiliar and terrifying a prospect that almost anything can prompt a general alarm. Perhaps there is simply some other sense of liberty or fear in their minds that rejects forsaking the free sea for the arduous ardor of breeding that will leash their lives to land. But land they do" (Letting Go).

The importance of this for Links is that if they land on *themselves*, that is, if they discover who they are and attain the inner peace they desperately seek, then they are able to escape being categorized as one of the marginalized, weird outlaws and can enter into a new subjectivity, one that is going to give them both the freedom to fly and the freedom to stay.

In Search of the "Good" Place

At this point in *Link and the Shooting Stars*, before Link boards the ship that will take him to where he thinks the shooting stars land, he does not know that he has this freedom because he does not know if he is good or bad, if he is a creative creature or a troublemaker. He does not know if he will be able to do what he feels he needs to do without causing others pain or if he will always be struggling between, on the one hand, feeling weak and submissive (but good) if he obeys the wishes of others (his father, his mother, and Gray, for example) and, on the other, feeling strong and alone (but bad) if he does what he wants to do, even as he changes his mind from one moment to the next.

He has been yearning so long for kindred spirits, for the company of creatures who are like him, that when he arrives at the dock where the boatful of animals is waiting (Chapter 7), he more readily accepts the man's classification of him as "weird" and "rebellious" than he does Mr. Tree's classification of him as a seeker. This is because until he met the tree, he never felt that he was a seeker and had never been called one, but many times in his life he has felt himself to be—and has been labeled as—weird, different, rebellious, and defiant.

In this moment Link embraces his weirdness and rebelliousness, believing that he is finally in the company of others who are just like him. Link is hopeful that he has at last located his "people," the group where he can feel the sense of belonging that he, and all Links, long for. Locating the tribe of the seeker, however, and understanding exactly what and who make up that tribe is no easy feat.

Nilton Bonder, in *Our Immoral Soul: A Manifesto of Spiritual Disobedience*, says that the soul is looking for a good place to inhabit, betraying the body that wants to stay in the place that is traditionally considered to be the "right" or "correct" place. He differentiates "good place" from "right place," defining the former as the place where the soul has more space to explore, more freedom, whereas the latter is the more rigid, confining place imposed by tradition, morality, and the rules that society sets for human behavior. The expanding awareness and the tremendous amount of information that comes with their gift of empathy makes Link children feel confined, causing them to feel suffocated by the expectation that they must subscribe to only one belief system, one way of feeling, thinking, and living. They are almost condemned from the beginning to feel like traitors because their souls (intuitions, insights) need to find this good place. But they don't know which place is the "right" good place, the one where their bodies will also feel protected.

Links go through different stages during their search. First, they feel suffocated by truths that they know or feel to be partial and narrow. Second, when they emerge from this feeling and start to feel the euphoria of freedom, they are capable of inventing or "jumping into" almost any truth. Third, they get depressed because they do not want to invent a truth that will leave them alone and with the feeling that even this truth is also incomplete and, therefore, unsatisfying.

Link the horse as well as Link children feel with the same intensity and force the need to preserve the spirit of the family, culture, and/or society in which they grew up *and* the need for change, always seeking a way to fulfill both needs. The challenge is that obeying one impulse (their need to find themselves) usually means rejecting the other (the status quo they were raised with). They wonder if this rejection—which over the course of their search may involve numerous moments of "destruction" of certain parental or societal mandates regarding behaviors, ways of thinking, values, etc.—is something bad on their part because it signifies rejecting or destroying that familial or cultural "spirit" or something good, because it implies that something better is to come. They wonder if the need to create something new is just an emotional and irrational way of challenging or opposing someone just for fun and for the feeling of empowerment that comes from doing this, or if it is something well thought out and planned that represents the needs of the family, culture, and/or society that produced them better than the existing traditions or status quo do.

After the euphoria Link the horse feels when he believes that he is on the verge of finding his people—those who have also been called "weirdo" or "crazy," as he has been called many times by Gray—he quickly learns that these animals he has been placed with in the shipping container are not at all like him. He realizes that, unlike him, they are actually mean because they treat others badly, steal food, and break the rules. He understands at last that, although he might be weird, he is not mean or bad the way these animals are.

In their early years Link children move freely through their environment. They are supremely creative and curious, interacting with complete strangers as if they were close friends, many times too quickly and without assessing very well if they will be trustworthy friends or if they will put them at risk in some way. This is clear in Link's behavior with the other animals when he first boards the boat. He brings to this situation his curiosity and innocence, believing that he will connect well with this new "tribe" and that they will embrace him as one of their own. But he learns immediately that this is not going to happen.

For Link children, many times these fast friendships will also come to a fast end. Like with many of Link children's adventures, in these friendships they will end up needing to be rescued because they have misread the signs and have plunged impulsively into these friendships without fully grasping or intuiting correctly who these "friends" are.

The Good, the Bad, and the Weird

How, then, does one define "mean" or "bad"? What makes someone be considered "weird"? When is someone guilty of having done something wrong, against others, and when is someone feeling guilty almost every moment of his life, just by thinking, feeling, behaving, in ways that are not considered the "right" ones (using Bonder's terminology)?

Link knows that others think of him as "weird," but he does not know what it means, and furthermore, even the weird animals that are supposedly like him, don't accept him as one of their tribe. The hyena makes fun of him, calling him a fool, which makes Link doubt that the ship is headed to the shooting stars. Once again, Link feels uncertain about his own convictions. He notices monkeys stealing food and tries to explain why he is different. He doesn't see himself as someone who is hateful or deliberately engaging in wrongdoing in order to "win" or to defeat or hurt others in some way. He knows that he is "not trying to do things to go against anybody," as he says to the monkey after the monkey tries to define for Link what "weird" means.

On the contrary, Link the horse and Link children feel deeply that they are fighting for justice. "It's not fair" comes out of their mouth as frequently as they are afraid of being accused of doing something wrong—that is to say, almost all the time, especially in conflictive moments of disagreement. In the case of Link the horse, the sentiment of "it's not fair" emerges when he is accused of ruining the race for the spectators by stopping to help Blue. In this instance the question of justice and injustice appears in the following ways: Link feels that he is doing the fair thing by stopping to help Blue, who will not be able to finish the race without his help. But he does not realize that this is unfair from the point of view of his father and the spectators, who have placed their trust in him to do his best to win the race and have something to lose if Link does not win. Finally, he feels that the accusations from his father and the spectators are not fair to him, because he was only trying to do the right thing, the just thing. How could he have known that it wasn't fair for him to stop to help Blue? He was obeying his mother's mandate to be good. Similarly, how could he have known that it wasn't right, or fair, to the children to gallop toward them and rear while he was trying to be a riding horse? He did not know that this would frighten them. He was only obeying his father's mandate to be strong.

How can Link children possibly discern and learn to distinguish when and why it is good or bad to be kind, when and why it is good or bad to be bold, when and why it is better to be very cautious or to be very curious? The deep empathy that Link children feel for each of their parents causes them to absorb in equal measure the different and contradictory messages they are exposed to. When they are chastised, then, they feel wrongly accused and guilty, even as they are protesting, often loudly and angrily, "It's not fair!"

The DDD that characterizes Link individuals and that, for Link the horse, accounts for the unpredictable and impulsive behavior of running in one direction and then another, allows them to escape from the immobility, and even paralysis, that they typically feel. Their DDD is a consequence of the difficulty they have reaching conclusions or making decisions due to the long periods of time spent weighing the pros and cons of each and every one of the options they have witnessed and absorbed their entire life. For Link the horse, as for all Link children and adults, all options not only must be considered but are also equally viable and possible when compared with each other. Links know that each and every option is good in some respects and bad in others, but this relativistic way of thinking and perceiving the world is precisely what leads to the inability to follow through on one idea, stick to a single purpose or plan, or determine what the correct course of action in any given situation is.

When Link is on the boat, confined with the other animals, he comes face to face with the truly mean behaviors that the others exhibit. These animals are intent on inflicting harm on others intentionally, purely for their own benefit. As he takes all of this in, Link realizes he does not like these behaviors and that he is different from these "weird" animals, although he has been relegated to the same part of the boat that they are in. He also understands that he does not want others to categorize him as "bad" or "mean."

Unlike these animals, Link wants to live in a harmonious, conflict-free atmosphere. He longs for a kind of paradise, a perfect place where everybody is happy, where he will not be accused of being mean or bad, or criticized because of his behaviors or choices, where he can be who he is for himself and for others at the same time, where he will not feel like a hypocrite if he hides some parts of himself, and where he will not feel mean or aggressive if he expresses the many thoughts running around in his head.

Link imagines a place—the place where the shooting stars land—where he will feel, at long last, like a "whole" horse. This desire for and dream of wholeness is rooted in a notion of integration within himself, an integration that is free of inner doubts or conflicts between different parts of himself. This integration would allow him to understand which Link is the one that is in control of all the Links inside him that make him who he is, that cause him to be Link the curious horse or Link the difficult horse or Link the weird horse. More importantly, this integration would allow him to feel at ease with himself and in the world, a sense of peace, without the constant fear of always being accused of having done something wrong, without the constant feeling of guilt.

Paranoid Guilt and Freedom

At this point in the story and in his development, Link knows that he is guilty of having put his cousins in a dangerous situation by insisting that they take the steepest path to the top of the mountain. In that episode, he tries to repair the damage he caused by running to the road and finding help. Acknowledging his guilt and responsibility, he apologizes and, through this experience, recognizes why others (Gray, for example) might consider him to be someone to be avoided. While he understands his guilt or responsibility for this particular dangerous experience at the mountain, he does not understand why he feels a deep and abiding guilt simply for being who he is.

Grinberg's concept of paranoid guilt, discussed in Chapter 5, is much more related to profound feelings of anguish and fear than to the typical feelings of sadness and pain that come with the kind of guilt that involves recognizing that one has done something wrong, whether intentional or not. Link children live constantly with the feeling that they are about to be "found out," that they will be discovered as having done something wrong and be accused of being guilty or responsible for something. This "something" is not necessarily well-defined. What Link children imagine they might be guilty of is not necessarily the reason or wrongdoing that provokes their parents' anger.

Ten-year-old Anita provides a clear example of how Link children use impulsive behavior and DDD as a coping mechanism for the internal tug-of-war they constantly feel, and how paranoid guilt can play out in their behavior. After a very full day at the beach with her family, Anita agreed to see a movie at home with her grandparents and her brother. While taking her bath, she suddenly changed her mind, saying, "No, I want to watch my own stuff on my iPad." She saw her grandmother react to this pronouncement by making a face, prompting Anita, sometime later, to say to her, "Well, if it's so important to you to see the movie together, I'll do it." Her grandmother responded by saying, "Thank you, Anita. I'm very happy about that because I really enjoy doing things with you, and we don't have a lot of opportunities for that because we don't live in the same city."

To the grandmother's surprise, Anita burst into tears and ran off to her room, saying later, "I told you that we could see the movie together if it was so important to you, but I was hoping that you would tell me I didn't have to. So I would feel free and wouldn't feel the pressure of having to do what you want. I don't want to see the movie with all of you. I want to see my movie. But I feel really, really mean. You sacrifice a lot to give me all the things I like, and I can't even leave a movie to do something you want to do."

Anita feels completely torn between her own desire in that moment and that of her grandmother, though her running off to her room in tears might on the surface appear to be an act of defiance. To complicate matters her grandmother's desire is also to some extent hers: Anita wants to gratify herself by watching a movie of her choice by herself instead of the one that the family will be watching together, *and* she wants to gratify herself by doing something that her grandmother wants to do with her.

While she can watch a movie by herself any other day when she returns to her own house, she will not be able to watch a movie with her grandmother because this is the last night at her grandparents' home. The grandmother handled this situation by staying calm and explaining to Anita that there is a solution for situations in which contradictory desires are in conflict with each other: She needs to prioritize, which requires patience and taking the time to assess the situation that is creating the internal turmoil and feelings of guilt in order to see clearly what the best course of action is, the one that will allow her to, in effect, have her cake and eat it, too. That is, she can watch the movie with the family and also watch the other movie she wants to see, just not in the same moment. Finally, the grandmother also tried to ease Anita's guilt by clarifying for her that it is not a sacrifice but a *choice* to gratify herself by gratifying her granddaughter.

In the end, Anita understood what her grandmother was saying and decided to watch the movie with the family, knowing that she could also watch the other movie by herself the next day. Even though she did not hurt her grandmother in any way, she *felt* she had hurt her and that this would translate into her grandmother not loving her because she was "mean." A key to overcoming the feeling of paranoid guilt that Link children live with day in and day out is for them to understand which part of themselves they need to take care of: the part that needs to feel free and independent or the part that needs to feel it is a legitimate part of a family or a community.

This process of discerning which part of themselves to prioritize is one that Links must engage in with each decision they make. This is a central and continual challenge for both Link children and adults, one that with every decision makes them feel that they are risking something important. They need to learn to differentiate between when the need for freedom and independence in any given moment will forever compromise the possibility of belonging and when it is just a momentary prioritization that will have no lasting ill effects on their relationship to the family or community. The reverse is also true: They need to differentiate between when the need to belong will compromise their freedom and when it is a momentary need with no negative effects on their future independence.

I want to insist here that the sensation that Link children experience of always feeling guilty, of feeling themselves to be mean or difficult or hopeless, in the sense of being an unresolvable problem—these feelings are *not* the parents' fault. It is not useful for parents or other caregivers to feel guilty or wholly responsible for the suffering of Link children. Again, Links are *born* gifted in empathy and are exposed to what is at times a conflictive diversity in their upbringing. Additionally, they "know" without being able to put into words about a sad, tragic, or complex situation in the family circumstance into which they were born, which transmitted to them a feeling of melancholy, of irreparable failure or brokenness, of hopelessness that from a very early age instills in them the sense that they have to repair this situation. They are constantly worried about each and every member of their family and community as well as their family and community as a whole. Parents must understand that their children's feelings of guilt are an almost constitutional part of their subjectivity and must not take on the burden of guilt themselves for something that they, as parents, had nothing to do with creating and have no control over in the present.

Paranoid guilt is an inherent component of the Link personality. Having such a complex subjectivity, constructed by so many diverse components, values, ideas, desires, goals, images of happiness, and concepts of good and bad, is the basis of having an eternal "immoral" soul, in Bonder's conceptualization—one that is always trying to find the good place, the place that is right for the soul, even if it is not considered right by the establishment, and along the way passing through many wrong places. I borrow Bonder's notion of the immoral soul not to say that Link children are immoral but to show how their souls, more than those of others, are compelled to seek out the ultimate place where they can feel free, while continually struggling with the need to belong to the family or community, even as they reject familial and community traditions and expectations.

After his experience with the mean animals on the boat, Link knows definitively that he does *not* belong to this group of creatures and that, as a result, he does not deserve to live life as an isolated or excluded being. Nevertheless, he has yet to discover what kind of "good" horse he is or where his own "good" place is. He, therefore, must continue searching for himself. He must continue pursuing the elusive landing place of the shooting stars, wherever this pursuit takes him and, like the albatross, wherever the winds may carry him before he finally lands in the nest of inner peace, the place that will feel like Home.

Chapter 8

Different Strokes: The Nonconformist Nature of the Link Child

Once Link is freed from the container where he was trapped with the wild, mean animals, he experiences yet another turning point in both his development and his journey. Mr. Brown, the owner of the circus where Link will spend much of his youth, declares unequivocally that Link is "not as beautiful as some animals, nor as weird as others." Sensing something "special" about him, he chooses to take Link to his circus, not quite knowing what the young horse will do or how he will fit in with the rest of the circus family.

This moment is key to Link's journey of self-discovery and self-understanding because, for the first time in his life, someone who neither knows him nor loves him (as his grandmother and Pink do, for example) accepts him for who he is. He may not be not well-defined or easily definable, as Mr. Brown's comment indicates, but Link feels validated for who he is, although he does not yet know who that might be. Even though he was released from the container occupied by the animals who are classified as "wild" and "weird," he realizes that Mr. Brown perceives him as trustworthy and unique, as a horse with potential to contribute and do good rather than a horse that belongs with the mean, marginalized animals. Link, in fact, is not even capable of belonging to the category of "outlaw" or "wild." Yet he feels tremendous relief at knowing that he does not have to resign himself to being a "bad guy" or an "outlaw," to being one of those who are condemned to permanent exile and its accompanying loneliness. Someone—Mr. Brown—has "seen" him and chosen him, which means that he must have some value.

Link, then, finds himself at the beginning of his autonomous life, responsible for his own choices, faced with the consequences of his actions and decisions. He understands that he is capable of doing bad things *unintentionally*, which causes others to label him as "bad." This in turn causes him not only to feel angry due to the injustice of not being well understood but also to do bad things *intentionally* to take justice into his own hands. Because he is always accused of being bad, regardless of if his bad actions are intentional or unintentional, he ends up feeling unlovable and that he deserves to be rejected. Now, however, embarking on a life that is not only independent but distant and completely different from the life he had with his family on the ranch, he must discover how to do good things and be good *intentionally* so that he can feel himself to be lovable and worthy of being loved.

In "Discoveries at the Circus" (Chapter 8), while still taking in his new surroundings and the new humans and animals that will become a part of his life, Link meets Ms. Zebra. This encounter is paradigmatic in Link's development for two main reasons: first, because he learns from her that he does not belong to the category of beings who form part of a homogeneous group, that is, whose personal choices and life decisions are coherent and consistent with those of the homogeneous group; and second, because he discovers that not all living beings are like him or are preoccupied with the same things that Links devote their full attention to. Although it may be hard to believe, Links always react with astonishment and incredulousness when they discover that not everyone feels and thinks the way they do.

In his conversations with Ms. Zebra, Link discovers that, even though he might want to be, he cannot be like her and her kind: those who follow the laws that mark them from birth and who know that they will be rewarded for not straying from the paths that others lay before them and designate as the "right" paths to follow. When Ms. Zebra suggests that Link choose just one talent to focus on, after he has shared with her that he has several different talents, he says, "I can't choose and I don't want to choose just one thing because it would not feel like me anymore. I don't feel like I fit into any one box but that instead I can fit into many different boxes." Later in the conversation, she shows Link her family's place in the Circus Hall of Fame, pointing out that she is descended from a long line of circus performers and affirming that she always knew that she was going to dedicate herself to carrying on the family tradition.

Link is increasingly uncomfortable and frustrated in this conversation, acknowledging his confusion about who he is and who he is meant to be, and feeling distressed that some creatures, like the zebra, have known their whole lives who they are and what they are meant to do, whereas he has been mired in doubt and uncertainty from a very early age. Despite his discomfort and confusion, however, and due to feeling that the circus owner has in a strange way validated him, Link feels calm and trusting enough to dare to think in an honest way about what and who he is, without getting defensive or going on the counter-offensive, as he would have in the past. Ms. Zebra is completely different from him, but he allows himself to learn from her. He takes in her words without feeling attacked and, therefore, without feeling the need to blame her in order to purge himself of a sense of guilt for not living up to some ideal.

Reading between the lines, using what we know about Link's personal growth and developmental journey thus far, we can discern Link's perception and assessment of himself in his conversations with Ms. Zebra. Link realizes that yes, he is unbearably impatient and demanding, that he wants things to happen immediately and in the way that he wants. He realizes that it is true that he gets angry and is capable of volatile reactions when he thinks or feels that others do not understand him, accept him, or value his ideas to the extent that he thinks they should be valued. He also realizes that learning something new, or even learning this about himself, has had to be done his way and not the way recommended by anyone who has tried to teach him and help him incorporate new (more efficient, more appropriate, less costly, less risky) ways of resolving a problem or of getting out of a situation in which he feels trapped. Recognizing that he lacked important information or was incapable of doing something was so intolerable to him that he would transform it into a decision: "I don't want to," "I don't need you," or "Nobody can help me the way I want to be helped." In the conversation with Ms. Zebra, Link begins to understand some key things about himself precisely because he and the zebra are so different from each other. Whereas he has always disobeyed, she obeys. Whereas she has inherited and followed the path of a clear family tradition, with family members and ancestors to encourage and guide her, he inherits family traditions in conflict with each other. Whereas she feels free right where she is (at the circus, with her family), with no need to be anywhere else, he feels trapped (or afraid of being trapped) and is always searching for another place that he idealizes. Whereas Ms. Zebra feels inner peace, Link feels inner turmoil.

Link also realizes that on the ranch he was lonely. He realizes that he had to leave the ranch— leaving behind his grandmother's understanding, Pink's admiration, his mother's protection, and his father's resources—because none of this would do him any good as long as he was still struggling between, on the one hand, feeling vulnerable (and unworthy) if he recognized that he needed help, wanted to be loved, and wanted to "belong," and, on the other hand, feeling powerful (and admirable) if he believed that he was "free," that he did not need anyone, that he could be alone, and that he always knew more than anyone else regardless of the topic.

Links as "Different"

Thanks to his experience on the boat when he is trapped below with the truly bad animals, the lawbreakers—those who wish to hurt others for their own gain in order to have power over them through creating fear—Link begins to understand that he is not bad *like that*. It is true that he does not belong to the category of children who are easy to take care of, those who are grateful when they are being taught something, who return the love they are given, who share with others a sense of belonging, who are privy to the family codes and unspoken mutual understandings. But he is also not a monster who should be banished from the community, who deserves to be expelled or treated like a dangerous element just because he is different from his peers or because it is hard for his parents to understand him.

He begins to realize that, yes, he is hard to understand. Not even he truly understands what he wants. He only knows that what his family circle was offering him did not satisfy his creative needs and was not sufficiently stimulating for his curious, inquisitive nature. And that what they asked of him—that he be a racehorse *and* a riding horse, for example—was too much for his limited capacity for discipline and for tolerating the inevitable frustrations in the course of any kind of learning.

His experience on the boat and his conversations with Ms. Zebra at least allow him to understand that he is *different* from others, but not *bad* out of meanness or out of a desire to cause harm. He knows that he is not filled with hate, but with confusion: He truly does not know who he is or who he wants to be or is capable of being. For the first time in his search for where the shooting stars land, where Link trusts he will discover who he is and where Home, that place of inner peace and ease, is for him, Link accepts that, however much he might have gotten angry with Gray, challenged his mother and father, or declared categorically that he knows what he wants and where he is going, in reality he does not know who he is or what he is looking for. He sums this feeling up when he says to Ms. Zebra, "It's all so confusing. . . . I really don't know where to look for more clues about what I ought to be."

In addition to deepening Link's exploration of his identity (Who am I?) and his concern with finding his place in the world (What am I meant to do in life?), the conversation with Ms. Zebra also helps Link to see that these questions that preoccupy him do not necessarily preoccupy everyone else. As is the case for Link the horse, for Link children and adults it is extremely difficult to accept that these concerns that consume their time and energy and send them on a quest that seems to be endless, full of failure, and fraught with frustration and an existential sense of nothingness or emptiness are not the concerns of most other people. These concerns, in fact, are not universal or even "normal," in the sense of being commonly experienced. The interesting thing is that Link children from very early in their childhood and Link adults (whether or not they know that they belong to a group of people called Links) feel themselves to be different.

This difference from others is painful for Links because they feel left out, like they do not belong and, therefore, are not lovable enough to have the right to belong. They also know that their "difference" often makes others feel uncomfortable. Because they feel unlovable, they do not trust any embrace (attention, caring, etc.) they receive from others (their parents, for example). In order to not feel that they are "bad," they deem the embrace insufficient, telling themselves that they do not feel cared for in the way they would like. That is, they feel unlovable, so they project this onto others and end up accusing others of not caring for them well enough or loving them sufficiently. They are constantly moving back and forth between feeling guilty for being so hard to understand (accusing themselves of being sick, crazy, ungrateful, and bad) and feeling angry at not being understood (accusing others of being rigid, authoritarian, selfish, and bad).

What the outlaws (like the bad animals on the boat) and the conformists (like the zebra) have in common is that they do not spend time doubting their decisions. Both follow to the letter the instructions that teach them to be what and who they are. The *raison d'être* of the outlaws is to transgress the laws of society, whether or not they are just, while the *raison d'être* of the conformists is to uphold these laws, whether or not they are appropriate for the circumstances and whether or not they are fair.

In stark contrast to either of these groups, Link children and adults are full of doubts. They have doubts almost all the time about everything. Their work, then, is to determine who the "I" is who must put together the needs and desires of all the I's that are present and active in each moment inside of them, in order to make the best decisions. And the best decision will always be the one that includes most of the needs and desires in a way that no damage will be done and that considers and prioritizes the most essential, important part of their being. Although it involves much time and effort, trial and error, falling off of the path, desperation, shame, guilt, and, most of all, fear (sometimes disguised as rage), it is possible for Links to create their own way of being that is neither immoral nor moralistic, neither selfish and individualistic nor capitulating and dependent. It is possible for them to be neither a sinner nor a saint, neither an outlaw nor a conformist. It is possible for them to be nothing more and nothing less than... a Link.

Links as Nonconformists: Alexandra

Alexandra, a young Chilean architect living and practicing in New York, offers a real-world example of what Link the horse is currently just beginning to understand about himself. She describes herself like this:

> Since I was very young, I have been extremely sensitive to noise, loud TV and music volume, and shouting. These things saturated my senses and, as much as I enjoyed the company of others, I never really liked big crowds. I wouldn't say I am a solitary soul, but I'm not a "social animal" either. I love small group gatherings that allow me to connect sincerely with others. Crowds overwhelm me, and even when the atmosphere might be entertaining and fun to others, it can many times feel empty and meaningless to me. I simply feel disconnected, out of place.
>
> I have always lived in my own world.
>
> I was different. People would give me a look for asking them to turn the volume down or the TV off or to stop arguing, trying to convince one another about politics and religion. What was wrong with me for not accepting all of that as part of my everyday experience? This sense of difference wasn't just my perception of reality; people agreed. I still remember my father calling me "delusional" because of the ideas and statements I came up with not only as a child but in my youth.
>
> But wanting a more peaceful, harmonious and sensitive world around me was not all. I was also different in my physical

appearance. I was petite and short. Other children called me "shorty" since even for them—the small citizens of the world—I was way too tiny. I've always had a different conception of life that somehow required stepping on a path very different from that of others. I never walked the path of the masses, but interestingly enough I've always managed to adapt very well to what was expected of me: I was the best student, the one who behaved properly and was worthy of imitation—oh, how many times I was held up as an example to others—the trophy winner, the captain of the teams. And right there the dissociation was manifesting. A "dissected soul" if such a term could actually be used. I carried that feeling around all these years but became aware of it only once I moved to New York. I was always so focused on not disappointing others that I managed to trick myself into believing that I was doing exactly what I wanted. After many weeks of crying in Ithaca, I began the search into trying to understand why, if I've always been successful in whatever I endeavored, I had not been able to feel true to myself. Was that not my real "I"? What had I been doing all those years? Was it just the need to make those who surrounded me happy? Was that my purpose in life? How much would I have to give to others to finally feel I was giving enough? And how not to feel guilty every time I sensed I couldn't really give what the other person wanted even though I was giving all that I had to offer? Was I a traitor because I left my home country and with it my family and friends? Was there a hidden soul of mine worth finding? All these questions to be answered. I began to realize that a lot of what I had been doing until that point in my life didn't truly resonate with me. Still, all of those patterns and beliefs were very much engraved in my being.

A real internal battle began. And with it, the quest to find (and eventually protect) my authenticity, my uniqueness.

Since then, I have been going back and forth, having one part of me wanting to follow what I enjoy and feel is right for me and the other thinking about the affections that I left in Chile and feeling guilty because of it. Knowing that here in New York I am not a "delusional" being (and even if I happen to be one, I am just one more amongst an innumerable group of them, so in reality my uniqueness doesn't stand out as something outrageous). I have heard and read many times "follow your heart." But here is the big dilemma: Which of these two is the call of my heart? To stay in New York and continue with my search to find, understand, and honor my uniqueness or to return to the place where I was born knowing that sooner rather than later (and with a bunch of battles in between) I will end up surrendering to what others expect of me, to their way of approaching life? If it's the former, I pay the high price of being away from my family and close friends; if it's the latter, I pay the price of losing my authenticity, freedom of expression, my wings, or an equivalent expensive price of having to constantly fight to defend those values.

Is there a right answer? If so, I have not found it yet. I go through some days of feeling very lonely, of not knowing if staying here is, in the end, the right decision, of not understanding what the real purpose is behind all this struggle.

Alexandra, a Link adult, has arrived at a place of profound understanding of her life path and the dilemmas she faces. The way this self-exploration manifests in a Link child or adolescent, however, is different because a young Link, as we see with Link the horse, has not yet arrived at this level of self-understanding and recognition regarding what must be done in order to resolve the internal struggle. Lori, a 12-year-old American girl, responds to a question about why she says "no" to almost everything that she is asked to do or is offered by saying, "To be rebellious is to be different. I want to be unique." Ironically, she already *is* unique, or "different," but because her difference from others, the feeling of not "fitting in" that she has no control over, causes her to suffer, she finds ways of being different that are of her choosing, such as behaving rebelliously or making choices that she knows will shock those around her, including her parents.

Lori's insight into her own behavior, while not the more developed insight of an adult, provides a key for parents to understand their Link children and to learn to choose their battles in the process of raising them: Link children are *already* different. They already think and feel in ways that are not the common, accepted, traditional, established, and easily recognizable ways, the ways that have been proven to be "right" as opposed to marginal, risky, or even dangerous. To claim their uniqueness, Link children do not need to exaggerate their disagreements with others or their difference from others to the extremes that they often resort to. Their motivation is not to hurt or endanger themselves or others but to suffer less by "joining" a group that they imagine to be full of people like them (just as Link does with the wild animals on the boat). What Link children and adolescents do not realize, however, is that even once they seem to "belong" to the group of people they feel are like them, they will still be different, they will still suffer, they will still not feel at ease. In fact, they will suffer more because their strong sense of ethics will make them feel even guiltier and less worthy of being loved and accepted by groups that are unique, distinctive, creative, and original (as opposed to marginal or conventional) and that recognize them as desirable members.

Some of the most frequent exhausting and unfruitful battles between Link children and their parents occur when the children do not feel "felt" enough by their parents. This misunderstanding between Link children and their parents about the best ways to make decisions or to solve problems is a constant source of conflict, rage, and anguish for both. This is something that Alexandra, for example, feels when her father labels her as "delusional," although she has proven many times in different situations that her "delusional" ways are more successful than her parents' more conformist or mainstream ways.

Links as Nonconformists: Paula

"I don't want to wear any uniform. I don't want to cover myself in anything that doesn't allow me to be myself. I don't want to define myself as a housewife, psychologist, architect, or any other label," my youngest daughter Paula would say, distressed, toward the end of her teen years. Once, at one of our regular Saturday lunch gatherings with family and friends, when someone asked her, in a pleasant and interested tone, what she was going to study—a question that should have warranted a serious response—Paula answered, to the consternation of all the adults present, "I'm studying how to live. Do *you* know how to live?"

From a very young age, Paula was always searching for her truth, which responded to her need to find her "essence" and the meaning that life held, not just for her but for the world. She wanted to exist simply for the sake of existing. Her tremendous curiosity, her capacity for enjoying nature and dance, her close relationship with her grandmother (my mother), her enjoyment of adventures that demanded physical dexterity with her father, and the laughter and tenderness that she generously shared with everyone she lived with signified for her being in the world "just because."

She did not want to define herself using restrictive, predetermined professional titles. Although from a young age she knew she wanted to be a dancer and a healer, becoming just an artist or a just a therapist did not allow her enough space to express her deep passion for living an integrated and artful life and her search for a meaningful life in every single moment of existence.

Some years earlier, after attending a Jorge Donn concert, during which he danced Ravel's *Bolero* with his well-known genius, Paula cried for hours on end, saying, "I am neither Jorge Donn nor Maya Plizetskaya. What am I going to do *now*?" She had discovered that night that her passion for dance, although it was coupled with countless hours of practice and a true effort to learn, was not enough to create the magic that she wanted to bring to the world.

"Magic" for Paula did not involve dabbling in the supernatural. She wanted each moment of her life to shine in a special way, to emanate a light or a "natural" energy that would allow those around her to be able to appreciate the beauty of the world in each of its elements. She wanted to be able to provide others access to something ineffable, something akin to a supernatural experience far removed from the typical, often robotic, gestures and actions of everyday life.

But how could she achieve this if she did not possess an inherent "gift" for a particular artistic activity? How could she achieve this if she also did not want to "dress" like a priestess or guru and did not want to acquire the liturgical elements of any kind that would help her use the words and actions conducive to the creation of magic? How, in short, could she live?

"Between suffering and nothingness, I choose suffering," said Faulkner. Similarly, Paula's unspoken, though lived, response was for many years this: Between a world without magic and a life spent searching, I choose to continue searching, although I might not know what for or how or where. Paula's insistence on continuing her search led her to find what she was looking for: the capacity to help others appreciate the world's beauty and to experience the ineffable in their daily lives.

Paula's refusal to settle for a world void of magic and to remain true to her convictions illustrates not only the nonconformist but also the exacting nature of the Link personality. Links desire precision. They want the pieces of themselves and of their lives to fit together in the exact way that they are supposed to, which can translate into behavior that is "picky" or meticulous or, as in the case of Paula, desires and goals that must be an exact expression of who they are, so that they do not feel like they are "faking it" or conforming to others' ideas about who they should be.

When I was 12 years old, my mother told me that she would not be able to take good care of me if I veered from the paths that she had chosen. As a mother who felt herself to be like a hen taking care of her chicks, tucking them under her wings in order to protect them, she did not know how to care for a child like me, who would take off flying like an eagle, venturing toward horizons and skies where she was unable to follow.

The challenge for my mother, for me as a mother, and for all parents of Link children—who are drawn to their mates because of their difference from each other (the "opposites attract" model) and because of their profound conviction that there is not just one truth—is to uphold what they think is good for their "difficult" child when the child tells them that something is not only not good for them but that it is not what they want and, in some cases, they even feel it is *bad* for them. This is the moment when, in their attempts to not be authoritarian, parents are stripped of their authority to care for their child. Without intending or realizing it, parents fall into the manipulative game of threats and punishments, defending their position by saying, for example, that they are the ones with the financial resources and that, therefore, the child must obey them. But in this twisted dance, the child ends up convinced that they are the victim, or "the good guy," in the realm of emotional power, casting their parents as the victimizers, or "the bad guys." This of course causes the parents to feel bad, guilty, inadequate, and powerless. Paradoxically, deep down, it also causes the child to feel guilty and like the "the bad guy" because they know they are hurting their parents.

Both my mother's mistake with me and my mistake with Paula was feeling too afraid of not being able or not knowing how to shelter, care for, and protect our daughters from the dangers of the world. Regardless of how much my mother gave me, or I gave Paula, the recognition that we were different people and the implications of this difference were too colored by the fear of having failed as mothers and by the guilt of not having been able or known how to produce more "normal" daughters.

Link children, of course, must go through their own moments of "recognition" as they move along their challenging life paths. Link's acknowledgement at the beginning of "Discoveries at the Circus" that he does not in fact know who he is and, therefore, does not know everything (in contrast to what he has always tried to project to others) is crucial to his development. This important step on his journey of self-exploration is what allows him to finally begin to learn. This moment is critical because Link children have a very hard time admitting that they do not know what they want, although they expend much energy trying to make others believe that they do know what they want. Riddled with inner doubts, they behave as if they have a monopoly on absolute truth, although they are just looking for their own essential truth. When their certainties seem to be questioned, their shame, anguish, fear, and guilt increase. Blaming or accusing others can become a habit to free them from the humiliation they feel for having made a mistake or gotten something wrong.

If blaming or not trusting others becomes a habit, the Link child will have serious difficulties with any learning process and with tolerating the inevitable frustrations that come with learning. Therefore, it is critically important to detect the moment when these children "break," that is when they realize they do not know everything and cannot do everything by themselves. On a profound level, they are confronted with the knowledge that they cannot count on either the certainty and pride of belonging to or falling in line with family histories and traditions, like Ms. Zebra, or the certainty of the "right" to hate and harm others that protects the outlaws. They also cannot count on the patience and humility that would allow them to ask for help, nor can they accept the pleasures and conveniences of mutual interdependence. It is in this moment of recognition or "breaking" that Link children (like Link the horse with Ms. Zebra, Mr. Brown, and most significantly and later in the story, David) allow others to enter. They allow those to enter who until now they may have rejected out of fear of having to obey; of not being allowed to be who they want to be; of being led down paths that they would not choose if they were alone, free, and completely independent; of not achieving what is expected of them; or of disappointing others if they allow themselves to be loved and cared for by them. In short, they reach a point where they allow another to take them by the hand, so that they can finally learn.

Chapter 9

Coming into One's Own:
The Link Child's Need for Legitimacy

At this point in Link's journey, Mr. Brown has been responsible for two important turning points for Link. First, like Link's uncle who saves him from the rushing current of the river, the circus owner has come to his rescue by "saving" him from another failed attempt at finding where the shooting stars land. However, he sees Link as "special," as a being who has talent and potential, even if it is not yet clear what those are. Just before arriving at the circus, Link goes from feeling sad, ashamed, and like a failure because once again he is wrong about where the shooting stars land to feeling that he may, indeed, be special, though he still does not know in what ways. Second, when Link talks with Mr. Brown about his role at the circus, he feels happy because for the first time in his life someone seems to understand that, although he may be impossible to categorize, he is a "wildcard" who will be useful for many things that require less specialized, more generalist abilities. For the first time Link feels legitimized for doing what he most enjoys doing and what comes most naturally to him—many different things simultaneously—and it is exactly this quality that Mr. Brown seems to need him to possess. Neither Mr. Brown nor Link fully knows yet what they have to offer each other, but finally someone believes that Link's condition of being indefinable could be useful. For the first time Link sees that being a "Jack of all trades and master of none" might also be a virtue and not just a defect.

Although Link does not ask to be rescued or brought to the circus, he is grateful for Mr. Brown's help and direction. Feeling a sense of relief, he takes on the jobs that the "most important" person assigns him, the adult who holds the power at this moment in his life. Why does Link obey him? He could choose to escape from the circus or to refuse to follow Mr. Brown's orders. At this point in the story, however, Link has already experienced several very painful situations as a consequence of insisting on doing everything the way he wants, often in reaction to a limit or accusation that someone else has tried to place on him and without taking the time to think things through. He is now starting to realize that, as much as he wants to be free, he also wants to belong. As much as he believes that he can get through life completely alone, he has relied on the help of strangers to be able to stay alive and well since leaving the ranch. As much as he needs to be creative and to follow his own thinking, desires, and ways of moving through the world, he also needs to feel contained, protected, supported, and embraced. He needs to feel accepted for who he is to be able to feel taken care of so that he can tolerate being embraced without feeling suffocated.

So rather than continuing to struggle with the constant emotional up-and-down of, on the one hand, feeling great when he does things his way and they turn out well, causing him to feel powerful and even better than others, and, on the other hand, feeling terrible when things turn out badly, making him feel powerless and humiliated, he chooses to follow the paths that his "boss" tells him to follow. For the first time in his life, the limits that someone imposes on him give him a feeling of relief rather than entrapment. For the first time in his life, following directions is more desirable than figuring things out for himself and doing things his own way.

In order to change a habit, to free oneself from a repeated behavior that seems to act of its own volition, eluding our control because it presents itself as more powerful than our willpower, it is essential to give up the pursuit of instant gratification in favor of a more systematic approach toward achieving desirable outcomes. This is difficult for Links because they do not know how to think about or process their intuitions, and they also do not know what will satisfy them in the long run. Deep down they are afraid of not knowing what they want, not knowing how to learn, not being as smart as they think they are, and the certainty that something is missing— something they cannot identify, cannot find, and about which they cannot ask for help. They are unfamiliar with the habit of thinking systematically, seeking out information, and reflecting on their intuitive ideas. And they do not understand that patience is fundamental to the process of seeking.

Letting Go of "My Way"

Link children, like Link the horse, display a habitual impatience and impetuousness about doing things their own way, which provokes conflict with their parents and with others who try to take care of them. In Link's case, he wants to find where the shooting stars land *now*. He wants to cross the river *now*, because he thinks of himself as an adult—self-sufficient and independent. At the race he wants to be admired *now*, in spite of having disappointed, and even betrayed, many others, because according to his understanding of things, winning the race was not the priority (although he implicitly agreed to this when he decided to participate). He wants to be loved *now*, in spite of having inspired fear in the children he was supposed to entertain, because according to his understanding of the situation, he had the right to run fast (although he had been told that this skill of his was not the reason he was hired).

The fundamental, mostly unconscious feeling of Link children is, "Either I do it my way or I feel abandoned, disrespected, unloved, and misunderstood." The truth is that neither Link children nor Link adults completely understand themselves because they do not yet know or understand all the characters (the I's) that make up who they are, or how they relate to each other, or how to resolve the contradictions and the different needs of each of these characters.

Only when Link the horse confronts the fact that "his" way can end up in tragedy, can lead to a painful or even dangerous situation (Gray's injury as they are climbing the mountain, the consequences of which are painful feelings of guilt and anguish; the threats from the wild animals on the boat, which provoke in him feelings of fear and distress), does he become aware that something might be wrong with his way of wanting to enjoy life, which is *Now, the way I want to, the way I think is the "only" way.* He begins to understand that insisting on having and doing things his own way can result in something more negative than positive, more impoverishing than enriching, and more frustrating than satisfying.

Why do Link the horse and Link children have such difficulty understanding and accepting that their parents and caregivers might know less dangerous and less costly ways of achieving good results in life?

As I have said, one of the reasons is that from a very young age their empathic understanding leads them to perceive that each of their parents has their own truth, both apparently valid and considered to be "the best" by those who share it, which leads to the child's not being able to believe completely in either truth. This leads to their not trusting their parents or caregivers. In fact, they are more dedicated to noticing when and how their parents and other authority figures make mistakes rather than in giving themselves over to their protection.

The case of eight-year-old Pierre is instructive here. His father takes him to the pediatrician on his bicycle with the child seated in the basket. Pierre complains, saying that his bottom hurts and that for the ride home he wants to take a taxi. His father tells him that they can't because the taxi won't hold the bicycle. Pierre says, "Then I'm going to go alone in the taxi, and you can go home on the bike." His father responds saying that he can't leave him alone in the taxi because that's not safe. Pierre says, "So then you can just follow me on the bike." Irrefutable arguments.

Another irrefutable argument is what Pierre says after a fall that, unfortunately, results in a broken arm: "You didn't teach me to skateboard well enough. Look at the blood that's coming out of me! You're irresponsible. I already found a pharmacy that can treat me. Google it to see where the nearest one is. . . . You didn't even come outside with anything to disinfect me with."

A third episode involving this same child illustrates another reason that it is hard for Link children to accept (or even listen to or try to understand) the ways of life and good, sensible decision-making (which for them are boring) that their caregivers propose to them: the desire to find "magical" moments during which they feel at one with their surroundings and at peace with themselves and with others. Pierre is with his father in a plaza in Paris, and he is bored. He looks around and sees a man performing magic tricks, for which he is receiving coins that people put into his cap. Pierre starts flattering him and asking him how he does the tricks. The audience is enjoying this little boy who seems like such a know-it-all. The man realizes that he is attracting more people to his show by having the boy take part in his tricks. This goes on for over half an hour. When the show is over, having earned applause and many coins in the cap, Pierre says to the man, "I want my share. I should get half because I brought more people to watch you." The father does not know if he should be embarrassed or proud, and the street performer does not know if he should be angry or laugh at the completely irreverent, but also completely pertinent, demand of the child.

The methods that Link children have of finding ways to entertain themselves—following literal and figurative shooting stars by trying to decipher the clues that their amateur version of evidential thinking tells them to follow—lead them, at times, to unusual, unknown, magical places, in which apparently without effort, without the risk of danger (because clear warning signs do not exist), without any logic that would appear to regulate how to live life, they feel a sensation of flow, of being one with the universe, of being in the moment, where their incessant questioning and doubting cease and life makes sense. These moments of flow serve to ease the permanent existential anguish of these children, who from an early age, before they are even capable of grasping this information, perceive the limits of time (death) and the finite nature of beautiful moments and experiences, and the limits of space (being trapped in the confines of a single body that is able to do some things but not everything and that is also definitively separate from others). Moments of flow bring respite and relief from their perpetual confusion between imagination and reality, between "knowing" something through their feelings and intuitions and knowing something through thinking about it and studying it.

For Link children, this constant state of "knowing" but not knowing what they know or understanding how they know what they know is intolerable and results in tremendous self-doubt. Their self-doubt is exacerbated by reactions from others (as evidenced in the story by Gray and Ms. Zebra), who do not believe them or trust them because they are not able to say how or why they know something. They *feel* what they know, but they do not *think* what they know and, therefore, cannot explain their intuitions and convictions to others in a way that others can accept and trust. The doubts and accusations that others hurl at them of not knowing something, or even of lying, only deepen the frustration and anguish that Link children constantly live with.

Searching for Home

It is understandable, then, that Link children want to devote themselves to finding more of those moments—moments of glorious intimacy and flow—in order to temporarily erase their metaphysical anguish and profound frustration and so that the everyday "I," the corporeal I that exists in time and space, does not need to demand, fight, or cry, because the permanent, transcendent I, is fulfilled. These moments of flow that provide Link children with a sense of calm and fulfillment, the moments where they can feel at ease and "themselves," allow them to feel that they are safe, protected, appreciated, and loved. These moments, however fleeting they might be, provide Link children with the sense of Home that they are fervently seeking (and that they will continue to seek as Link adults), although they cannot yet articulate it as such.

A constant challenge for Link children and their parents is that the search for this feeling of being at ease, for Home, compels them to seek out experiences that to them feel interesting, exciting, novel, and challenging because they hold the promise of this calming Home. The parents, however, believe that their children will put themselves or others in danger if they do what they insist on doing. So two radically different sets of feelings are in play at the same time. Whereas the child feels excited, confident, and completely determined to do what he has in mind, the parents feel afraid and worried and that they must rein their child in. Their fear, worry, and frustration easily erupt into anger when the child does not listen, which then provokes the child's anger, setting in motion a vicious circle and making the child feel deprived of the excitement and feeling of ease that he is seeking.

When Link children experience these moments of Home, they feel embraced by life and that they exist in worlds that are immense, in an infinite universe. But when they do not find their place and places in the world, they feel bereft, empty, surrounded by darkness, and trapped in a black hole. Oftentimes Link children and adults are erroneously diagnosed as bipolar because when they find their space of flow, a feeling of complete happiness akin to euphoria takes over them; but when something goes badly for them and they begin to doubt themselves and everything around them, the anguish they feel is so intense that they cannot find words to express their pain and fear. In between this emotional heaven and hell, there is nothing.

Both Link children and Link adults who do not know themselves well enough to know how they think, feel, and act lack the emotional capacity to handle the inevitable frustration that is part of any learning process. There is no space for the temporary, normal sadness provoked by the awareness of the things that are missing or that they do not yet know. There is no space for the normal sadness of having to let go of people or things that no longer serve the purpose they once served for them, such as friends, collaborators, or jobs. Because Link children cannot tolerate this "normal" emotion of sadness, they cannot experience a healthy process of letting go or of saying goodbye. As a defense mechanism, they resort to blaming, criticizing, and arguing in order not to feel the impotence, frustration, and fear that are unavoidable parts of life.

In the emotional world of Link children, there is no developmental depression of the kind that psychoanalyst Enrique Pichon-Rivière describes. This "healthy" depression occurs when the child realizes that the person who takes care of them, (breast)feeds them, and whom they trust is the same person who frustrates them and whom they begin to distrust when they do not receive the food (the breast) right when they demand it. According to Pichon-Rivière, this moment of realization is necessary and fundamental to a child's healthy development. By contrast, Link children constantly go through either melancholic experiences of profound self-accusation and paranoid guilt or fits of rage and accusations directed at everything and everyone around them or both.[5]

Sadly, sometimes Link children must find themselves in very painful and dangerous situations before they can accept or tolerate dependence and the limitations and lack of freedom that they feel dependence comes with. While parents or caregivers must not relinquish their authority when their child is going through something painful, they must also not abuse their authority by denying their Link child any participation in making decisions. On the contrary, it is essential that they use these situations to appropriately value and legitimize their child's innovative ideas and to contextualize them. This allows the child to have good self-esteem, which does not mean feeling that they are the best but rather learning what their strengths and weaknesses are, where they can be supportive and where they need support, when their ideas are good and original, and when they are a product of their imagination with no basis in reality. Understanding and knowing themselves better will serve as an antidote to the peaks of euphoria and the depths of despair that they typically experience, when they feel alternately on top of the world or inside a bottomless pit. In other words, self-knowledge will allow them to feel good about themselves in a healthy, balanced way, understanding what they are good at and not so good at, instead of continually vacillating between feeling that they are the best of all or the worst of all.

---

5 "Link" as a concept appears in Pichon-Rivière's work but is used in a completely different way and is unrelated to the concept of the Link personality.

Learning How to Learn

In his learning journey, Link the horse makes important strides, learning that he is fast (like his father always told him he was) and helpful (like his mother always told him he was). He is also beginning to learn that there are activities in which the two virtues can be joined by an "and," where, together, they result in better performance, rather than an "or," where they cancel each other out. The most obvious manifestation of the harmonious simultaneity of these two virtues is when he runs fast to seek help for Gray after the rockslide accident. The feeling of harmony also occurs in the first scene of the story, when Link is happily inventing games to play late at night with his friends, a moment when he is excited and inventive but is not putting himself or others in danger. His game of linking the stars with imaginary lines to make shapes is true not only to his name but to the core of his being, since it is a moment when he is operating in the realm of "and" rather than "or," when he is feeling most himself as a Link, most at Home.

Link's progress thus far in his journey of self-awareness, coupled with his frustration at not being able to identify what his own singular talent is, allows him to approach David Green, the circus's lighting technician, to ask him to teach him how to operate the light show. He is finally ready to ask an adult to teach him how to do something. Link desperately wants David to be his guide, his mentor, but he can only dare to have this desire to apprentice with him because he knows that David thinks that Link is special. He is able to trust David because he senses and intuitively knows that David will not ridicule him for being different, will not scold him for wanting to try new things. He senses that David will, on the contrary, accept and even appreciate his unique, "crazy" ideas as positive contributions to the work. This allows him not only to enter into the mentor-mentee relationship but to develop trust and closeness with David the longer he works with him.

Like Link the horse, once Link children know what they know, know what they don't know but can learn, and know what they don't know and can accept without shame what will be very hard to learn because they lack the necessary skills to carry out activities that are not solely based on intuition, they can trust and surrender to the care of others. They can stop being afraid and stop being constantly on the defensive. Although they will encounter difficulties that will continue to appear throughout their lives, they can begin going down the hard road of adjusting themselves to the discipline that any learning process requires.

The encounter between Link and David occurs under perfect conditions: Neither David nor Link feels fear. Link is not afraid that David will want to discredit him as Gray did and as (very subtly) Ms. Zebra did or that he will want to attack him and take advantage of him the way the mean animals on the boat did. More importantly, Link does not feel the profound, unarticulated fear of being accused of being bad, being abandoned, or being unloved.

David, in turn, has nothing to lose or gain with Link. He does not need Link to rise in standing or to augment his self-esteem. He knows who he is, and he is at ease with himself—an important part of why he is able to be an excellent mentor to Link. If Link does not follow his instructions, David will not doubt himself or his authority and expertise (the way parents of Link children typically do). He will simply think, "Poor Link, what a shame that with so much intelligence he doesn't give himself the gift of being able to receive what I have to teach him." David's attitude will allow Link to question his own authority and need for power in a way that is healthy for his development. Link will realize that refusing everything, refusing to depend on someone, to learn from others, to obey rules, to accept the rules of games that aren't invented by him—none of this will make him feel strong. And above all, he will realize that constantly rejecting what others offer or propose does not make him feel at peace because it means he must always be on the defensive and, ultimately, alone.

Since fear is not present as the predominant emotion in the relationship, the feeling of trust between Link and David can grow. This is a necessary condition for Link to be able to look at himself more calmly, more honestly, and more joyfully, as well as to feel enthusiasm about his quest to follow the shooting stars that will take him to the Home within himself, to the place where all of the Links inside him, all of his "characters," or I's, and innermost needs, can live harmoniously, in the space of "and" rather than "or."

Link's decision to work with the light show mirrors this longing for an inner connectedness, a place where the various Links are linked together as one. It is no accident that Link gravitates toward an activity that involves everyone: Through the light show he has a unique power to make every single audience member feel that they are a special and necessary part of the performance. Through lighting everyone up, he converts them all into participants in the magic. "You are the magic," says the ringmaster to the audience. True to his name, Link creates a way of connecting with many people at once as well as a way for them to connect with each other by having them all participate in this communal magical moment.

With David, Link learns that his name is not strange, ambiguous, and undefined. He learns that he is not just a wildcard who only exists as a pawn to be manipulated in the games of others, but that, precisely *because* he is Link, he has the ability to bring together dissimilar elements from different universes—and the power to create new ones. He also acquires the new name of "Light Magician," which legitimizes him and defines him as one thing and as having a singular talent. It gives him a concrete (if temporary) identity rather than being considered a Jack of all trades, as he is when he first arrives at the circus. In stark contrast to Ms. Zebra's telling him that his name is strange when Link first meets her, David's support of Link's development allows him to own the identity that his name reflects as something positive and valuable.

Nature vs. Nurture

The Nature-Nurture conflict is never more evident than in Link individuals. Beings like Ms. Zebra, who move through life along a less conflictive path, experience very little if any tension between nature and nurture because for them there is a concordance between the two that allows for a harmonious parent-child relationship. Links, however, must constantly struggle with the inner tug of war between nature and nurture that affects their pursuit of the wholeness and harmony that they need. That is, they must struggle between what they know instinctively, deep down in their being (through their extraordinary capacity for chameleonic empathy and strong intuition), and what they know from their upbringing, which is in part that no one absolute truth exists—no single law, rule, or life path that can be completely trusted.

"Nature" allows Link the horse to know that enjoying the feelings that come from showing kindness toward others (which provides a sense of belonging and connection) is as good as enjoying the exhilarating feelings that come from running fast (which provides a sense of independence and freedom). In the past, however, he was confused by "nurture" when his innate kindness and speed came with the high cost of being rejected and being accused of being a bad horse (at the racetrack and on the ranch with the children), which resulted in his feeling that he was neither likable nor good. The fundamental identity conflict for Link children is that they reject (by nature) being domesticated (through nurture) and therefore are unable to access the benefits of being "tame," which would help them not feel like outlaws, which would allow them to feel just weird or different rather than wild and bad.

At the circus, however, because he has evolved to a place where he can tolerate the sadness of his failures and because he has had the good fortune of encountering David along his path and of recognizing him as a mentor, Link is ready to "take on" an identity. Through his ability to connect, in this case by seeing—through his sensitive, perceptive way of looking at the world—the colors of the audience and through the speed with which he links it all together in a new configuration, he becomes the Light Magician.

One of many important and influential conversations with David occurs after the first light show, when he has adopted this new identity. Link says, "I wish I could see my own colors as easily as I can see those of others." Although he is crying, he feels relief in his tears because the light show and the connection with the audience give him a purpose, a sense of belonging, despite his lingering uncertainty about who he really is, about not knowing what his own true colors are.

Link's heartfelt declaration during this conversation, "You are the very first person who understands me even better than I understand myself. You don't judge me at all," indicates the critical importance of trust for Link children. They need to know they can trust the authority figures in their lives—most often their parents—to not judge them, to accept them, to offer them the precise embrace that they long for. This trust can only exist, however, if Link children feel that their parents demonstrate stability, certainty, and confidence in their parenting as opposed to uncertainty or vacillation or incoherent contradictions related to setting limits or expectations for their child. Therefore, it is extremely important for parents and other authority figures to behave with confidence, to own their legitimacy as *good* parental authorities, and to feel and act on the certainty that placing limits on a Link child is necessary, although the child might resist. The best way to reduce the child's resistance is to accentuate the positive and creative things that the child succeeds at doing precisely due to being a Link, a "connector," a "unifier," without even realizing that this is who they are.

During his debut performance as the Light Magician, Link experiences an important challenge, a moment that illustrates how far he has come on his path toward feeling at ease with himself. In the midst of the flow and harmony that Link is experiencing as he mesmerizes the crowd with his light show, a man yells from the audience that he is a fraud. In stark contrast to how he would have reacted in the past, Link handles that situation well and calmly, showing his increasing maturity and ability to control his impulsiveness. The audience rewards him for this by clapping and cheering once again in support of his calm answer to the accuser. Link's calm reaction, however, could have just as easily been a defensive or even volatile one rooted in fear. While it is true that Link's positive connection with the circus audience and his way of handling the accusing comment indicate his continued progress towards integration, he is still, like most Links, tortured by the impostor syndrome. A lack of confidence, anxiety, doubts about their thoughts, abilities, achievements and accomplishments, negative self-talk, feelings of inadequacy, dwelling on past mistakes, and not feeling good enough are long-term companions of both Link children and adults. The attitude of "I know," "I can do it by myself," "I don't need help" is a defense mechanism against their deepest fears that the contrary is true. But these contradictory feelings—those associated with fear and anxiety and those associated with confidence and "know-it-all" behaviors—are completely sincere.

It is important to understand that Link children are not narcissists, nor do they have outsized egos. Their egos are nothing more and nothing less than a link, a place of perpetual emptiness that only has meaning if it joins together opposite elements in harmonious ways. Therefore, praising them or emphasizing the positive will not transform them into unbearable, pedantic people if this praise is accompanied by offering them new challenges and integrating their individual achievements into community achievements, that is, if it is accompanied by a recognition of family or community heritage or legacies, or the learning processes and experiences of people who are or have been in their life (like David with Link). This is essential for Link children to be able to grasp the concept of being an individual and being part of a community at the same time. Being "for myself" and "for another" at the same time, arriving at the place where they can accept their own vulnerability and not be afraid to show it, allows them to enjoy relationships of mutual caring and openness. These relationships bring with them the place of Home that will give Link children a feeling of inner calm and ease with how they are in the world.

Link's experience as the Light Magician allows him to feel more integration within himself as well as connection and integration with others, that is, some measure of ease that Link children and adults yearn for. The tremendous affirmation Link receives from the audience, however, is not enough to allow him to fully reach the comfort zone he is so desperately seeking—that place of peace and Home. In other words, he does not yet fully know how to be the "link" he is destined to be. While Link declares to David after the success of his debut as the Light Magician that he feels "at home" in this identity, saying, "So maybe this is what I have been searching for all this time," his inherent restlessness and boredom will soon take hold of him again, ultimately causing him to leave the circus to pursue another path toward Home.

Chapter 10

In the Zone: The Link Child's Addiction to the Search

As Link progresses toward a deeper understanding of what he knows how to do well, and as David's trust in him grows, Link is able to create *his own* magic show. David's trust authorizes Link to explore things through trial and error, without demanding that he understand the intricacies of the technology in order to control the lights in a deductive or analytical way but by allowing him to experiment with the light board through his use of evidential thinking. Link's magic show is a place where what he wants to do coincides with what others want him to do: Playing with the lights entertains the public, makes money for the circus owner, provides some prestige to David as the supervisor of this new successful performance, and allows Link to have fun and be creative. Everybody wins.

Everybody continues to win when David, knowing that Link gets easily bored when he is successful at something, encourages him to collaborate with Susu, the accordion player. David's idea is a gift to Link because it provides him with another outlet for his creativity, another place where he feels he can be fully "himself." To create a new show with Susu he needs to concentrate on the challenges of learning something as part of a team and of coordinating and harmonizing different desires and ideas into a single multifaceted performance. He has no time to get bored.

Despite things going so well for him at the circus, Link's frustration and restlessness take hold of him two more times while he is there. The first is when he pitches his idea to Mr. Brown about having audience members hold flashlights so they can participate in the light show, only to feel the sting of rejection and denial of something that Link feels he *must* do in order to fully express himself and his creativity. Again, as a Link, he is the inventor of new games, the one who proposes innovative, new ideas. What he and Link children cannot tolerate, however, is the rejection of their ideas by others, whether they are peers or adult authority figures.

The second time he feels intense frustration and restlessness is after months of performing the new show with Susu. His creative work with Susu is a key moment in Link's journey for a number of reasons. Like David, Susu is an adult he can trust and whose calm and quietly self-assured manner radiates an inner peace and ease that then envelops others, including Link. He and Susu "link" with each other in a profoundly creative way, producing the most successful synchronized show the circus has ever had by combining music, movement, and lights in harmonious and beautiful ways. This work with Susu is not only a soul-saving outlet for Link's creativity; it also symbolizes and embodies where Link is in his development and his journey. The harmonious integration of disparate elements (music, movement, and lights) is a place of peace, a symbolic home that Link is able to inhabit for several months and one where he feels affirmed, validated, and recognized. He actually experiences the feeling of integration more fully in this work with Susu, both because, externally, he is linking or joining different elements together to create a whole, and because, internally, he is able to integrate more of his "I's" than he has ever been able to in the past.

Addiction to the Search

In spite of these positive, affirming experiences, Link grows restless and bored. If he is not creating something new or able to act on a new idea, he is unhappy and feels the need to leave, to move on to another adventure, a new chapter in his life. This pattern of experiencing affirmation and success followed by feelings of boredom and restlessness is typical of Link children and adults. For someone like Ms. Zebra, receiving praise is assurance enough that she is in the right place; it legitimizes her and her (relatively easy) life path. For Link, even after he receives tremendous praise upon excelling at the light show and exhibiting his originality and creativity in various ways, the feeling of success or legitimacy wears off. It is temporary, and he must keep seeking.

This urgent need to be constantly seeking out new experiences (in the form of a new job, new relationship, new place to live, etc.) is what I call "addiction to the search." The ultimate challenge for Links is knowing when to not continue searching simply because of their addiction to the sensation of almost euphoric joy that comes from feeling that they are being nourished by the world rather than feeling alone and nourished only by themselves. The challenge is also knowing how to recognize when they have found what they were looking for and when to stop chasing something new. Incorporating and integrating something recently learned is more important than escaping the boredom that is bound up with depression, but Links do not yet know this. How to stop searching is what Link the horse, Link children, and Link adults need to learn.

At this point in his search, Link the horse is afraid. He has already managed to become the star of the circus as the Light Magician, and he has already shared a new form of stardom through his successful show with Susu. Now, however, he wonders what will happen if his inventions dry up and disappear. He knows that he does not know as much about lighting as David or as much about music and dance as Susu. He knows that he was not born and raised in a family (like Ms. Zebra) that has been dedicated to performing "magic" in the circus for generations. It is true that sometimes in his life he creates moments that are unique, sublime, and magical. It is true that he manages to turn ordinary situations into extraordinary ones. But Link has no idea how he does this. Therefore, he does not know if he will be able to re-create those magical moments either for the many others who love and appreciate them or for himself—an uncertainty that causes him to feel afraid. For Link, repeating the magic means losing the magic because he loses the taste of the unexpected, the surprising, the new, what transcends the limits of time and space. The absence of that feeling is terrifying.

This fear of failure goes hand in hand with a fear of disappointing others and not living up to expectations, all of which leads to his feeling that he must "escape" from the circus in order to escape the unbearable fear that he carries around inside him. He feels he must escape the fear of Ms. Zebra's anger that might be accusing him of having lied to her when he said he had no skills, the fear of depending too much on the circus owner because he gave him a name and a place in the world, the fear of David's sadness at being abandoned if he wants to change professions and if he no longer needs him as his mentor in the field of lighting.

Given his inability to *admit* that he is afraid, however, Link uses the pretext of blaming someone else to justify his escape, saying to David after he announces that he must leave the circus, "Besides, I keep asking Mr. Brown if he will invest in flashlights for a different show idea I have, and he keeps saying no. I think it's finally time for me to go." Blaming someone else and chalking his desire to leave up to boredom allow him to not confront the tremendous difficulty he has with embodying a single identity. Limiting himself to just one identity would feel like a spiritual death, a killing off of the other "I's" that are clamoring to be expressed, revealed, and also legitimized. Because of his fear that his true self (all of his "I's") will disappear and no longer exist if he commits to one endeavor for too long, Link abbreviates his life processes, moving in quick succession from one pursuit to the next. This existential fear, coupled with his fear of failing and disappointing others, propels Link to flee from the success he has enjoyed and from the demands and responsibilities that come with it.

With all addictions, the element of immediate gratification or instant relief is fundamental to detonating, instilling, and perpetuating a behavior that takes over the ability to make good, well-reasoned decisions. For Links the unconscious thought process goes like this: *I am not the one choosing to do this. Rather it's the object of my desire, the thing that is attracting me like a tempting serpent or a singing mermaid, that is making me do this.*

Finding the Flow State

In the case of the addiction to the search that Link the horse as well as Link children and adults suffer from (following all of the literal and metaphorical shooting stars that appear on the horizon), what provides the instant gratification and relief is the state of "flow," that profoundly fulfilling but fleeting space that allows them to exercise their ability to find the perfect connections or encounters, the ones containing the ideal combination of different elements existing in harmony with each other. The flow state, or the feeling of Home, is the catalyst that sparks the need in Links to be perpetually embarking on something new. The experience of newness allows them to continually arrive at an "Aha!" moment or a "eureka" of discovery.

The concept of flow, developed by Mihaly Csikszentmihalyi and sometimes referred to as being "in the zone," is characterized by complete absorption in what one does and a resulting loss of the sense of space and time. This flow state is created in a particular relationship between one's skills and the challenges in the specific activity that the person decides to focus on. Putting into practice one's own natural abilities to conquer the challenges that arise in a given process and maintaining a delicate balance between, on the one hand, the risk of entering the zone of anxiety (stress) because the challenges appear to be much greater that one's abilities and, on the other hand, that of entering the zone of boredom (lack of interest) because the challenges are too small for the abilities—this is all part of the experience of flow.

What is the ability or skill that Link children feel to be most characteristic of them, that flows most naturally from them? Understanding a wide range of experiences (feelings, different ways of communicating, etc.), surprising others with their tremendous capacity for making unusual connections, discovering details that are imperceptible to a less trained eye, and feeling sensations of fullness and transcendence that are generally ineffable because they are so unexpectedly unique. For Link the horse, the experience of working, creating, and performing with Susu is the prime example of participating in something ineffable, his own quintessential experience of Csikszentmihalyi's notion of flow or being "in the zone."

If Link had been able to count on a different unique, well-defined ability—his speed, for example—he would have been able to find his flow state in the athletic competitions in which running was the measurable element. Or if his unique, well-defined ability had been the ability to take care of others, he would have been able to find his flow state in his particular way of caring for others, also a measurable element. But given that his most defining characteristic is his extraordinary capacity for global empathy (feeling others' feelings to be his own), neither running faster nor caring better for others gives him the peace he desires, the peace that would allow him to forget his metaphysical anguish and to get outside of his own head and body, the places where the unease takes up residence.

Link the horse and Link children feel at constant risk of drowning in a sea of questions, doubts, fears, conflicts, contradictions, insecurities, and uncertainties—the shifting currents that form and epitomize the selfhood of these individuals. Searching for a shore to land on, arriving Home, is the goal of all seekers. Home signifies the safe haven, the place of ease that you land on that confirms for you that you were not crazy for engaging in the search that got you there. Each time a seeker experiences the feeling of flow, they feel they are Home, that harmonious place they are seeking where they feel they are one being, integrated. Paradoxically, however, they feel that they fully, truly exist only when they are seeking.

Recall that Link children are almost always overcome by a sense of metaphysical anguish due to the constant awareness of the limits of time (death) and space (loneliness), and due to the need to find meaning in life and a way of inserting themselves into this world. Looking for the place of stillness, the balancing point that stabilizes the needle on the many scales that all need to be balanced at the same time, can become addictive, and in fact, the risk of it becoming addictive is almost constant.

Recall, too, that the way Links resolve problems is through trial and error, and the way they learn is through evidential thinking: following clues that will only be revealed as the correct ones (as opposed to false ones) if and only if they reach their destination. Therefore, what is better than always being at the start of a new search, when the process of connecting the dots, of making meaning out of signs and clues, already produces the feeling of being capable of success? What is better than always being the unique one, the first, the pioneer, the one who escapes insulting comparisons and can move around with the freedom of being "one of a kind"? What is better than exercising the ability to quickly understand a complex situation that requires innumerable simultaneous interpretations in order to forget about the painful internal conversations that tell them that they are never "good enough" at activities that are measurable?

These moments of perfect flow are only present at the beginning of a search, the beginning of a new task, new relationship, or new challenge. Almost immediately afterward, it is inevitable that the Link child will experience anxiety and/or boredom. Learning processes, after all, are not linear but full of highs and lows, plateaus, errors, and, potentially, joy when one finally understands or masters something. For Link children, the lows of recognizing an error or admitting they do not know something (which implies that they depend on someone who knows more than they do), are not just the normal lows that most people experience but the feeling of not existing, of forever being dependent, of being a total failure, of being eaten alive by the black hole of nothingness.

From Omnipotence to Despair

More than anything else, these children feel bad and guilty. This is because when they begin any given process they feel completely certain that they can do it alone, that they do not need help. They actually think that they already know how to do whatever they set out to do. Their capacity for imagination, coupled with their ability to understand a scene through global empathy, is so powerful that it makes them feel that a problem is already solved. But when they confront difficulty or an obstacle that provokes frustration or the need to stop what they are doing, they go from feeling all-powerful to feeling completely powerless.

This feeling goes hand-in-hand with fear because they realize that 1) they do not know how to do what they were certain they could do or 2) they can do it once but cannot repeat it because they do not understand the methodology or steps required to carry the action out. They have no patience for taking the time to learn the steps, although doing so would allow them to be able to understand how they carried the action out in the first place and would ensure that they are not simply operating at the mercy of luck. The powerlessness and fear that all of this provokes makes them feel angry, which causes them to blame those around them for their failure. This, in turn, leads to their feeling guilty and that they are "bad" for having lashed out at others.

Being powerful in various ways causes them to act as if they were omnipotent, especially after spending much of their lives rejecting teachers and mentors because they did not trust these authority figures enough and out of fear of being criticized, belittled, or deemed "less than" (not smart enough, not good enough) by them. This feeling of omnipotence comes from not knowing their own limits or the limits of any given situation. For Link children, limits do not represent a necessary and desirable containment or restraint designed to protect and help them during a learning process. Instead, limits are transformed into a condemnation to exile, to complete and utter failure. Nothingness.

This happens because they have not learned, nor have they been taught, to understand or know what they know. They are not able to describe what they know in a way that would make them feel that they can trust the knowledge that they feel they possess. Therefore, they cannot transform their ideas, which they think are brilliant and wonderful, into a tangible project that would make their creativity and intelligence visible to the world. They also cannot submit to the learning processes required to attain the confidence and mastery they seek because they cannot tolerate the internal contradiction and tension between knowing something quickly (as they do, through intuition and global empathy) and what for them feels like an impossible slowness that is required to learn something by carefully thinking it through. Very quickly they fall into despair. They abandon their ideas and can become apathetic and paralyzed, anesthetized and numb. In some cases they may even contemplate suicide as a form of escape.

Although it might appear to be the opposite, Link children do not believe in themselves. And if they believe in a part of themselves, they feel they are betraying other parts. The defense mechanism against this constant feeling of doubt and insecurity is to launch themselves into risk, into action, without pausing to think, because on some level they believe that if they do, they will remain paralyzed forever by the fear of failure and/or fear of being accused of betrayal. This way of running ahead as a reactive way of keeping danger at bay causes them to adopt pedantic positions, to appear to be people who are "full of themselves" and who do not ask for permission to do what they do.

Another difficulty they must encounter is feeling overwhelmed by the imposter syndrome, the fear of being discovered as fakes, as not knowing what they are supposed to know. This intensifies the fear of being punished for being bad. The self-sabotage of Link individuals is inevitable if they adopted this attitude of omnipotence (which typically manifests as arrogance) without realizing that it was not necessary and without understanding that what they know (and it is true that they know a bit about everything) is more than enough if they delineate clearly their rights and responsibilities. It is important that they not take on tasks intended for "specialists" for which they need to know a lot about a certain thing. There have always been and will always be people who serve as the Link child's teachers—whether the child learns from them through their chameleonic ability to imitate, their global empathy, or their oppositional defiance. These teachers, like David, support them in coming into their own healthy and developmentally appropriate "power." When these children take full stock of and are duly recognized for their abilities, they are able to begin to move beyond the feelings of powerlessness, fear, and guilt.

Link's self-sabotage is evident in his conversation with David when he announces he wants to leave the circus. Both are frustrated (like parent and child)—David because Link refuses to listen to reason and wisdom as a result of his usual attitude of "my way or the highway," and Link because he feels hemmed in, limited, and anxious, causing him to resist David's guidance. Although David keeps telling him that Home is not about an external place but an internal feeling, for Link, Home still equals where the shooting stars land—what he imagines to be an actual, physical place. Furthermore, David recognizes the impulsive error that Link is about to make when he invents a mistreatment on the part of the circus owner (the refusal to let Link follow through on his flashlights idea) to justify his need to leave. But what triggers Link to feel compelled to keep seeking his "fix," the feeling of flow and freedom that Links are addicted to?

It is the frightening thought that he has "arrived" and that this means he will have to stay there at the circus as the Light Magician, doing what the public and the circus owner want, for the rest of his life. Link and the majority of Links I have worked with do not want their being, or essence, to be defined by a single way of existing. Any single way of being seems to them to be a betrayal, in the sense of being a rejection and diminishing of the other options. For Links, this feels like an amputation of vital parts of themselves. They experience success, then, as a kind of death.

Being loved and thinking that this affective dependence condemns him to having to be how someone else wants him to be in order not to betray or abandon the person who loves him is another element Link must grapple with in this struggle. The idea of not being able to repay or reciprocate the love he receives and of betraying this love terrifies him. He prefers to put himself in a position of being the one who is tossed aside or abandoned and to show that he is not deserving of this privilege of being loved, rather than "stealing" something that he feels he does not deserve or that he feels is exaggerated or usurped.

Finally, Link is afraid of becoming too full of himself, too powerful. He has always struggled against systems by disobeying orders and locating himself as a "victim" of the powerful "bad guys." If he is the one who now has power, however, he thinks that he will become a powerful bad guy, someone who feels he has the right to lord it over others. Yet at the same time, he does not want to lose the privilege of being the one who accuses, denounces, and points out the incongruences of the systems, although adopting this role might mean that he will remain on the outside as opposed to being on the inside. And being on the inside, of course, while providing a sense of belonging, means that he must accept the established rules of the game—even if the rules are dictated by him. Accepting any rules—even his own—makes him feel suffocated because he still feels trapped and deprived of the absolute freedom that he longs for. He must continually negotiate between, on the one hand, his need for freedom and the ability to live authentically, as his "true" self, and, on the other hand, his need to belong and to be accepted and loved.

Given these beliefs about himself and his relationship to his surroundings and the many situations that arise in life, it is almost inevitable that Link convinces himself that leaving is a necessary act of survival. But as with any decision that is made from the impulsive, rash behavior that characterizes addiction, Link the horse does not just leave the circus but, without realizing it, also abandons a part of himself. He could, however, leave the circus taking with him the best of what he has learned, making the decision from the reflective behavior that characterizes an accurate evaluation of the situation.

Keeping a Healthy, Loving Distance

As we know, David is not afraid and does not despair when he sees that Link urgently needs to discover on his own his purpose in life. Unlike most parents, David, who has no history with Link and, since he was not the one who raised him, no reason to feel guilty or that he has done anything wrong in shaping Link, is able to feel a healthy involvement with Link but not an unhealthy fusion with him. He cares about Link and sympathizes with him, but he is able to maintain a healthy emotional distance, focusing on the big picture instead of each annoying or infuriating confrontation. David does not feel responsible for the difficulties and complexities that Link experiences when choosing the best possible ways of living his life. Because he does not feel responsible and, therefore, does not feel guilty, he is able to recognize the enormous richness and potential of the creative life that Link internalized as his own from the diverse models that he was exposed to growing up. This is beneficial to Link as well as to David himself, because Link can also experience pleasure in a learning process that is less guilt-ridden and less conflictive.

In contrast to an objective mentor like David who can approach challenging situations with Link with equanimity, parents of Link children continually face these dilemmas: How to exert authority without being authoritarian? How to be democratic and respectful of your child's desires and strong will without putting yourself or your child in danger? How to be for yourself and for your child at the same time? How to teach your child to reconcile their various desires, to integrate their different "I's" into a single harmonious "I"? While it is difficult for parents to have David's detachment during the daily conflicts with their Link children, characterized as they are by tantrums and angry outbursts (often from both parent and child), it *is* possible and is, in fact, the challenge that parents of Link children need to be taking on.

Up until now Link has been searching in a disorganized and fearful way for his reason for being, the sense of purpose and meaning that makes life worth living. Link's dilemma is that he still does not know what a "good life" will look like for him. Link children also experience this dilemma, unable to settle for the lack of satisfaction that they know their parents experience in their own lives, whether it stems from their fundamental differences and problems with each other, their professions, or other aspects of their lives. When their parents insist that they have to get an education, get a job, aspire to a certain kind of life—in short, conform to societal expectations and norms—Link children cannot abide this, representing as it does for them the unhappiness and dissatisfaction that they perceive in their parents' lives. It is safe to say that Link children feel happy in infancy and early childhood because their parents are happy and united around this special being they have produced, in spite of their differences. But once the children register that the differences between their parents have become a catalyst for conflict rather than a basis of attraction, they begin to be feel unhappy and insecure, emotions they externalize in "bad" behaviors, as we have seen.

The challenge presents itself more virulently in those moments when what you think is good for them is not what they think is good for themselves and vice-versa, and when you do not want to use your authority as the one with the financial and legal power over them to impose your will on them. In spite of the anger, anxiety, and extreme anguish that you feel when you cannot contain, protect, calm, embrace, or even love them the way you would like to and the way you know that they need you to, *your love is always present*, as is your emotional commitment. You desperately want to give them what they need so that they can find, in their own lives, what is best for them. The reassuring news is that, despite their rebellious behaviors, *Link children know this.*

❖ ❖ ❖

The risk for Link of, once again, not finding the landing place of the shooting stars is huge, given that until now his movements were "push" migrations, motivated by the desire to leave various places. What David wants for Link is a positive "pull" migration, which he demonstrates by proposing to him that he work with Sia at the space center, thereby encouraging him to go to a place that might be a better fit for him than the circus. David understands that this would keep him for a longer period of time in a state of flow, given that he would have to use more skills than those needed to perform well in the circus light show. He understands that the space center work would involve multiple learning processes in which Link would at last be able to see his own colors through daily discoveries and measurable progress. While at times David feels frustrated with Link's impulsive decisions, he is not afraid to let Link go or to let him pursue his search in his own way. In fact, by encouraging him to move on to a new challenge, he helps him get closer to the fuller self-knowledge he is seeking.

Link will continue to benefit from this healthy detachment of caring, compassionate authority figures in his life, most immediately from his encounter and training with Sia, the head of the space center. His experience during the training and the eventual journey into space, which he is chosen to lead, ushers Link further along in his quest to find the internal harmony that he longs for: a less fleeting place of peace and Home that he can at last find within him and claim as his own.

Chapter 11

In Perfect Harmony: Learning to Be a True Link

Link's "flight" from the circus, motivated by a combination of push and pull factors, leads him to what will be the greatest adventure of his young life as well as the most profound experience thus far related to his development and to his quest for a sense of inner peace, belonging, and validation. This adventure is his experience at the space center with Sia and her team of experts, from whom he will learn more than he could have imagined. The transformation that Link experiences during this period of training and the subsequent travel into outer space are central to his growth process and the integration of his different needs and contradictory desires.

As discussed in the previous chapter, Link's departure from the circus is rooted in a fear of being forever trapped in a single identity, in addition to the fear of disappointing others. He therefore behaves in the most typical Link way: Out of fear of disappointing others, he disappoints. Out of fear of abandoning people, he abandons them. Out of fear of not being able to or of not wanting to perform in a way that will satisfy the expectations that he himself created in the circus audiences and in the circus owner, he is responsible for tremendous dissatisfactions. He therefore feels the need to escape, to break the ties of belonging that bind him to the circus community.

NO ONE IS TO BLAME

David's calm way of understanding and interacting with Link allows him to propose to the intrepid horse a way out that is less painful for both Link and those who love him at the circus. David understands that going to the space center will provide Link with work that he knows how to do and is perfectly suited for: connecting different systems, translating, interpreting, and conjoining dissimilar elements. Link is on the verge of going to a place that will allow him to travel to where there are many shooting stars, to where he will be able to see them simultaneously up close and from a distance. He will be able to see his own search in the "big picture," to understand it from a broader perspective, and to be able to feel that his quest is connected to this larger whole. In short, he will understand that he is not alone and that his journey serves him as well as others.

This movement toward integration and a sense of belonging or feeling at ease with himself and with the external circumstances of his life is related to the following questions that all Links pose constantly to themselves: If I am not for myself, who will be? If I am only for myself, what am I? And if not now, when? This is the mantra that expresses the conflict that Link the horse, Link children, and Link adults who do not yet know they are Links experience. This is because who they want to be may not coincide with who those around them want them to be. The two main feelings that this conflict provokes are anger (related to powerlessness, submission, feeling suffocated or stifled) if they feel that they are doing more of what others want them to do than what they themselves want to do, and guilt (related to selfishness, abandonment of others, and betrayal) if they feel that they are doing more of what they want to do than what others need, want, or expect of them.

The central need and desire that Link the horse, Link children, and Link adults who do not yet know they are Links share is that they want the two things at the same time: to be who they want to be and to be who others want them to be. When, after their long search, they achieve this, they have arrived Home, the ultimate destination of the shooting stars (the quintessential metaphor for Links themselves), where they can softly land and at last rest, the place where the constant questions about the meaning of life recede (for a little while, anyway).

Link allows himself to experience what he does at the space center only because he has reached a stage in his development where he is finally able to discipline himself to learn something new that he is neither familiar with or controls in a methodical way, requiring perseverance and dedication, and to stick to it, rather than bouncing around from one thing to another. Links typically find it hard to discipline themselves and do not accept discipline at all when it is imposed on them because, being autodidacts, they always insist on learning by themselves. They prefer this to the feeling of imprisonment they experience when they are forced to follow instructions or manuals.

My daughter Paula taught me this lesson when, at the age of 16, after studying for two months with a friend of ours who was a brilliant writer and an exceptional teacher, she refused to continue. Our friend was disappointed because she thought that Paula was unusually insightful. But Paula's decision to stop attending the private lessons initiated a pattern that would repeat itself later when she decided to discontinue photography classes after only three sessions with a well-known artist who had also praised her work. Paula said to me in no uncertain terms, "Don't pay for me to have any more classes with the best teachers around. I don't want you to spend money on things that I already know that I don't like enough to continue with."

That was a hard moment for me because she had convinced me with her curiosity, interest, and intelligent questions that she *was* interested in literature, then photography, and before that, ballet, and before that, music. To her credit she always, since adolescence, insisted on living "authentically," in a kind of community system based on exchange, a desire that we, her parents, looked upon with benevolence, telling ourselves that sensitive people are always utopian. We took her desire for this more egalitarian economy and way of living much more seriously, however, when, at the age of 30, with much effort and a high degree of commitment, Paula was able to realize this desire by choosing to live in a small community that operated in this way.

What, then, leads Links to dive deeply into something, study, and discipline themselves enough to stay the course? Finding the task, idea, or project that combines the possibility of using most of their skills and abilities in service of an interest greater than just their own. That is, being the same person, at the same time, for themselves and for others. Transforming their constant and innumerable contradictions into creative, unique, original, and integrative paradoxes.

What allows Link the horse to accept the rigorous discipline that is necessary for him to prepare for his new job as the coordinator of the journey into space? Two elements are always present in any transformative process, in any shedding of an old habit or way of thinking and choosing a new one: the push factor and the pull factor, both of were in play with Link's decision to leave the circus. The push factor is rooted in failure, in what makes one have to abandon a place because of the threat of death, whether real or symbolic. The pull factor is rooted in hope, in what one hopes will be salvation, the possibility of a new life, whether real or symbolic.

By the time Link the horse arrives at the space center, he has reached the limit of the "my way or the highway" way of being. He has experienced the bitterness of failure, pain, disappointment, disillusion, shame related to his mistakes, and guilt related to the accidents he has caused. Through his experiences at the circus, especially his apprenticeship with David, he has also enjoyed the pleasure and affirmation of success, pride in his abilities, the certainty of some of his hunches and intuitions, and the satisfaction of doing a job well and of meeting or exceeding others' expectations.

He therefore does not want to go back to the place of "my way or the highway" that he has just managed to get himself out of. Toward the end of his time at the circus, Link could easily repeat that mistake if he were to leave the circus in anger, feeling that he is misunderstood and underappreciated, because of an irrational fight or because of feeling himself to be a prisoner of someone else's wishes. He would once again be trapped in the negative script that tells him, "There's no place in this world for you, Link." Thanks to David, however, Link does not fall back into that mode, and he has something to look forward to with the prospect not only of working with Sia and the space center team but of reaching the shooting stars by traveling to outer space. He has enjoyed the peace of belonging and the pleasures of reciprocity—of learning that if he respects and listens to others, it is more likely that he will find someone who also respects and listens to him. Because of this, he is able to feel motivated to explore completely territories that are unknown to him but that others have mastered. The space center experience will provide him not only the vastness of outer space, that is, the possibility of seeing himself from the outside, but also the opportunity to be simultaneously the Link that he wants to be and is able to be while being the Link that Sia asks and needs him to be.

A fundamental question remains: What makes it possible for Link to get to this place where he is on the verge of giving full expression to his idea—finding the landing place of the shooting stars—previously a utopic fantasy, but now suddenly a concrete, realizable goal?

Link experiences a *mutation*. He experiences a profound leap in perspective as a result of the accumulated lessons of his journey that have been crucial to his development while on the path toward integration and feeling at ease with himself and with those who accept him as he is. This mutation is precisely what allows Link to finally feel he can be for himself and for others at the same time, in the same place.

Like Link the horse, only when Links experience a process in which they can resolve their contradictions, finding new ways of feeling integrated, without cognitive dissonances among their different values, can they create a life in which it is possible to be for themselves and for others at the same time. They need to find a way to exist that allows them to not feel weak, miserable, or captive to the desires of others when they choose to pursue their need to feel that they belong somewhere. However, this place must also be the place that allows them to not feel mean, violent, or treacherous, to not turn into people who constantly reject and criticize the values and ways of life of those who are not completely like them when they need—within this space of belonging—to also pursue their profound need to feel free.

It is important to note that the process of mutation does not need to happen in every area of a Link's life and that different mutations will happen at different times in their life. Links may experience the longed-for sense of ease, calm, and integration in their professional life, for example, but not in their personal life, or vice-versa. Mutation means that Links can comfortably accept that their inner lives are filled with an infinite range of contradictory feelings and can acknowledge that, for them, ambivalence and uncertainty are normal feelings that they bring to any decision-making process. For Links, the key is to seek out solutions that are integrative, that transform contradictions into paradoxes that they can "be" with from a place of ease rather than anguish, shame, guilt, fear, and doubt.

Links as Kaleidoscopes

Using a kaleidoscope as a metaphor for Links, we can say that their selfhood is made up of many little colored pieces of glass. They vary in shape, size, and color, but they are all contained within the same structure and reflected by the same mirrors, which allow the wonderful effect of simultaneous multiple reflections that seem to speak to each other. The person using the kaleidoscope experiences many constantly changing, unique, and magical manifestations of color, shapes, patterns, and light as the pieces organize themselves into different configurations. Just as operating the kaleidoscope allows one to experience the beauty of ever-shifting visual mysteries, the beauty of Link individuals lies precisely in their paradoxes, in the changes they undergo as they move through their developmental journey. The moment that the person stops moving the kaleidoscope is the moment that the little pieces fall into place, finding their "right" space (using Bonder's terminology) in the multi-mirrored structure. But if we were to look through a kaleidoscope without the element of the multiple mirrors, we would only see a bunch of disorganized, chaotic, maybe even unattractive pieces of glass with no understandable logic. It is precisely when the movement stops, at the exact point when the mirrors can simultaneously reflect all the colored pieces, that the originality is fully revealed in the fascinating creation of a reality that seconds earlier did not exist. So it is with Links: Before they "mutate" the world sees them as chaotic, unpredictable, unpleasant, and strange. After their mutation, when they arrive at a place of peace within themselves, the world is more able to appreciate their beauty, originality, and "difference."

Links can mutate only once they understand that they are supremely empathetic and learn to distinguish their feelings from those of others. Understanding what feelings are theirs and what feelings belong to others (even though they themselves are feeling these feelings) allows them to say "no," first to themselves and then to another person, from a healthy place and not from a reactive, oppositional place. Pre-mutation, Links feel that they can only be free if they are not doing what the other person wants them to do. Their symbiotic relationship with others (due to their global empathy) does not permit them a sense of belonging that is their own; they feel afraid of not being able to leave the symbiotic relationship, afraid of never getting out from under the desires of the other person—a tremendous key force behind their defiant and challenging behaviors. Yet Links tend to prolong the symbiosis because they do not know what their own desires are: what it is that they want as separate from what others want.

Mutation, then, is a paradoxical movement: Links must feel more secure about themselves in order to stop taking refuge in their defense mechanisms (being in constant fight mode or behaving arrogantly); yet they must also understand and accept that they need others. Only by letting go of their arrogance can they strengthen their identity, and as they strengthen their identity, they are able to move away from the behaviors that leave them feeling alone. It is a virtuous circle.

As seekers of the metaphorical landing place of the shooting stars, Links must learn when to stop their search, when to say no to their entropic tendency to continue moving, seeking, and questioning each and every truth, in order to be able to formulate their *own* truth. As with kaleidoscopes, this truth is made up of multiple, sometimes contradictory pieces, but if it organized from a rigorous, constant, and honest dialogue among all of these pieces and sifted through cenesthesia (the feeling of inhabiting one's body that arises from various bodily sensations), it will give Links a view of their specific reality that can be considered *their* truth, and it will allow them to make the correct decision in any given moment. Cenesthesia is key in this process, because it allows Links to prioritize the relevance of each bit of information, each bit of truth related to the objective they are trying to reach, which is to be at peace with themselves, to feel at ease. In other words, they need to stop moving the kaleidoscope (themselves) when they arrive at a place where the pieces reflect congruence and connection among what they think, what they feel, and what they do; that is, when their head, heart, and gut are in harmony with each other and their whole self feels at Home.

Finding the best moment to stop is difficult for Links because it is based on this key question: Who am I among my many I's? How do Links recognize the right moment, the one they can trust and count on as the moment when they find the truth they have been seeking? This is a tricky question because the trust that they are looking for is precisely the trust that they will find by looking carefully, rigorously, and in a disciplined way at each unique reality from all points of view, from all the I's that make up the kaleidoscopic identity of Links.

The analogy of the albatross from Chapter 7 is helpful here. Just as the albatross may not seem to know how to fly but can glide her way across a vast ocean, Links may not know what they want and they may lack personal ambition, but they can reach more goals than the average person thanks to their capacity to glide within and among many points of view and life's many styles and forms. Links must learn to differentiate between the information or signals that come from their gut and the information that comes from what Antonio Damasio calls "false maps of the mind," which refer to the ideologies and values that they have been taught that are in conflict with their own needs and feelings and that have caused them to mistrust and deny the information that their bodies gave them when they were children.

The mutation that Links must experience, then, is the passage from behaving and being considered and treated like "different," undesirable children because they are so challenging to deal with, to behaving and being considered and treated like different, but very desirable, adults because their complexity makes them so useful and valuable.

For Himself and for Others

Link's progress in his own mutation process is most evident in his experiences at the space center, where he is finally able to commit fully to a rigorous training program so that he can learn the challenging and complex job of leading the team that will travel in space. The most crucial moment arises when he is in the spaceship and perceives that he and his team are possibly in danger. Rather than listen to Sia, who, from her position on the ground at the space center, tells him that there is nothing to indicate danger, Link disregards her assessment based on his own reading of the situation. This scene is important and key to understanding where Link is in his own mutation process. He disobeys Sia because in this moment he knows and feels he must put greater trust in his own bodily sensations—his gut and intuition—which will allow him to avoid a horrific accident. He is able to trust his intuition in this moment because he feels confident about what he learned in the formal training he underwent to be the leader of the expedition. He is able to integrate his intuitions (feelings) with his knowledge (thoughts), relying on his creativity *in relation to* his training instead of relying on his creativity with no solid underpinning of the knowledge required to successfully carry out a project. In this crucial moment of integration of head, heart, and gut, Link understands that he is not imagining things, that he actually *knows* the truth of the situation through the combination of his intuition and his training. This is a critical moment of integration for Link, one in which he feels a coherence among what he thinks, what he feels, and how he acts.

As the leader of the spaceship's team, in this moment especially, Link is able to harmonize for his own benefit and the benefit of others his capacity to be autonomous: sufficiently independent to be able to think for himself, and sufficiently dependent, or connected to others, to be able to sense the fear of his crew. In short, he is the "link" between the danger (which is felt or sensed) and avoiding the danger (which is thought and action).

When Link is able to express in words and with logical, comprehensible arguments why he acted the way he acted in that moment of peril, he does not need to fight, as he did when he was younger, when he still had not taken the time or made the effort to profoundly understand his actions and when he lacked the words to make himself understood because he did not yet understand himself. Having experienced the mutation process, he now knows that when he gets angry, it is because he feels vulnerable. He knows that the defense mechanisms he previously used—hiding his doubts from everyone, including himself, and exaggerating his certainty about things—no longer serve him and are no longer needed. He understands that studying, learning, and respecting the conventions of any learning process gives him, paradoxically, the freedom to act in a creative and intuitive way without fear of being accused of being an impostor or delusional. Now he is able to say, "I know this, and I don't know if I know that, but I have some ideas that seem like valid possibilities. Would you like to hear them?"

Link the horse and Link children need to feel that they are wanted, accepted, understood, and embraced by their parents in all their complexity and contradictions, and that their parents can help them to figure out the creative element—that unique, original, imperceptible something that is contained in their ideas but that, because as children they lack the rational, conceptual, and linguistic understanding to explain it, gets expressed as impulsive behavior, tantrums, or evidence of oppositional defiant disorder.

This profound need to be understood by others is satisfied in Link's relationship with Sia at the space center. Like David, Sia appreciates and values Link's many versatile qualities and abilities. She and others at the space center understand that his kaleidoscopic way of being in the world, his ability to make connections and grasp things that others do not always see, is an asset to the work they are doing at the center. Link has the freedom to act on what he feels is right, even as the "experts" on the ground are telling him to do something else. Rather than being criticized for this, he receives well-deserved praise. Rather than being considered defiant or insubordinate, he is valued for knowing the right thing to do in that moment, for listening to himself rather than others. But Link is only able to arrive at this place of receiving appreciation and respect because he has made important profound changes in himself. He has learned how to learn—to rely on others to give him knowledge and information that he needs to be successful in his work—and he has learned how to unlearn behaviors that were keeping him stuck in a place of defiance and, as a result, marginalization.

Now that Link has experienced the mutation process, he can begin to fully understand himself as a "Link"—as a being who has value and who has much to offer precisely because of his difference from others, his quirks, his intuitions (rooted in global empathy), and his ability to make helpful, valuable connections that most others cannot make. He can now do what was unthinkable throughout the course of his long search: He can return home to the ranch, the place where his journey began, the place where so long ago he left behind those who love him the most.

Chapter 12

Arriving Home: Linking to Self, Linking to Others

Freedom. Belonging. Peace. Home.

The relationship among these concepts is potentially complex for anyone who has struggled to define themselves in relation to the family they were born into or raised by and in relation to the community or communities they find themselves a part of. For Links, the tug-of-war-like tension is even more distressing and taxing. How do Links find not only a home, but the deeper feeling of Home, when they feel the continual pull of freedom and independence from everything traditionally associated with home? How do they live a life characterized by freedom—a need that all Links share—when the need to feel a sense of belonging and not feel marginalized by others is equally strong? How and when do Links ever find the peace in their lives that allows them to let go of the addiction to the search so that they can explore and choose their places of belonging from a less anguished and, therefore, less provocative place? How do they find the peace that allows them to dedicate themselves, with patience and commitment, to mastering where they are in their journey, both in relation to themselves and to the project or pursuit that they are involved in at that moment?

A hallmark of the Link personality is the urge or need to leave stable places behind. Links both nourish and are nourished by the various cultures, communities, and groups that they insert themselves into.

Their search, then, does not end. The difference is that when they are operating from a place of feeling at ease with themselves, they will stop and stay somewhere for the amount of time that is necessary and agreed upon by them and those around them rather than just pausing as if they were nomads and then moving on precipitously to the next project, job, or relationship. When they do finally move on, they will do so in a thoughtful, caring way. They may be leaving, but they reflect on and understand why they are leaving and demonstrate care for and seek understanding from those they are leaving. Their leaving takes the form of a careful closing of a chapter, rather than abandonment.

The process of mutation, as Link the horse makes clear, does not happen quickly or without real effort and the development of tremendous self-awareness. It requires time and entails struggle for Links, as well as demanding patience and understanding from those closest to them. At the end of the journey, however, lies an invaluable reward: the feeling of finally being at ease with themselves and with others, which allows them to contribute their unique gifts and talents to the tasks, problems, and challenges that they will continually confront in life. Link's journey home to his family is highly symbolic, encompassing not only an emotional reunion and welcome but also his own personal "landing." He at lasts finds Home, belonging, freedom, and peace—what he was searching for all those years, even if he did not always realize consciously what he was searching for.

On the heels of his triumph at the space center, Link's most fervent wish is to return home. After years of making his way from one place to another, one adventure or experience to another, he comes full circle back to his roots—the ranch where he was raised and nurtured by those who love him more than anyone else in the world. Feeling the importance of this return home, he insists on leaving the trailer that is taking him to the ranch and walking through the familiar landscape of red mountains, the same beautiful mountains where his journey first began in a state of confusion, self-doubt, and sadness. The rockslide those many years ago caused Link to feel that he was not only different from others but, in fact, a dangerous presence in others' lives, given the emotional and physical harm he had inadvertently caused his cousins as they were climbing the mountain. Upon returning home, however, after all his work to try to be less difficult for others to understand, he can trust that he will be more easily accepted in his "difference" and more readily appreciated for his "weird" contributions.

Link's need to finish his journey on foot is important because it allows him the time to take in the landscape and prepare himself emotionally and mentally for reuniting with family members and friends, whose reactions to his sudden reappearance he cannot predict. It also allows him to seek out Mr. Tree, the grounded voice of wisdom who was the first to give Link the name of "Seeker," validating his impulse to leave his home and continue with his journey of finding his purpose. Link prioritizes expressing his gratitude to the tree, and the tree, in turn, recognizes that Link has learned from his many adventures and experiences and is now able to make wise decisions. While the tree is forever rooted in one place—the way he is meant to live out his own purpose—Link is meant to live out his own purpose through freedom of movement. Their means to the end goal of integration and purpose may be radically different, as is the number of years of life experience that each has, but Link and the tree have ended up in the same meaningful realm, if not in the exact same place: Both are good, wise, and discerning, and both know much about who they are and what they have to offer to those around them. They both understand that the world needs them, that they have a purpose. Link undoubtedly still has much more to learn about life than the elderly tree, but they have in common a grounded sense of self that was absent from Link when he first set out on his journey.

Most importantly, Link understands and accepts that he took the path he needed to take to get to where he belongs, the place where he feels truly accepted in his individual idiosyncrasies. As a Link, he could not have done it any other way.

When Link arrives home, he is surprised by the warm and effusive welcome that his family and community give him. While not everyone is thrilled to see him (Gray, in particular), he is now able to accept that he will still experience rejection in his life for being the way he is but that he can choose not to identify with the rejection and not take on the role of the crazy, weird, or bad one that others assign to him. Equally important, he has learned to be humble enough to learn from his mistakes, recognizing that, despite his good intentions, he is still behaving arrogantly with Gray by presuming that he knows what he should be doing with his life. Link is able to listen to Pink gently admonish him for this, pointing out that he needs to recognize when he is in a situation where his help is needed and useful and when, not only is it not useful, it is not wanted. Link has learned much during his journey and has returned to the ranch having changed in fundamental ways. Like all of us, however, he still has much to learn about relationships and about himself. The mutation that Link experiences is essential for him to understand that in the course of his life, rather than desperately seeking answers in confusing contradictions, he will need to transform these into intriguing paradoxes.

The most significant aspect of Link's return to the ranch is the peace he feels being there, in stark contrast to the restlessness, defiance, and need to break free that characterized his sudden departure years earlier. He can only feel this peace, however, because he has experienced the mutation that allows him to feel at ease within himself. His inner calm and self-acceptance, hard-won after many years of searching, in addition to his humility, opens up space for him to apologize to his parents for the pain he caused them by disappearing without a trace so long ago.

It allows him to "own" the arrogance and cockiness he exhibited when he still lived at the ranch. It allows him to show his parents how much he loves them and to understand that, although he is different from his family, he is not a bad horse, he is not being cast out from the sheltering fold, and he deserves to be a part of his family.

The importance of peace runs throughout the message his deceased grandmother leaves for him in the seashell. She acknowledges that it was also hard to "make peace with the parts of me that seemed to be in conflict with each other." Among other lessons his grandmother shares in the seashell message, she says, "[Y]ou can use your skills to be a peacemaking link, connecting the beautiful parts within yourself and also building strong relationships by connecting with others." Grandma's words capture the essence of what it is to be a Link who has mutated and the reason that Links are called Links: When, through the mutation process, they are able to integrate the contradictory parts of themselves, they have the capacity 1) to make connections that others do not (Link as the leader of the space mission, when he intuitively knew that something was wrong); 2) to bring disparate elements together to form pleasing wholes (Link as Light Magician at the circus); and 3) to be a peacemaker—a mediator—in situations where opposing views are at play and there needs to be reconciliation or compromise.

The path of a Link child typically begins with strife, defiance, arrogance, sadness, anger, inner turmoil, and feeling like an outcast. But after experiencing the mutation process, adult Links can land in a place where others appreciate them for their creativity, out-of-the-box thinking, originality, capacity for making connections that others do not readily make, ability to unite people, and—ironically, given where they started—their calm presence in the face of conflict or danger. The calm that they feel inside them does not prevent them from expressing excitement, enthusiasm, or other strong emotions. It just allows them to express these intense feelings from a place of ease within themselves rather than a place of self-doubt masquerading as arrogance or a place of powerlessness that causes them to feel the need to wield power over others.

In the closing scene of *Link and the Shooting Stars*, after Link has been back home for several months, contributing his unique skills and talents to the community, Link and his father one night are gazing up at the sky together. His father lets him know how much he loves him and how proud he is of him, despite not having understood him in the past. This moment of love and deep connection with his father contributes further to the peace that Link feels. When he looks up at the constellation that he considers to be his reflection, he sees two stars shining more brightly than before, mirroring this newfound link to his father. In this moment he accepts fully that being a Link is how he is meant to make his way in the world. He understands that the connections he has made in his life with and for others are precisely because he is and has always been a Link, an "essential go-between."

At this moment, a shooting star passes through the night sky, affirming his sense of himself and his identity as a Link. His father, for the second time that night, offers Link *the precise embrace*, bestowing his blessing on Link for him to feel the freedom to stay or to go, without judging his son, without labeling him. Link's feeling of warmth, peace, and fullness lingers after his father walks away to let him ponder the immense night sky in solitude. Link realizes that, whether it is his family home or the space center or any other place where he feels appreciated without feeling afraid of being rejected or of having to be someone he is not in order to be accepted, "he would always have a place to land."

Link's return to the ranch, his childhood home, allows him to finally understand and *feel* that the home he left is still his home. More profoundly, his return to the ranch symbolizes his return to himself, though it is in many ways a self that is vastly different from the one that left the ranch years before. The essential Link qualities are and have always been there, however. The difference is that now they can be fully appreciated by those who love him because the masks of anger, arrogance, defiance, and rebelliousness have been replaced by humility, patience, and respect for others' ways of being and living. The inner fear, self-doubt, and paranoid guilt have been replaced by inner peace.

The ranch provides shelter, warmth, comfort, and love from his family and community, a wonderful home that he can return to again and again. The space center and no doubt other places he will venture off to in the future are also places he can call home. Yet no physical space, family, or community is the Home that he has been seeking. The Home he has been seeking is precisely the peace that, after his long search, he feels within him. He finally understands that the feeling of belonging is something he can carry with him from place to place, something that comes from the inside, rather than something granted from the outside by others. He can belong and still be free.

At the end of the story, Link sees one more shooting star as he is lying under the night sky in peaceful solitude thinking about his own trajectory. The star seems to give him a smile and a wink as it shoots through the resplendent sky, bestowing upon Link the ultimate affirmation: Link the shooting star has landed. Link the shooting star has found himself and his inner peace. Link the shooting star has finally found within him what he needs to feel truly free—his Home.

Chapter 13

Parenting with Compassion: Learning How to Give the Precise Embrace

As a parent, perhaps you feel some comfort knowing that your child's mystifying and exasperating ways of being have an explanation and a name. You may even feel relief knowing that you are not alone and that many other parents in the world are also struggling to understand how to best parent their Link children.

But you may be asking yourself: *Why me? Whose fault is this—mine or my partner's? My child scares me. It's as if I don't recognize her. I feel sometimes that I don't know how to love her and that she doesn't love me. How do I help my Link child feel better? How can I love my child in the way she needs to be loved?* As a Link adult, you may be asking yourself similar questions: *What did I do wrong? Why am I like this?*

The goal of this book, and this chapter in particular, is not to prescribe actions and behaviors but to help parents and adult Links understand, accept, and *trust*—despite their fear—that they have the capacity to understand the complexity of Link individuals. My hope is that it will also help to guide adult Links, as they continue on their journey, to that place inside them where they trust themselves. Trust and creativity, in spite of the fear and uncertainty, are at the heart of all of this.

A key part of the learning process for parents is to fully understand and accept that the difficult situation they find themselves in with their

Link child is also unbearable to the child. The challenging work of trying to understand what is going on in every interaction with their child and what underlies the anger and conflict, without giving up during moments of crisis in the relationship with their Link child, will create space for the child to tolerate, understand, and accept himself. Throwing one's hands up and declaring, "I give up!" is an option parents have when they are feeling despondent, guilty, and like they have failed. The purpose of this book is to help adults who care for Link children to understand that they have other options for dealing with these complex beings, who are not better or worse than other people, just different. Giving the Link child (or adult) the precise embrace, in the place where they are hurting the most *and* when they exhibit their most challenging behaviors, helps to teach them to appreciate their multifaceted, contradictory, and difficult way of being and to stop judging themselves so harshly. It lets them know that, while they may be difficult, they are not crazy, bad, or dangerous people.

Just as Link the horse's mentors help him throughout his search, parents have the ability to give their child the tools they need to help them make their way in the world and to perhaps make their child's journey Home—the place of ease and peace that they seek within themselves—less painful, less fraught with danger and risk, and less frightening and anguishing. Teaching them to establish priorities related to what they want as an individual and what they want as a member of a community alleviates the fundamental tension that Link children and adults suffer from—a tension rooted in their perpetual internal struggle between their need to be free and their need to belong. For the child to achieve this they must learn to take care of others (satisfying the need to belong) while learning to take care of themselves (satisfying the need to be free while also being accepted, idiosyncrasies and all). Parents can play a critical role by legitimizing that these contradictory needs require creative solutions that honor the validity of both.

Preventing the "perfect storm" that produces a Link child is not possible. To recap, the perfect storm comprises four circumstances: 1) being born with an extreme capacity for empathy, 2) being exposed to very different and often contradictory values and points of view, 3) understanding that one's parents are good people but not being able to fully trust them to take care of them as they would like, and 4) experiencing a family trauma either in utero, infancy, or early childhood.

The Link child is born into and shaped by these inevitable and uncontrollable circumstances. Accepting this inevitability is necessary if parents are to be able to forgive themselves as parents and forgive their child for being so different and difficult to understand and satisfy. *No one is to blame. It's nobody's fault*—not the parents', not the child's.

As human beings and as parents, we cannot do everything, and we cannot do everything right every time. The dynamic between parents and their Link child is one of trial and error. There are no maps for raising these children, who are unique in their idiosyncratic difference. You will sometimes enjoy the feeling of having gotten it "right" with your child, of giving them what they need and reaping the reward of their good, loving behavior in that moment. Other times you will feel that you have failed when, despite following to the letter suggestions and advice on how to embrace such a complex being, it doesn't seem to be working because your child isn't cooperating or responding the way you hoped. Trial and error is an inevitable part of this journey, as it is of any journey, process, or experiment in which there are neither maps nor guidebooks from other parents of Link children. Therefore, hurt and missteps are inevitable, as is the almost mystical joy of discovering the precise embrace, well given and well received. For this reason, it is so important for parents to be compassionate with themselves as parents as well as with their child, who suffers because they are the way they are.

This chapter is not a list of prescriptions or instructions. It is an embrace that attempts to be precise by reaching the place of pain, sadness, worry, and guilt that parents of Link children suffer, as do Link adults until they learn to transform their negative contradictions into positive paradoxes.

Working with Global Empathy

It is important for parents to acknowledge that guilt is somewhere, somehow always in play. Guilt rumbles around in our minds and bodies, sometimes quietly and surreptitiously, sometimes noisily and deafeningly, insisting in unpleasant ways that we have done something wrong. In the case of parents of Link children, guilt cries out, "Why do I feel afraid of my child? Why do I get so angry with them? What did I do to make my child this way? What did my husband/wife/partner do to make our child this way?"

Similarly to Link children themselves, the intense frustration and anger that their parents feel mask feelings of fear—fear that they do not understand their child, that they cannot do anything right in relation to them and are, therefore, failing as parents. And like their Link child, parents find it easier to deal with their own anger rather than the profound sadness and despair they might feel in relation to the parent-child dynamic. Anger, torturous guilt, and accusations directed at oneself, one's partner, or one's child are attempts to hide the fear of failure, heartbreak, and powerlessness.

Link children's global empathy causes them to not only sense this parental guilt but to incorporate it into themselves as their own, which makes them feel truly bad, like failures who are condemned to exile and being alone. One of the most effective things a parent can do to help their Link child is to help him understand his emotions, including guilt (which Link children feel all the time as paranoid guilt, and which is impossible to overcome and makes it impossible to feel like a good person). By encouraging the child to be curious about his emotions, distinguish them from those of others, and name them, parents are able to support their Link child in his journey of self-exploration and help him understand the consequences of his innate global empathy, the original cause of the jumble of confusing and contradictory feelings inside of him.

Helping Links Understand Their Feelings

Link children's global empathy makes them feel all the feelings of others as their own. They do not realize that the sadness, fear, or anger that invades them can belong to someone who is physically near them and that these emotions cannot necessarily be explained as natural reactions to the situation in which they, and not the person nearby, find themselves. Basically, they do not have a clear understanding of the difference between themselves and the other person. They are sponges that soak up the emotional energy that emanates from people who are important to them, or they are chameleons who take on others' emotional shapes and colors.

Links, more so than most people, are also highly susceptible to emotional contagion. Whereas global empathy is innate and defined by a profound incorporation of others' emotions as one's own, emotional contagion is brief and superficial. The child is "infected" by others' emotions, mannerisms, accents, etc. and adopts them as their own; but unlike their experience of global empathy, they know their feelings or "imitations" in that moment are not theirs. While most people have moments of emotional contagion (such as being susceptible to infectious laughter when not being in a good mood), unlike Links, they do not experience this in addition to global empathy. Links must continually deal with both.

Since their emotional reactions are often explosive and unrelated to the circumstances in which they appear, it is to be expected that parents or other people involved in the situation do not understand what is happening or the true cause of a fight or an attack of anguish when nothing on the outside seems to justify it. Link children and adults who do not yet know how to distinguish between what they feel as a result of their own situation and what they feel as a result of global empathy often find themselves involved, or even trapped, in confusing situations characterized by misunderstandings, trial and error, and categorical affirmations and negations in which they do not know how to express themselves and from which they do not know how to escape.

One way that parents can help a Link child (or that others can help a Link adult) is to clarify for the Link individual what they are feeling and then communicate transparently and honestly that the anger, fear, sadness, or whatever else they may be feeling is not coming from the Link person but from them, from something not necessarily related to the actions of the Link child or adult, and that the emotion the Link person is feeling is a consequence of their high level of global empathy. Links need to understand that feeling the emotions of others does not mean they are to blame for having these emotions. They are, however, responsible for the ways they react to this emotional "contamination." They need to learn that fighting, attacking, and accusing are not useful ways of dealing with the confusion and distress caused by their global empathy.

As we know, despite behaving as if they are constantly rebelling, Links are so obedient that if someone important to them, due to their own conflicts, needs them to behave a certain way—whether it is being completely servile and complacent or being angry, resentful, or complaining—they will comply, believing that they are acting on their own volition when they are actually succumbing to the unconscious will of the other person. Link children and adults want to be loved and harbor a perpetual fear that they will not be. Therefore, in order to please, they unconsciously do what they think the other person needs or wants them to do, although this action might be precisely what makes them not be loved or otherwise works against them. If Links could understand where this emotional impulse comes from, they would not react in the automatic way that they do when they are indiscriminately obeying their global empathy.

To complicate matters further, although the child assimilates the parents' emotions as their own, they do not always read the emotions correctly, so that a parent's mild frustration about something unrelated to the child might manifest in the child as a fear of being blamed that is so extreme that the punishment they imagine can reach tragic proportions.

Another important mechanism that makes it difficult to understand Link children and adults is the projection of their own feelings onto others. If they feel angry about something, although they may not know why, they might believe that their parents are also angry, although the parents may be trying to reassure the child that they are calm and content. Links also feel that they do not love the way they should, that they cannot stand, or even hate, their significant others, parents, teachers, or friends. This is the origin of the paranoid guilt that constantly plagues them: the fear of retaliation because they think that, ethically, they should be unloved, not tolerated, and hated for feeling what they feel. It is important to remember that a characteristic of these complex individuals is their deep commitment to the truth, that is, to ethical conduct, justice, and what is right.

Calm, patient conversations with a Link child when the moment of crisis has passed help the child understand that what the parents are feeling does not always have something to do with what the child has done. Parents can clarify for the child that their feelings are different from those that the child thinks they are feeling. It is also important for parents to make clear to the child that they do not need to take on the parents' feelings as their own or to be responsible for those feelings. If, however, the parents' feelings of anger, fear, powerlessness, and desperation have been provoked by something the child has done, it is important to work with those feelings until they are transformed into compassion, love, trust, and calm.

Of course, it is necessary to help the child connect not only with the negative feelings of dislike they feel for their parents, produced by the frustrations that arise from the parents' attempts to care for them, raise them, and protect them, but also with the positive feelings of gratitude and love that arise from recognizing the affection, effort, and patience of these same parents in their attempts to care for them, educate them, and protect them. This recognition, rooted in the ethics of Link children and adults, is highly curative and restorative in the process of integrating their emotional complexity.

Helping the child understand how to "cleanse" themselves of others' emotions consists of making clear to the child which emotions belong to the parents and working with the child to explore what their own emotions are, separate and differentiated from those that the child imagines that the parents are feeling. Over time, this helps the Link child establish healthy boundaries between self and other, allowing them to see that it is not their responsibility to take on everyone else's emotions and that doing so is detrimental to their own wellbeing as well as to their relationships with others.

Another way to help a Link child differentiate or discriminate between their feelings and those of others is to encourage them to be curious in the realm of emotions. Curiosity is generally an attribute that Link children already have. Exploring emotions together through questions and conversation shifts the focus of this quality to include what is invisible and inside them. It is helpful to extend this to the visible world that they live in and are typically curious about. The questions do not always need to be "heavy" or based on occurrences in daily life. A lighthearted, playful approach could be useful here: "When you're really mad, what does it feel like in your tummy? Does your tummy feel wiggly or still?" Or "When you're really sad, where do you feel it in your body? Mommy feels it in her heart, like a giant animal wants to burst out of there." It can also be helpful to talk about the feelings of different characters in a movie, a show, or a book that the family shares together. Analyzing the personalities of the various characters in the *Harry Potter* or *Star Wars* series (about which much has been written), for example, is extremely valuable for discovering how a child understands their own feelings and motivations as well as those of others. Three other children's films are also helpful in this regard: *Moana*, *The Emoji Movie*, and *Inside Out*.

Teaching children how to name their emotions is a helpful corollary to the previous two actions. Calling an intolerable feeling "anger" or "hurt" or "fear" is a way to begin reducing the pain and, with time, to learn to distinguish between anger and fear, frustration and humiliation, sadness and calm, and euphoria and joy. "I feel angry!" allows for exploration in a way that a tantrum or other volatile behavior alone does not. It creates the conditions that allow children to share what they are feeling in a clearer, less explosive, less desperate way. The act of naming is also an act of taking control, of having dominion over something. The more a Link child or adult can name their feelings and connect them to their bodily experiences, the more they will understand that, despite the almost constant swirl of confusing, angst-producing feelings inside them, they are not reducible to these feelings, nor are they condemned to being confused and hesitant people. On the contrary, they are characterized by a supremely enriching complexity.

Setting Consistent Limits

Setting limits is one of the most challenging responsibilities of good parenting. It is particularly challenging for parents of Link and other "difficult" children because of the exasperation and exhaustion that characterize the parent-child dynamic when the child is typically defiant rather than compliant during the learning process. Parents may even feel afraid of whatever outburst, tantrum, or other angry reaction might be sprung on them next if they dare to admonish, correct, or deny the child something they want. It is much easier to buy the child the candy or toy than to calmly explain to the child why they cannot have the candy or toy during this visit to the store. It is much easier to let the child stay up past an established bedtime than to fight with the child to get them to go to bed. For parents of adolescents, it is much easier to let the child shirk their household responsibilities than to continually remind, nag, and implore, since these approaches often result in a fight and, in the end, prove to be useless for achieving the desired outcomes.

Yet it is not only the child's behavior that makes setting limits especially difficult for parents of Link children. Parents of Link children tend to value difference and diversity of ideas. They tend to believe in (or at least allow for) different truths. Their relativism makes it hard to set limits because so often the parents do not know where the correct place to "draw the line" is. They themselves are filled with self-doubt about what appropriate limits are for a child or adolescent and, because of who they are, feel compelled to allow the child freedom in general as well as certain specific freedoms (the freedom to try different things, even if that thing is not good for the child, the freedom to eat the amount of candy they want, the freedom to not have to stick to a rigid schedule, etc.).

The fundamental confusion for liberal-minded parents is how to distinguish between the limit that protects the child and the limit that threatens to destroy a child's spirit. When parents are confused about limits, whether overtly, through moving the line they set so that there is no firm, consistent rule or expectation, or more covertly, through agonizing over a decision in the moment in relation to their child, their Link child perceives and assimilates this confusion. This is detrimental to the child because the child then has no compass, no guide that indicates to them how to behave. When the parents keep moving the line, they create tremendous confusion in the child, both because the line keeps moving and because the child feels the parents' confusion as their own confusion. The lack of compass heightens the feeling for Link children that they cannot trust their parents and that it is better for them to take care of themselves.

As challenging as it is, parents need to set consistent limits for their Link child because without reliable limits, the child cannot understand what the rules, or the "code," of any given situation are and, therefore, they cannot understand when they will be chastised for something they have done or might do. Setting consistent limits does not mean clipping the child's wings so that they do not have the freedom to be who they are. It also does not mean being overly strict and depriving them of all free-doms. Authoritarian, overbearing parenting does not produce healthy children. For the Link child, especially, authoritarianism will only result in more anger, resentment, and rebellion because they will feel stifled and trapped, deprived of any way to express their creativity and independent thinking. Above all, they will feel that they have the right to behave badly because they consider the contradictory, everchanging orders from their parents to be unfair and, therefore, not credible.

Parents need to set limits that simultaneously protect the child and allow the child the freedom to figure out what they need and what is good for them. In order to do this, parents need to decide for themselves what risks they are able to tolerate and willing to let their child take. This allows them to determine more precisely the appropriate amount and type of freedom for the child to enjoy. When situations call for very strict limits (such as not running into a busy street or not lighting matches without adult supervision), it is important that parents let the child know that the limits are not there because they do not trust the child but because they know what the potential dangers are, including the unintended consequences. The child, however, thinks they have all the information they need before engaging in the risky behavior. When parents adhere to the limits they have set for different situations, the child will more readily understand that there are lines they cannot cross, no matter how much they protest. Conversely, when parents give in to the child's every desire, out of fear that they will engage in objectionable behaviors if they do not get what they ask for, it tells the child that this behavior works, gets them what they want, and, as an added bonus, gives them power over their parents, rewarding their manipulation.

Perhaps this situation sounds familiar to you: Six-year-old Andrea asks her mother for candy, but her mother says she can't have any more. Andrea asks again, and, again, her mother says no. Andrea continues, over and over, to ask, with her requests escalating into pleas and whining, pushing her mother, who has been trying to stand her ground, to the point of exasperation so that she finally gives in to Andrea's begging and lets her have more candy. When Andrea is with her babysitter, she tells her that when she asks her mother for candy over and over, she knows this drives her mother crazy and makes her mother finally give it to her. Not only has the six-year-old learned to manipulate her mother, she is also fully aware that this is what she is doing.

While Andrea may be getting her way and feeling she has some measure of power over her mother because she can "make" her do what she wants, she is also feeling confusion—both her mother's confusion about whether to let Andrea have candy and the perpetual confusion that this leads to: What is okay and what is not okay in any given situation? Because the mother does not stick to "no" in this situation, and because she does this repeatedly as a result of her own confusion about limits and of allowing herself to be swayed by her child, she creates a situation in which Andrea has too much freedom and no firm, reliable boundaries. Paradoxically, the absence of boundaries does not provide Andrea with true freedom, a freedom that is rooted in feeling secure and certain. Instead, over time, it creates uncertainty and confusion about how to read and interpret different situations and how to behave in order to achieve her goals.

Setting limits does not mean denying the child everything all the time, but it does mean keeping things in balance and being ethical and consistent regarding when and why something is granted and when and why it is not. Link children need to feel justice and fairness in situations. And they themselves want to be fair but know that sometimes they are not. However, they do not know how to defend themselves from what they perceive to be unfair behavior from their parents. This exasperates them, which makes them act unfairly toward their parents. Another vicious circle.

For Link children, limits are not just about rules set by their parents. They also feel resistant to conventions, such as those they might encounter at school or in other social situations. When a Link child resists a common, accepted convention, getting to the heart of the matter with the child is helpful. This means talking with the child about why certain conventions exist and why they need to follow them. They can explain to the child that rather than the stifling prisons that Links feel them to be, conventions offer them the key to their own freedom in any culture or group by helping to ensure that they are not further marginalized or harshly or unfairly judged by others. Accepting certain conventions does not mean that they give up their authenticity. It just means that they understand that to be able to exist authentically in a world made up of structures and expectations, they need to know which limits to respect if they want to belong instead of being excluded. They need to understand the codes and follow them so that they can truly be their authentic selves in ways that are beneficial to them and to others. If they remain constantly marginalized because they refuse to enter the world of conventions at all, then they will not be able to discover and create with unfettered freedom who they want to be in life. For Links, the pain of not being able to gain access is more difficult to bear than the feeling of being trapped and unable to leave. Their fear of constant rejection due to their rejection of others is the true prison. If parents take the time to understand their child's resistance to convention and to talk with them about the consequences of that resistance, their Link child is more likely to comply. Consistency is key, however. If parents let their child's continual defiance of conventions slide, this will make the child's path even more full of doubt and confusion and, therefore, harder.

Addressing Contradiction and Conflict

Just as Link children incorporate their parents' guilt and confusion, they also incorporate the disagreement, anger, rejection, and even lack of love that parents from different backgrounds in conflictive situations tend to display toward each other. Parents may feel they are living out a tragedy in relation to each other, and they unintentionally transmit this feeling to their children. Classical tragedy is often rooted in more than one misunderstanding or misinterpretation of events. In the case of the vicious circle that parents and Link children experience with each other, there is a double misunderstanding: 1) Link children "see" and "feel" beyond what they can understand (the double-edged sword of global empathy), but they think they understand everything; and 2) they accuse their parents (either overtly or through their rebellious behaviors) of being blind, ignorant, indifferent, insensitive, and of not understanding anything at all. How can families avoid this tragic misunderstanding?

Revisiting Why You Chose Your Partner

In order to begin to leave the realm of tragedy, parents need to remember what brought them together in the first place, even in their worst moments of estrangement and conflict, even after separations or divorces. This allows them to view their Link children as the beautiful result of a meaningful intimate connection rather than as a constant living reminder of their lack of connection. If parents do this, Link children will discover and connect more easily with that part of themselves that is pleasant, loving, and worthy of being loved. They will be able to find harmonious ways of blending their contradictions more quickly, without the need to take the winding, tortuous, and even dangerous paths that often seduce Link children (and adults, pre-mutation).

213

NO ONE IS TO BLAME

How can parents accomplish this? They first need to recognize that the constant tension between freedom and belonging that the Link child struggles with is also to some extent their own struggle and something they have in common with their child. After all, parents of Link children flew in the face of conventions and expectations by choosing a partner who was not the expected partner, who signified difference rather than sameness or compatibility with the family norm. It is important to let their child know that he has this in common with one or both parents, so that the child feels that he has a family that, in some way, through some specific tie, he belongs to.

Parents also need to have honest, revealing conversations with each other in order to rediscover—or discover for the first time—what exactly brought them together. What do they have in common? What do they love and respect about each other? In particular, what do they love and respect about each other *in the realm of their differences*? The latter question opens the door for parents to acknowledge and appreciate the qualities in each other that are different from themselves—both the traits they value and those that infuriate them about their partner and contribute to the ongoing conflict between them. It also gives them the opportunity to genuinely appreciate each other's qualities as they manifest in their Link child, even if these character traits are not their own. When the traits that the Link child has inherited are positive, albeit different, this is not such a challenge and, in fact, parents can feel happy that their child has inherited something "good" from their partner that they themselves do not have. But when the inherited traits or learned behaviors are "negative"—the aspects of the partner that irritate or infuriate—acceptance and appreciation are of course much more difficult.

Regardless of the negative or ambivalent feelings parents might have toward each other, they need to take care to not transmit their profound dislike of certain traits and behaviors to their Link child because this causes the child to feel bad. Link the horse, for example, observes his parents exchange a wordless look with each other on the heels of their disagreement about whether he should be a racehorse or a riding horse. This look makes him feel confused and even worried that he might be a traitor, a fraud, and, therefore, a bad horse for wanting to be like both of them and please both of them. If Link's parents had reassured him, however, that the look had nothing to do with him but instead with the conflict between them, Link may have still felt worried (due to the atmosphere of conflict), but at least he would have known that he was not bad and not responsible for the look. Beyond this, when parents explain to the child what the differences between mom and dad are and when they approach these differences as possibilities—as interesting components of the family dynamic rather than solely as catalysts for conflict—it provides more clarity, stability, and richness for the child.

In addition to working with their differences, parents need to also identify what unites them, which they can do by revisiting what they have in common and talking about this with each other. Even if the main attraction initially was to their differences from each other, rediscovering what they have in common (if it has been buried over time) will allow them to find concrete places of connection that will benefit their Link child. Perhaps it is music, travel, sports, food, politics, a hobby, or another shared passion. Perhaps it is several shared passions, despite the estrangement or anger they may feel toward each other.

Something besides difference drew them to each other in the beginning. Recapturing this, even just as a basic recognition (not necessarily as a rekindling of love or desire), and regularly incorporating it into their interactions with each other and into domestic life will allow parents to begin the process of opening up space to give their Link child the precise embrace. This is the space where they can meet their child's needs precisely, where they and their child feel a meaningful symbolic kinship that goes beyond belonging to the same family simply because of biological ties. It is the space where they can all feel that they belong to the same "club" and are united because they are connecting with each other in ways that resonate deeply for the child, confirming that he belongs in this family, that he is "one of them" and not an outsider.

Making the effort and the time to regularly nurture and celebrate what parents have in common and what unites them instead of what divides them and creates conflict will allow parents to move forward with themselves, each other, and their Link child. Parents will feel much better if they forgive themselves and give themselves permission to have made the unconventional but autonomous, creative, and appropriate choice that they made based on their desires and needs at the time they chose each other and that laid the groundwork for creating together the child that would later become "difficult." This self-authorization by the parents will go a long way toward the child's not needing to act out her own inner conflict and toward her being able to stop fighting on the "outside" because she will no longer be fighting on the "inside."

For Link children, then, the longed-for feeling of legitimacy and validation, the feeling that they have the right to be different, begins with the parents themselves. Link children need to feel understood and embraced by their parents in all their complexity and contradictions, but this is a hard need to satisfy if the parents feel themselves to be full of contradictions and in perpetual competitive conflicts with each other. It is also hard for parents to give their child what they need when they are afraid of the constant accusations and criticisms that their child hurls at them because of the incongruences that they perceive in them as individuals and as a couple. Instead of being able to offer their child the precise embrace—the response, reaction, or gesture that will reach their child precisely in the way they need it in the very moment when they are attacking their parents—parents, understandably, counterattack, provoking the child to double down on their own attack because they now feel they are being accused of being bad and must have their guard up even more.

In short, if parents actively work on their conflicts with each other and their own internal contradictions and self-doubts, they will be much more capable of giving their child the longed-for precise embrace. By doing this work together, the most important part of which is rediscovering what they have in common and what they appreciate about each other and ensuring some manifestation of this is a regular part of their lives, parents will be taking a huge step toward being able to give their Link child what they need.

Cultivating Trust by Adopting a Healthy, Loving Distance

Suggesting that parents maintain a certain distance from their child may strike some as wrongheaded or counterintuitive. If I am trying to be closer to my child and have a better relationship, why would I want to distance myself from my child?

A healthy distance is necessary for parents to be able to observe their child's behavior in addition to connecting with him emotionally. It allows them to feel compassion for their child instead of judging him. In the most difficult moments especially, it is important for parents to take a deep breath, take a step back, and understand that although their child is yelling at them, *it is not their job—nor in their or the child's best interest—to yell back.* The child is doing everything possible to bait the parents, to drag them into a situation that is rooted in the child's own pain, confusion, and anguish. The natural tendency is to slip into the vicious circle and engage on the child's level of anger, tantrum, and outburst. To be the grown-up in the situation requires distancing oneself from the turmoil in order to be able to "hear" what is really going on. It requires not taking the child's anger or attacks personally but seeing beyond them to understand that he is in pain and that what looks like baiting is really a cry for help. If parents begin from a place of sympathy and/or empathy (instead of their own reactive anger and frustration), they will be able to show compassion for their child's pain and give him the precise embrace.

Showing compassion toward one's child means, in part, taking the time—especially in the most challenging interactions—to understand where the anger is coming from. Anger is often a mask for fear, worry, self-doubt, and pain. Anger is the language that Link children use because they are not able to articulate the emotions that are torturing them deep-down, either because they do not yet have the words to do so or because they are so caught up in their emotions that they cannot step outside of them in order to identify them, examine and explore them, or express them in calmer, more appropriate ways. Their volatile ways of communicating what they are going through are often the only recourse they have in that moment.

Their anger also stems from frustration. Link children desperately want something that they think they know how to get, but since they do not know everything they need to know to obtain it, they do not get what they want. The tension between their uncontrollable desire and the feeling of tremendous powerlessness unleashes intense despair, the best way out of which is through anger. They get angry with themselves, with the world, and with those who brought them into the world without the magic wand that would have allowed them to immediately transform their creative ideas into reality.

Links' struggle between belonging and freedom produces a complex relationship to dependence and independence, which necessarily translates into a complicated relationship to their parents. This, in addition to having to make sense of contradictory messages from their parents, makes them feel that if they rely on their parents they will not be well taken care of and will, additionally, not have the freedom to take care of themselves in ways that they believe are better for them and in the ways they convince themselves they would be able to if they were completely independent. They do not want to need their parents because they feel that if they need them, allow themselves to be cared for by them, or obey them, they will cease to be free, to be themselves. They also feel hemmed in because they believe that to deserve their parents' love they must behave in socially acceptable ways and not embarrass their parents in public, conduct that is many times hard to sustain.

Helping Links Understand Their Guilt

For Link children these complex navigations and feelings are inextricably bound up with guilt: guilt about defying their parents' expectations and rejecting their parents' attempts to give them what they *need* when they do not give them what they *want*. They also feel guilty because they do not know if they are good or bad, generous or selfish, intelligent or just "street smart"—someone who takes advantage of others' mistakes to get what they want. Being Links, they feel they are only ever "in-between"— not one thing or another, always vacillating among opinions, desires, decisions, and actions, while never being completely certain about which of these are their own. They live continually in an amorphous space of doubt, which they transform into "certainty," or assertions and declarations that are overly provocative or aggressive, in order to feel stronger. It is important for parents to understand, however, that the goal of Link children is not to annihilate or erase the person they are interacting with but to pacify their own uncertainty because their constant self-doubt and not knowing who they are cause them to feel perpetually afraid, insecure, and ill at ease.

One of the most important things a parent can do for their Link child is to help them understand the constant guilt that they feel. As in Chapter 6, Segismundo's words are helpful in understanding the notion of paranoid guilt: "[W]hat horrid crime was perpetrated at the time when I, offending you, was born? At last I grasp why cosmic scorn should be my portion after birth…. As being born, I've come to see, is mankind's greatest sin on earth." Because Link children live with this paranoid guilt as a core part of their being, they do not know how to distinguish between "normal" or "depressive" guilt, which is the sadness they feel at not having been able to avoid hurting a loved one, and paranoid guilt, which is the almost constant feeling that Link children and adults have that they will be challenged or accused of something that they are not even aware of. Paranoid guilt is also responsible for Link children and adults feeling that they are bad or selfish when they want or do things that others consider different or strange. These are desires and actions that they defend in aggressive ways, not realizing that this defensive way of being, which comes across as an attack, is what makes others label them as "bad" and, therefore, what causes them to be punished.

Parents can help them to understand, in both parent-child interactions and peer-to-peer interactions, when it is appropriate to feel guilty because they have done something that is clearly wrong and that they regret doing. This can be done by teaching them the possibility of making amends, asking for forgiveness, and forgiving themselves, and by helping them understand if it was an accident or an unconscious way of showing displeasure toward someone whom they love. Parents can also help their children understand when it is unhealthy, in addition to inappropriate, to continually operate from a place of defensiveness and lack of trust.

As previously discussed, Link children also feel guilty about how they love others. They are afraid of being "found out" in the realm of love because they are afraid of not loving people the "right" way. Their constant negative judgments of others, including the accusations they level at others (especially their parents) of being bad, make them feel continually at risk of being accused themselves of being bad, unforgivable, and condemned to being abandoned, excluded, or rejected. Parents can help their Link child to avoid this self-fulfilling prophecy by helping them to understand that their guilt, fear, and other negative feelings do not mean that they do not love their parents or others. While it is difficult to hear accusations from one's child, in these instances parents can help their child by not taking what they say personally or reacting with anger and by focusing instead on the child's pain that underlies the accusations. This healthy distance allows parents to help their child understand their feelings and to let them know that they are capable of loving others and of doing so well and the "right" way.

Providing Unconditional Love

The unconditional love a Link child so often needs means that, no matter what, their parents will not abandon them without trying to understand why they broke the rules so blatantly. Parents need to convey to the Link child the certainty of unconditional love through forgiveness, but not excuse the behavior by downplaying the infraction committed or by avoiding showing the child the negative consequences that their actions may have caused. In contrast to paranoid guilt, depressive guilt, which is the sadness one feels about having done something undesirable, is a feeling that helps to repair, to connect someone with their abilities to heal, to be reborn, to learn. This allows the child to learn to take responsibility for their actions and anticipate the responses to their interactions with others and with the world, removing from the responsibility the tremendous weight of the fear of condemnation and abandonment. It is important for parents to understand that provocative behaviors are ways of asking for the precise, pure embrace, where love is differentiated from responsibility.

Because Link children typically do not know how to ask directly for help, they opt to forge ahead into situations and encounters, not realizing how emotionally vulnerable they are. It is important for parents to learn to read the Link child's subtle signs of distress before they turn into a full-blown explosion or meltdown. This requires a heightened attentiveness, an awareness that allows them to be attuned to their child's emotional needs in a way that is not distressing or smothering but calm and trusting. For example, if a child is at a birthday party but is clearly feeling marginalized or overwhelmed and seeks out their mother or father, giving them unconditional love means not dismissing the child as timid, fearful, or unreasonable but instead offering them the emotional safety net they need in that moment. It may also be the case that the child feels insecure but does not seek out help, in which case the adult who notices this social discomfort can embrace the child literally and metaphorically, letting them know in some subtle way that they are not alone, that someone has "seen" them and understood them. Paradoxically, teaching a child that there are ways of being dependent that do not suffocate or debilitate them will help them search for ways of being independent that do not involve mistreating, rejecting, or abandoning others.

Of course, meltdowns—including instances of full-blown anger—cannot always be avoided. Yet parents can still be there to provide the precise embrace that their child needs—maintaining a compassionate distance that allows them to assess the situation (that is, understand and honor their child's pain and interpretation of what they are going through) and act in a way that benefits the child. The case of Josh, a Link college student, is a good example. Josh and his friends were out drinking one night, and one of the friends was very drunk and fell, hitting his head hard against the concrete floor of the bar, causing him to have to be rushed to the hospital. At the hospital, Josh lifted the friend to put him onto the hospital bed since no medical personnel were doing it and the friend could not stand on his own. In doing so, Josh twisted in such a way that he severely injured his back (having had too much to drink himself). When he returned home for the summer, he was in the kitchen making a meal and talking with his mother, getting angrier and angrier as he talked, saying repeatedly, "Why me? Why did this have to happen to me? Why is my back not better yet?" Josh felt he was being punished for trying to do the right thing by helping his friend into the hospital bed. He was also talking angrily about how the injury was ruining his post-graduation plans: Because of his back injury and not being able to lift things or to bend his back more than an inch or two, he would not be able to work as a waiter over the summer, which he was counting on doing in order to make enough money to achieve his goal of moving to California for a year.

As his anger escalated, he began slamming things around in the kitchen and raising his voice. He threw a serving spoon. His mother was listening sympathetically but also telling him to not get so angry, that it wasn't helpful. She realized, however, that she needed to change course and approach the situation differently because it was only getting worse. She did two things: She set a limit by saying, "No matter how angry you get, you do not throw things around in my kitchen." Josh snapped out of his anger long enough to apologize for that. She then said that she understood why he was so angry and frustrated at the prospect of not being able to make enough money to live independently and move away. Rather than continuing to say things like "Try not to be so angry," she met him where he was and allowed him to let his anger and frustration out—verbally. It was clear that the feeling underlying Josh's anger was fear—fear of never recovering from his injury, fear of not making enough money to be independent, and fear of not being able to leave his hometown, where he was feeling trapped. She stayed calm as he talked about his fear, though he was doing so in an angry way, and she began saying supportive, understanding things that encouraged him to express what he was feeling. Suddenly, his explosive anger turned into tears. At last Josh's vulnerability had come out of hiding, which opened up space for her to give him a long, tight hug as he cried on her shoulder—a literal embrace that he could receive only after she had given him the precise embrace of seeing, understanding, and accepting him where he was feeling most wounded and vulnerable. Showing Josh compassion was the key here, rather than telling him to not be so angry.

As hard as it may be, it is precisely during these moments that parental compassion is most needed. By distancing themselves from the volatility, parents are able to open up space inside themselves to calmly listen, gently probe, ask elucidating questions, and, ultimately, help to guide the child toward a calmer place so that they can identify and explore the frightening emotions that are consuming them and that they cannot handle. This action of distancing oneself from the drama, remaining calm, and helping the child to understand what they are going through so they can arrive at a place of some relief, some easing of the pain, is the most compassionate thing that a parent can do for their child in moments of intense suffering.

It is possible that the notion of the *precise embrace* still seems abstract, and you may be wondering how you can provide this essential way of showing love to your child. When a Link child receives the precise embrace, they feel that you are seeing them in the exact place where it is the most painful to be who they are. This is the place where it is so difficult for Link children to accept themselves that they torture themselves with shame, guilt, fear, or other emotions that, inappropriately understood or acted on, can be very destructive. The precise embrace is what an important adult in the child's life can offer the child to validate their feelings and help them understand themselves in a realistic way, distinguishing their persecutory fantasies from dangers that actually exist and that the child detects but does not know how to explain.

Sometimes words are called for, sometimes not. Josh's mother, for example, could offer the precise embrace by continuing to be attuned to his emotions—including his ability to truly hear her—saying to him something along these lines: "You're feeling this pain because you want something for yourself, but when you were drunk you didn't think about what might happen if you picked your friend up off the floor to put him onto the bed. You were trying to do the right thing, but you weren't taking good care of yourself. You made a mistake, which has had serious consequences. But mistakes are part of learning process, and I know you will get through this."

Providing a child one's own version of the precise embrace, using the words that feel right in that moment (and that are age-appropriate for the child), opens up a space for the child to also be able to accept the literal, physical embrace that is best offered once the worst of the storm has passed, when they feel deserving and worthy of receiving that loving gesture.

Cultivating a healthy, loving distance also means truly understanding and internalizing that the emotional world of a Link child or adult is more complex, mysterious, and agonizing than one can imagine, given that they perform so well in other areas of life. It means letting go of the assumption that one might have about what a "normal" child is like and knowing that not only extreme social injustices, deprivation, or child abuse justify feelings of pain, unfairness, anger, or hopelessness.

225

The metaphysical anguish that Links suffer from—the confirmation very early on of the inevitable limits of time and space—is a completely valid reason for the psychic pain that Seekers suffer from, as described by Boorstin. This is not to say that Link children never feel happy or joyful—of course they do. When Link children feel validated in what they discover or create and are affirmed in their originality, they feel relief from the anguish of feeling alone in their "strangeness."

Honoring that a Link child is a unique being with a complex inner life that is not easily accessible and that, therefore, can cause parents to mistake a panic attack for a manipulative tantrum, makes it more possible to feel and show compassion for the child when he cannot express his suffering intelligibly, since parents are not trapped in the feeling of powerlessness caused by not understanding their child perfectly well.

Links are different, though not in the way that Andrew Solomon in his book *Far from the Tree* discusses. Links do "fall far from" familial idiosyncrasies, but their differences reside in how they experience emotions—all blended together and everchanging—and how they construct their identity, their sense of who they are. Solomon discusses the need for generosity, acceptance, and tolerance to form part of the definition of what it means to be human. I would add that parents, teachers, and other adults who are close to Link children need to fully develop these qualities to avoid making these children feel so strange that they think of themselves as abnormal, as incomprehensible, indomitable creatures.

In *Link and the Shooting Stars*, for example, David's behavior toward Link, even when Link exasperates and bewilders him, is respectful, generous, and accepting, which allows him to help Link move along in his journey toward himself. David does not take Link's rejection of a career in the light show personally, although he trained him to do this work and is his primary mentor. Appreciating and valuing a Link child as their own person and taking a step back to allow them to be that person, as David does with Link, is the most loving, compassionate, and effective way to help the child move beyond poorly established self-esteem, which manifests as behavior that vacillates between too arrogant and cocky and too insecure and fearful.

Making Sense of Fear

Learning to really listen and not just hear is crucial to being able to discern what is going on behind the accusations typical of a Link child. Learning to listen is also the key to overcoming various fears parents might have in relation to their child. These fears might include being afraid that anything they say might trigger a volatile reaction, causing them to feel like they are walking on eggshells around their child. Parents may also be afraid that if they say "no" to their child in response to a desire, whether in an attempt to protect him because the child's demand could be dangerous, or simply because they are not in a position in that moment to satisfy the demand, it will cause a painful situation or interaction. Understandably, they prefer to avoid this.

More deep-seated fears might include fear of who their child is or may become; fear of what truth might lie behind their child's accusations; and fear of their own anger that might get unleashed in destructive ways toward the child. Finally, parents may also be afraid of the pain they will feel upon causing their child to feel emotional pain, or even trauma, by denying them what they want. This is because parents understand that for a Link child denial makes them feel misunderstood as well as angry or frustrated. This aversion to making the child feel bad may cause parents to feel paralyzed or passive in relation to when, why, and how to place limits on their child, or, conversely, it may cause them to react more explosively than the situation warrants in order to mask their own pain at causing their child to suffer.

When parents listen openly, they are able to ask appropriate, helpful questions without judging either their child or themselves and are able to allow their fear and guilt to fall away because they are focused on understanding their child rather than on any shame they might feel related to their child's "strange" behaviors. Asking questions like *What is my child's reaction hiding? What is my child trying to say? What truth might there be in the accusation?* opens up space for parents to review their positions and allows them to show compassion toward their child rather than being stuck in counterattack mode. Moving past the feeling of being attacked and getting defensive with a child to a place where parents are able to listen openly and honestly to what their child is trying to say is critical to overcoming any fear, guilt, or shame they might be feeling with respect to their ways of relating to their child. Instead of passively suffering without understanding, parents can move toward a proactive way of being by connecting this child who seems to have been born so far from the "the tree" to the emotional, calming ties of belonging.

Rather than falling into denial or counterattack mode in reaction to what their child is saying, parents can choose to help their child understand what they want to denounce by exhibiting the patience, sincerity, and respect of someone who is acting as an interpreter. That is, they can create and teach the child a language that allows her to understand what she feels, so that she can grasp and have more control over what is going on inside her and be able to express it.

For example, if the child says, "You are always mean to me and never let me do what I want. It's not fair," an exasperated parent might retort with something like, "I am *not* mean to you, and I *do* let you do what you want a lot of the time, but you're irresponsible and I can't trust you because you never listen to me." This kind of response ensures that the vicious circle of attack and counterattack continues and does not open up space for the child to be able to express more concretely what is really going on inside.

If, on the other hand, the parent responds by helping the child understand why she is so angry and why she receives everything as undeserved mistreatment, the vicious circle can be avoided. Saying something like this creates an opening for calm dialogue: "I understand that it feels unfair to hear me say, 'No, you can't do this.' In this case, I am saying 'no' because I am responsible for you, and I don't want you to get hurt or find yourself in a dangerous situation. I am saying 'no' to take good care of you and because I love you, not because I'm punishing you or because you've done anything wrong or bad." Because Link children do not trust that their parents know how to take good care of them, this kind of conversation may be somewhat difficult and may require several calm, patient attempts until they understand. If the child keeps resisting and arguing, then the best recourse is to try to pacify them in other ways, such as through distraction, and wait until the storm has blown over before offering the calm explanation.

It is helpful to return to the anecdote in Chapter 9 about Pierre, the young Link boy whose father will not let him ride alone in the taxi when he complains that his bottom is sore from riding in the basket on his dad's bicycle. His father explains to him that it is dangerous for him to be in the taxi alone with the taxi driver because the taxi driver might take him somewhere else. Pierre proposes a clever solution which is for his dad to follow them on the bicycle so that he can make sure the taxi driver takes him to the right place. How does a parent deal with this kind of logical (from a child's point of view) "solution" from an insistent child?

In the moment, perhaps the best the father can do in this situation is to acknowledge that the child's bottom hurts (validating what the child is experiencing, which is different from what the parent is experiencing) and say that next time they will not take the bicycle into town but that right now the only solution is for them to get home on the bike as quickly as possible. In a calmer moment, once they are at home, the father could explain to Pierre that there were elements in play that Pierre did not understand or foresee. For example, a bicycle cannot go as fast as a taxi, and even if it could, when the traffic lights change, the bicycle could be caught by a red light and lose track of the taxi that has moved ahead with a green light. The point is not so much the arguments that parents use to help their child grasp more fully a situation that they think they already understand, but to ensure that they take the necessary time to do the important work of explaining the situation to their child so that the child understands why they are being denied what they want and does not interpret the denial as punishment.

One of the main principles that parents need to accept is that by establishing rules and limits and insisting that their children adhere to them, they are being good parents, not bad or selfish parents. When a parent denies a child what she wants, it is likely because what the child wants is not good for her or will harm her, not because the parent simply wants to deny the child's wishes and desires. Situations may arise, however, when a parent does behave selfishly because they do not feel like being bothered or playing with their child in a given moment. We are only human. It is important, then, for parents to ensure that when they set and insist on limits it is for the child's good (which may also benefit the parent, of course) and that they do not behave in an overly authoritarian or unfair way toward their child.

An even deeper layer underlies Link children's difficult behaviors, necessitating an understanding on the part of parents in order to be able to deal with these behaviors patiently and respectfully. When Link children exhibit a "symptom," they are actually pointing to something that they feel needs to be exposed and dealt with in the family. Links are typically the most sensitive members of the family, which means that one of their functions in the family unit is akin to that of a fuse (to borrow Enrique Pichon-Rivière's instructive and useful analogy describing the key role that the most sensitive family member plays in a family system). Just as a fuse in a circuit box "blows" when too much current enters the line, Link children react, often explosively, to something that is not working well in the family system, although they may not be able to articulate what the malfunctioning element is. This sensitivity also allows them to be the strongest member of the family because their symptoms (rage, accusations, etc.) are alarm bells—powerful warning signs that something is not right in the family. Their intolerable behaviors are attempts, whether conscious or unconscious, to protect the family from further harm. Just as when a fuse blows one must check and correct something else in the electrical system, when Links "blow," they are announcing that there is something in the family dynamic (beyond themselves) that needs to be dealt with, healed, or even completely transformed. By approaching the "fuse box" fearlessly, parents are able to get to the bottom of what is bothering their child and of what the child is trying to say about a larger familial problem. As difficult as it might be to hear this truth from their child, parents need to be honest with themselves that something is going on that needs to be addressed and that their Link child's behavior is revealing something about them in particular. Only when parents recognize this and address these issues can the fuse stop repeatedly blowing.

Working with Anguish

As human beings we have parts of ourselves and others, even and often of those most dear to us, that we do not like, do not want to have to deal with, and do not accept. Carl Jung calls these aspects of our personalities the "shadow." But loving ourselves fully means working to understand our "dark side" until we can accept those parts that we deny and do not take care of precisely because we do not like them and find them intolerable.

Many Link children behave in ways that appear strange or weird to their peers and to the adults they interact with—teachers, friends of the family, relatives. Parents, however, can help their children by helping them to understand and work to integrate the dark aspects of their personality. Link children and adults have more dark, confusing aspects in their shadow, and repressing them carries the risk of their emerging in violent and unpleasant ways. Link children may feel marginalized at school and outright shunned. At home, then, it is essential that they feel accepted, embraced, and loved for who they are as whole beings, not just for the "good" or "normal" aspects of their personality. Along with accepting them as whole individuals, parents need to try to ensure that their child does not feel ashamed, guilty, or otherwise bad because they are different from others. They need to also learn to take care of, pacify, and embrace these challenging, repressed aspects, which the child herself feels to be unbearable.

Key to accepting the whole Link child is understanding that the way they experience the world is different from how most others experience it. Link children feel from an early age, without yet understanding it or being able to name it, an existential fear related to the limits of time and space, connecting them to an early awareness of the concept of finitude and death as well as the concept of separateness from others and loneliness. As explored in previous chapters, this awareness, however unconscious and unarticulated it might be, makes them feel alone, defenseless, and afraid in relation to the world. They also feel that they cannot rely on their parents to provide them with the stability they need related to their fear, even though they know their parents love them. The anguish they live with daily is much more extreme than the anguish we all experience from time to time. When parents accept that this anguish is an essential part of their child's identity, they are able to give them the precise, compassionate embrace that, while perhaps not calming them completely, opens up space for them to feel accompanied in their anguish.

Creating Stability Through Routines

By engaging in simple, reliable practices, parents can help a Link child better understand what they are going through, develop good self-esteem, and feel that their world is more stable. Although these concrete actions and activities are by no means a guarantee of smooth sailing throughout the parenting experience, they are likely to help the Link child find places of ease and calm more often.

The more a child feels that their parents do not fear them or reject them, the more they feel rooted in themselves and in the world around them, rather than afraid, self-doubting, insecure, and alone. Parents can teach children to manage their fears and frustrations, including the deep, existential fear of abandonment, being left alone, and death—the ultimate manifestation of aloneness, of complete and utter separation from others. Link children are both fascinated by the unknown and afraid of it. Providing them with concrete routines and daily practices in which they can learn to control their emotions and avoid sudden, explosive reactions will help them feel protected, embraced, and that they have a safety net of discipline, in the form of regular routines, that is rooted in love.

One simple daily practice is to ensure that you connect in a calm, loving way with your child at bedtime. Bedtime can be scary for children, especially for Link children, as this is the time when they move from one state of consciousness to another, from "being" or "living" in their waking life to suddenly disappearing into the mysterious abyss of sleep, or "dying." They might be plagued by strange, frightening dreams or nightmares; they might be afraid they will not wake up; and sleep, of course, is the time when children (and adults) are completely consciously disconnected from others and defenseless, even if physically they are not sleeping alone. Parents can help to ease their child's fear, unspoken or spoken, by making sure to spend time with them at bedtime holding them close, reading a story, encouraging them to share what they are grateful for or to feel proud of themselves for what they learned or accomplished that day, or by just asking them what is on their mind. Other evening routines, like dinner time or bath time, can be hectic. Bedtime, therefore, needs to be a time of quietude and comfort. Link children, especially, need to feel calm and protected before they fall asleep. They need to feel the safety net of love, regardless of what has transpired during the day.

The calming, curative, and integrative effects of human interaction with nature are evident in our own experience of it as well as scientifically demonstrated. This relationship causes a feeling of awe that activates the hormones that ignite feelings of wellbeing. Nature provides the double certainty that, like everything in the natural world, one is unique, and, at the same time, one belongs to the immense family of life.

For Link children and adults, daily contact with nature provides immediate relief, often more immediate and calming than a human embrace, even an embrace whose intention is truly loving. It is common knowledge that when a baby is "beyond" hungry and in full-blown crying mode, she is unable to latch on to the breast or the bottle, although this might be what she appears to most need in that moment. However, what she needs in order to receive the embrace, breast, or bottle is to pacify the internal feeling of turmoil or constriction in her belly so that she can trust again. The child reacts to these physical feelings with anger and interprets any kind of approach as a dangerous threat or attack. Likewise, when a Link child or adult experiences internal pain produced by their existential anguish, the key is to honor the feeling without judgment, which will help them calm themselves down so that they can then be soothed by another.-

A Link child or adult benefits from running freely and exploring open spaces like the beach, the woods, a city park, or their own back-yard. Noticing and appreciating the beauty and mystery of nature acts as a powerful calming force, returning the magic to the overwhelming presence of finitude, what is uncontrollable and uncertain. In its immen-sity and incomprehensibility, nature also calms because one can witness different continuous cycles of life and death: the renewal of spring, the abundance and harvests of autumn, the indispensable rest imposed by winter, and the vitality of summer. Noticing and truly taking in the small things—the sounds of tree frog choruses and bird songs, sights like wave upon wave crashing on the shore or the shimmery color of pigeons on the sidewalk, the smell of flowers, trees, and dirt, the taste of berries or apples they have picked themselves, the feeling of grass or sand under-neath their feet—functions as a ground wire connecting them to the earth, a huge space where they can both be themselves and be a part of life and belong to the world. This makes the world both interesting and manageable—a vast universe comprising millions of tiny elements that together make the whole. Just as Link the horse connects with the stars and the universe in a way that makes him feel cradled and protected when he is in the spaceship, when a Link child connects to nature in thoughtful ways, the anguish and overwhelming fear subside because nature provides enormous spaces of freedom without posing the risk of their falling into the abyss of the loneliness they so fear.

Link children reject any kind of tether that might threaten to take away their freedom. Yet daily, weekly, monthly, and yearly routines are key to helping them to learn that there is also a structure that gives shape to life. It is important that the rituals be chosen based on their meaning and content as well as the purpose that they serve in the life of the individual, family, or group. Otherwise, the rituals are just meaningless gestures. For Link children in particular, following basic routines gives them moments or events during the day that help to ground them and be in the present moment, connect with others, and know that, while the world may be constantly changing, the routines their parents provide them are a reliable, safe haven from the continual motion and flux of both the world that surrounds them and of their inner emotional life. It is crucial that both parents agree on the elements of the routine, make the routine clear to the child, and follow it consistently and with conviction about its meaning.

In addition to sharing a bedtime story and cuddle, having a regular bedtime and bedtime routine such as a taking a bath, brushing teeth, and putting on pajamas is also important in helping your child feel they can count on you to provide reliability and predictability, which for them means stability that protects them, makes them feel grounded, and eases their metaphysical anguish. When Link the horse is on the spaceship with the other animals, although there is no visible night or day due to the 24-hour darkness, their lives revolve around routines and protocols as if there were. In addition to providing stability for the crew, performing routine activities together creates regular opportunities for interaction and relationship-building. For Link children, routines like regular mealtimes (when possible); reliable before-school and after-school routines; family outings; holiday rituals; playtime routines; and routines related to artistic, creative, spiritual, and physical activities all help them manage their complex inner turmoil, in addition to making them feel a stronger sense of belonging to their family or another social group. Routines function in this way for Link adults as well.

Affirming the Uniqueness of Links

Link children feel what they think in their gut. There is no space inside them between feeling and doing. Therefore, they convince themselves that their truths are the only possible ones. This is perceived by others as arrogance, as contempt for more common, widely shared, and conventional truths. This complicates their interactions with their peers as well as their learning process, which demands respect for those who are trying to teach them. For parents (and teachers), the goal is to salvage and affirm the child's creativity and uniqueness while simultaneously helping the child to understand that these positive traits can be best nurtured by accepting that their original thoughts and ideas are connected to something bigger than themselves, to ideas larger than their own, to other original people whose "line" they can continue.

Affirming a Link child's uniqueness and creativity is key to building good self-esteem. If someone has good self-esteem it does not mean that they feel superior but that they know what they are good at, what they are okay at, what they are bad at, what they can improve with effort, and what they cannot improve, despite devoting much time, attention, and care, because of circumstances or conditions that have nothing to do with their desire or determination. For example, someone might desperately want to be a classical ballerina but never be able to do a split.

Since Link children's true "difference" from others might cause them to feel lonely and marginalized, especially at school and in other social situations, it is good to actively encourage their uniqueness and creative, out-of-the-box thinking while helping them to consider and incorporate additional information that will allow them to more easily carry out their ideas. While Link children may say brilliant things, they do not recognize on their own that they still have more to learn. By helping them understand this, parents and teachers can help them acquire an accurate perception of themselves in terms of what they know, do not know, and need to learn more about. They help them understand that having good self-esteem does not mean thinking of themselves as the best at something. Although Link children do not easily acknowledge that someone else may be right about what they know and do not know, these conversations help them on their path to self-discovery.

Sometimes a Link child's creative thinking can come across as manipulative, defiant, false, or stolen. This is because Link children (and adults, pre-mutation) sometimes present their ideas more as defense mechanisms stemming from insecurity, self-doubt, and inaccurate self-perception. They are not yet capable of understanding themselves as having creative and clever thought processes (springing from global empathy) that come from a quick, intelligent mind and that rely on evidential thinking. This is partly because, since evidential thinking is not something that is learned, Link children do not understand that it is characteristic of their thought process. And because it is not taught, adults typically do not take this way of thinking seriously in Link children, so they do not feel validated in their creativity. If parents and teachers help Link children to distinguish between the unique, creative part of an idea and the part that is so fantastical that it can become a manipulative lie, they can learn to think about their ideas simply as proposals that may or may not be accepted rather than as concepts they must impose on others.

For example, Melanie, a Link tween, asks her mother for five different cell phone cases for her birthday. Her mother says she only needs one and that she will, therefore, buy her only one and spend the additional money she was planning on spending to buy her other things because she considers one phone case to be sufficient. Melanie, however, persists, explaining to her that the reason she wants five different phone cases is that she sees each case design as expressing an emotion—like a mood ring—and that she wants the freedom to change the phone case daily depending on how she feels in the morning when she wakes up. Although the mother has never felt the need for more than one phone case, she appreciates the thoughtfulness and creativity of Melanie's explanation and of the desire itself and agrees to buy her five different cases. (For her part, Melanie knows that her mother loves her and has always encouraged her to pay attention to her emotions.) The more affirmation a child receives about their creativity, even when it appears in the guise of an undesirable behavior like defiance, the better the child is able to hear and respond appropriately to parents when they say "no" in other contexts. Bestowing more rewards and affirmation than punishments and denial will help a child feel validated and help build their self-esteem as well as their trust in adults.

Because Link children's defiant behaviors are understandably exasperating to their parents, it can be easy for parents to slip into thinking that their child is often acting on motivations and intentions that are self-serving or manipulative. Even when the child is being good or generous, parents might assume there is an underlying ulterior motive, something the child wants to gain, like friendship or attention. However, it is important for parents to acknowledge and focus on the child's generous and good behavior and intent, not the ulterior, "bad" motive that they suspect the child might have.

Helping Links Understand the "Rules of the Game"

In order to live and interact with others without continually fighting or being accused of being a traitor, a fraud, or a danger to other people, it is crucial to know the rules of the game that one is participating in at every moment and in every group situation, no matter how seemingly insignificant. The danger of not knowing the rules increases in proportion to the approval or recognition that someone seeks when they participate in a group.

For Link children raised in homes where the norms and expectations are not clear, not agreed upon, change too frequently, or are regularly set aside due to urgent needs or circumstances, thinking about the importance of the rules of the game—not just obeying them but understanding them—is nearly impossible. At the same time, the capacity for global empathy of Link children and adults frequently allows them to not only become involved but to stand out in group or institutional situations, causing them to constantly run the risk of being accused of being impostors, opportunists, or deceitful people. Unfortunately, these accusations are often correct—not because their intention is to cheat or deceive but because their intuition, imagination, and creativity lead them to perform extraordinarily well despite not knowing the rules of the game that they are playing. They might be accused of "faking it" when taking on a certain role or task, for example, since they are not doing so in conventional ways or with the deep knowledge base that allows most people to do their jobs well. They are relying instead on their gut and creativity, their own unique approach to the task at hand, which could be suspect and unreliable.

Certain creative or unusual behaviors or ideas might be appropriate to share at home in highly democratic households or those that reward individual creativity but would not be received well in the classroom or on the playground. For example, when Zach was in kindergarten at the age of four, his parents learned from his teacher that every day he was entering the classroom as a different animal. One day he would bound in as an energetic dog, another as a stealthy, growling tiger, another as a hopping kangaroo, and so on. While the other children settled into their seats, Zach was acting out his vivid imagination, feeling himself in those moments to be embodying those animals. Fortunately for Zach, he was in a non-traditional school that valued imagination and originality, whose teachers knew how to appreciate (and be patient with) these kinds of creative behaviors. Still, the teacher needed to set a limit for Zach so that he would know when it was time to stop pretending to be an animal and to sit down with the other children. Had he been in a conventional school, he would probably have been chastised and made to sit down immediately, without the space to let his imagination run free. Conventional, rigid learning environments are very difficult for Link children, but in many cases there is no alternative. If parents make sure their Link child understands that they, like all of us, need to modify their behavior based on what social situation they are in, this will help build good self-esteem in their child and help them to not be ostracized.

Helping Link children understand this does not mean teaching them to be hypocrites, play both sides, or repress what they feel. It means helping to prevent others from treating them like wild animals or untamable colts that must be castrated because they are dangerous. In most cases it means helping to impede the self-sabotage that Links typically engage in as a result of their fear of revealing how they feel and what they think. At times, then, in order to not be accused of being strange, different, or bad, they prefer to hide behind a cape, known in psychoanalysis as the "false self." This causes many intelligent creations, inventions, and changes to the (possibly stagnant) rules of the game to be lost because Links choose to censor themselves, sometimes prematurely. This is because they do not have faith that others will take their ideas seriously. This self-doubt prevents them from learning to defend their ideas or truths within the rules of the game they wish to be a part of.

Making Decisions

Link children need to learn to control their impulses and regulate their powerful emotions so they do not launch themselves headfirst into making decisions without carefully evaluating the pros and cons of the possible consequences. It is true that when parents try to help them with this, they rebel and accuse them of being authoritarian, old-fashioned, and mean. But it is precisely in those moments that Link children need the most patience, understanding, compassion, and careful guidance. Regrettably, if the relationship with the parents, teachers, or adults is so difficult that the children do not even try to listen to them, life will teach them "the hard way" the consequences of choosing immediate gratification over what, for Links, is tedious reflection. Link the horse, for example, learns the hard way that he needs to evaluate his decisions more carefully when he insists on taking the fastest, but more treacherous, path up the mountain, which leads him and his friends directly into a rockslide.

Making decisions, as we know, is a challenge for Link children and adults due to the many options that they think they have to choose from. This is why we say they suffer from Decision Deficit Disorder (DDD). This creates a level of definitive demand, as if making a decision were an all-or-nothing, lose-lose situation. They feel that they always run the risk of another option being better. They express the insecurity they feel within them as the impetuousness with which they rush here and there to decide something in order to escape the paralysis of indecision.

In fact, Links have multiple talents and possibilities for action, which creates even more confusion for them about which place, action, or option is the right one in any given moment.

The phrase "I know," which gets confused with "I'm bored," prematurely curtails the process of learning something new before they know if the topic, task, or activity interests them enough to continue with it. Links often decide too quickly that an activity does not connect them with their essence (even though, if they were to stick with it, it might) and abandon it because they feel the need to escape from the frustration, from the place of feeling ill at ease. Declaring "I'm bored" and moving on to another pursuit is also a defense mechanism even when they are passionately interested in an activity. It allows them to cover up the fear they feel of failing at what they are deeply interested in and/or of being confined to one discipline or pursuit. The problem with this is that they do not allow themselves to delve deeper into the learning process to learn if the activity or field that interests them will bring them the satisfaction that they long for and the feeling that it is connected to or expressive of their essential truth.-

Link children think that they already know how to do things, which in certain ways is true, since they learn things through empathy—through absorbing everything around them like sponges. They also learn through their keen senses, intuition, and chameleonic imitation—seeing, smelling, and feeling something in ways that make them feel they already know it or know how to do it. Finally, they learn through evidential thinking, which is not rooted in systematic reasoning but in trial and error with no way to first test out hypotheses. While these ways of knowing ensure that they grasp *much* of the information they need, they do not allow them to grasp *all* of the information they need to be able to really understand what an activity, encounter, or decision is all about. Link children's ways of knowing do not give them access to the intricacies of learning how to learn. When they say they know how to do something, they are reporting what they believe to be true. They know the external movements, the superficial layers of the thing, but they do not grasp it. They do not incorporate the knowledge or integrate it with their knowledge in other areas. This is another challenging problem for parents to resolve. It is better to delegate this responsibility to people who are respected as authorities in each subject. Then, if the children do not learn the rules of the "learning game" at hand, the consequence will be to not be able to play that game.

Unfortunately, declarations such as "What a shame.... She has so much talent in music (tennis, math, taking care of others)" are common among parents and teachers of Link children. Rather than discipline themselves to achieve mastery of an activity, Link children (and adults) prefer to abandon it and move on to something else where they will feel elated at the beginning, because of their ability to immediately grasp something through imitation, emotional contagion, or global empathy, until the moment of truth arrives: the recognition that they need to study, pay attention, and commit to just one thing, even if it is only for a brief moment. This leads them to conclude that it does not interest them, causing them to project a boredom that masks a profound sadness and fear that they will never be able to sustain a passion, to enjoy a feeling of pure and lasting satisfaction, or to have the security of feeling validated in whatever option they might choose. Link children have difficulty sitting down and focusing on something for a long time. Dividing the learning process into short increments of time will help them commit to understanding the fundamentals of whatever they are learning, making it less likely that they will abandon one pursuit for another in quick succession.

It is beneficial to the Link child when parents help them to pursue activities they are good at if the parents believe that their child will indeed feel the sensation of flow, joy, and pride once they move beyond the moments of failure and frustration that any learning process involves. They can give the child a space in which to cultivate self-control, decision making, and self-knowledge in addition to the pride that comes from doing something well and receiving affirmation and recognition from that. This is not to say, for example, that their child should play a sport or an instrument that the parents want them to play or that they clearly do not have an interest in or talent for. It is to say that it is important for parents to notice what their child enjoys, encourage it, and try to ensure that they stick with it even when they want to quit because they feel frustrated when it is time to move from one level to another (moving from comfortable effortlessness to the discipline and exertion that more advanced learning requires). Encouraging them also involves acknowledging and validating what they do know while pointing out what is still left to learn before they are able to do something well.

Finally, parents need to understand and accept that their Link child needs to safeguard their originality, even if this "originality" is not entirely original but comes from the parents themselves. Link children may view their parents' originality and creativity as boring, conventional, and limiting. This makes them feel the need to be even more original and creative, to surpass their parents in the originality department and carve out their own creative space and ways of demonstrating their difference from their parents and others.

My own experience and my work with clients have shown me that, as parents, you can trust that at some point in their life your Link child will be able to acknowledge and appreciate you and your own unconventional choices. Perhaps more importantly, you can also trust that every Link child will one day find their own way of being in the world and that they will not be afraid to recognize, and even celebrate, the manifestation of the originality that they possess.

Moving Forward

Parenting is not an easy job. Parenting a Link child is an even harder job. And being a Link adult who cannot count on "internal parents" to accompany him in his search is still harder. When it comes to parenting, there are no promises or guarantees, and there is certainly no such thing as the perfect recipe or "rescue remedy." For parents of Link children, learning how to take care of them takes years filled with confusion, mistakes, and missed opportunities. For Link adults, learning how to take care of themselves involves the same investment of time and the same pitfalls.

Through ongoing, careful analysis, however, parents can learn to detect what their child's behavior is trying to express. What action or event is provoking a reaction of rebellion, depression, or isolation from the child? What emotion or emotions lie behind the behavior? If parents can see their child's behaviors of fight, flight, or freeze as signs carrying messages written in invisible ink—messages invariably stemming from fear—they can then set about working with their child to reveal the hidden message, with understanding, compassion, respect, and love—*the precise embrace.*

I believe that Link children are a challenge that can be transformed into a blessing. The opportunity for parents to choose to learn alongside their Link child as they try to guide and teach them provides a path toward undergoing a profound change within themselves. My hope is that parenting a Link child can feel like an open space of possibilities, where parents can feel free to create their own forms of childrearing, trusting that they will not get lost on the road of trial and error as they strive to be the best parents they can be for their challenging and fascinating Link child. I invite all parents of Link children to keep as their loving mantra: *No one is to blame. It's nobody's fault.*

REFERENCES

Aesop. The fox and the grapes. In *The Aesop for Children*. Library of Congress. https://read.gov/aesop/005.html

Aron, E. (2002). *The Highly Sensitive Child: Helping Our Children Thrive When the World Overwhelms Them*. New York: Broadway Books.

Balán, S., and C. Cano. (2022). *Link and the Shooting Stars*. New York: IPBooks.

Bischof-Köhler, D. (1991). The development of empathy in infants. In M.E. Lamb and H. Keller (Eds.), *Infant Development: Perspectives from German-Speaking Countries* (pp. 245-274). Hillsdale, NJ: Lawrence Erlbaum Associates.

Bonder, N. (2001). *Our Immoral Soul: A Manifesto of Spiritual Disobedience*. Boulder, CO: Shambhala.

Boorstin, D.J. (1983). *The Discoverers: A History of Man's Search to Know His World and Himself*. New York: Random House.

———(1992). *The Creators: A History of Heroes of the Imagination*. New York: Random House.

———(1998). *The Seekers: The Story of Man's Continuing Quest to Understand His World*. New York: Random House.

Calderón de la Barca, P. (1636). *Life Is a Dream*. In B. Fuchs (Ed.), *The Golden Age of Spanish Drama* (pp. 195-269). Translated by G.J. Racz. New York: W.W. Norton and Company, 2018.

Carroll, L., and J. Tober. (1999). *The Indigo Children: The New Kids Have Arrived*. Carlsbad, CA: Hay House.

Chatwin, B. (1988). *The Songlines.* New York: Penguin. (Original work published 1987).

Csikszentmihalyi, M. (1990). *Flow: The Psychology of Optimal Experience.* New York: Harper & Row.

Damasio, A. (2003). *Looking for Spinoza: Joy, Sorrow, and the Feeling Brain.* New York: Houghton Mifflin Harcourt.

Ferry, L. (2010). *Learning to Live: A User's Manual.* Edinburgh: Canongate.

Festinger, L. (1957). *A Theory of Cognitive Dissonance.* Redwood City, CA: Stanford University Press.

Gardner, H. (1993). *Multiple Intelligences: The Theory in Practice.* New York: Basic Books.

Ginzburg, C. (1989). Clues: Roots of an evidential paradigm. In *Clues, Myths and the Historical Method* (pp. 96-125). Translated by J. and A.C. Tedeschi. Baltimore: Johns Hopkins University Press.

Grinberg, L. (1963). *Culpa y depresión: Estudio psicoanalítico [Guilt and Depression: Psychoanalytic Study].* Buenos Aires: Paidos.

Hanson, R. (2011). *Just One Thing: Developing a Buddha Brain One Simple Practice at a Time.* Oakland, CA: New Harbinger.

———(n.d.). Supporting positive motivation in teenagers. Rick Hanson, PhD. https://www.rickhanson.net/supporting-positive-motivation-teenagers/

Hoffman, M.L. (2000). *Empathy and Moral Development: Implications for Caring and Justice.* Cambridge: Cambridge University Press.

Iacoboni, M. (2008). *Mirroring People: The New Science of How We Connect with Others.* New York: Farrar, Straus and Giroux.

Jung, C. (1979). *Aion: Researches into the Phenomenology of the Self.* Edited by G. Adler. Translated by R.F.C. Hull. 2nd ed. Princeton, NJ: Princeton University Press. (Original work published 1951).

Kurcinka, M.S. (2015). *Raising Your Spirited Child: A Guide for Parents Whose Child Is More Intense, Sensitive, Perceptive, Persistent, and Energetic.* 3rd ed. New York: Harper Collins. (Original work published 1991).

Merriam-Webster. (n.d.). Empathy. In Merriam-Webster.com *dictionary.* Retrieved October 3, 2019, from https://www.merriam-webster.com/dictionary/empathy

Miller, A. (1997). *The Drama of the Gifted Child: The Search for the True Self.* Translated by R. Ward. 3rd ed. New York: Basic Books. (Original work published 1979).

Neufeld, G. (2020). Alpha children. Neufeld Institute. https://neufeldinstitute.org/course/alpha-children/

Neufeld, G., and G. Maté. (2008). *Hold on to Your Kids: Why Parents Need to Matter More Than Peers.* New York: Random House.

Orloff, J. (2018). *The Empath's Survival Guide: Life Strategies for Sensitive People.* Boulder, CO: Sounds True.

Pichon-Rivière, E. (1971). *Del psicoanálisis a la psicología social, Tomo II [From Psychoanalysis to Social Psychology, Vol II.].* Buenos Aires: Galerna.

Safina, C. (2011). *Eye of the Albatross: Visions of Hope and Survival.* Kindle ed. New York: Holt. (Original work published 2002).

Schairer, S. (2017, August 27). Empathy, sympathy, and compassion—What's the difference? Compassion It. https://www.compassionit.com/2017/08/27/empathy-sympathy-and-compassion-whats-the-difference/

Siegel, D.J., and T.P. Bryson. (2012). *The Whole-Brain Child: 12 Revolutionary Strategies to Nurture Your Child's Developing Mind.* New York: Bantam.

Solomon, A. (2012). *Far From the Tree: Parents, Children and the Search for Identity.* New York: Scribner.

Sternberg, R.J. (1997). *Thinking Styles.* Cambridge: Cambridge University Press.

Strijack, T. (2021, June 29). Adding the wisdom of play to the wisdom of trauma. Neufeld Institute. https://www.neufeldinstitute.org/adding-the-wisdom-of-play-to-the-wisdom-of-trauma/

Toguo, B. (2018, August 5-October 21). *The Beauty of Our Voice* [Exhibition]. Parrish Art Museum, Water Mill, NY.

Winnicott, D.W. (2005). *Playing and Reality.* 2nd ed. Abingdon: Routledge Classics. (Original work published 1971).

Appendix

Link and the Shooting Stars
Discussion Questions

The following discussion questions are designed to encourage an open, relaxed conversation between caregiver and child upon reading together each chapter of *Link and the Shooting Stars*. By using these questions to explore more deeply both Link's feelings and actions and those of the child, parents, family members, therapists, and others who work closely with children will perhaps better understand the Link child in their life. The questions will also help Link children, while reading the book with an adult, to better understand themselves.

Chapter 1
Why do you think Link felt frustrated and confused after his parents talked about his future?
How do you feel when your parents argue about you?
What makes you feel frustrated and confused?
Why did Link think he was going to disappoint his parents?
What do you think Link will choose to do?

Chapter 2
Why was Link's mom upset?
What do you do that upsets your mom?

Why did Link walk away angry?

If you were Link, what would you have said to his mom and Indigo?

What makes you feel angry and frustrated?

What things have you done that made your **parents angry or upset?**

Did you do these things on purpose, or were you being playful?

Did you feel they didn't understand you or listen to your explanation?

How did that make you feel?

Chapter 3

What do you want to be when you grow up?

What dreams do your parents have for you?

Does that make you feel confused about what to choose?

Why was Link's father disappointed in him?

Do you think it was a good idea for Link to stop racing?

Why was his mother happy?

Why was Link confused?

What would you say to Link's parents if you were Link?

When Link felt devastated, what would you have said to him?

Why did Link think he was a bad horse?

Do you feel that your parents are often disappointed in you?

Chapter 4

Why did Link think that he was crazy?

What are some things that you imagine?

Why is Gray reluctant to follow Link to the mountain?

Do you sometimes do things that your mom or dad tell you not to do?

Have you ever done things that the little voice inside you tells you not to do?

Why didn't Link like to hear that his ideas and actions might be dangerous?

How might Link be able to do things he wants to do without putting himself in danger?

Can you remember when your stubbornness put you in danger?

Chapter 5

When have you felt fear? What did you do?

Why does someone feel fear?

When have you felt bad about a decision you made?

What happened? What did you do to not feel so bad?

Why did Link leave his friends and family?

How did Link feel when he finally got to the top of the mountain and saw something different from what he expected?

Tell me about a time when you worked hard to achieve something and it turned out to be a disappointment. What did you do?

Do you feel that you have ever disappointed someone?

Do you feel that other people appreciate you?

Chapter 6

How was Link like a shooting star?

What was Link looking for on his journey?

Where do you feel most appreciated?

How was Link a seeker? Are you a seeker?

How is Link like the ocean? Tell me how you are like Link.

Did Link find where the shooting stars land?

Chapter 7

How did Link end up in a cage?

What could he have done differently to prevent this?

Who were the "weird "ones?

Why didn't Link think he was weird?

Why didn't Link belong with the bad animals? How was he different?

Have you ever been put in a group where you felt out of place?

How are you different from others?

Chapter 8

How was Link confused about his emotions?

What are some of your emotions that confuse you?

How is Link different from the zebra?

What box does Link fit into?

What box do you fit into?

Why did the zebra feel peace? Why didn't Link feel peaceful?

How are you different from your family? How are you the same?

What did Mr. Brown say that made Link feel calm?

Why do you think it made him feel better?

Chapter 9

Why did Link like David?

How do you feel when others judge you?

How do you judge other people?

Who in your life understands you the most?

Who doesn't seem to understand you at all?

What was the most important lesson that Link learned from David?

Chapter 10
Why was Link angry?

How does Link react when he doesn't get his own way?

How do you react when you don't get your own way?

How do you think Link might have resolved the issue?

Why did Link feel so close to Susu?

Why did Link leave the circus?

How does Link tend to make decisions?

Why does he make decisions in this way?

Give me an example of when you acted impulsively. How did it work out for you?

What does Link do when he feels stress or overwhelmed by a situation?

How do you deal with a stressful situation?

How does Link deal with his doubts and fears?

How do you deal with yours?

Chapter 11
Why was Link chosen for the space program?

What personality traits would make you ideal for the space program?

Why did Mr. Brown give Link a flashlight?

Why was Link successful in the space program?

What do you need to do to be successful in what you want to do?

Chapter 12
Why was Link able to solve the problem with the engine fire?

By linking all his life experiences, what had Link created?

Draw a constellation of your life experiences.

What do you think was the last thing Link had to do to make his constellation complete?

Where was Link's home? Why did he have many homes?

Chapter 13

Why can Link truly like himself now?

Who do you think influenced Link the most in his life?

Who has influenced you the most in your life? How did they change you?

Why did Link visit Mr. Tree again? What had Mr. Tree called Link when he first met him?

What is the meaning of "seeker"?

Why did Link choose to walk home rather than drive home in a fancy trailer?

Why did Link's dad think he would never return to the ranch?

What had prevented Link in the past from showing his parents how much he loved them?

Chapter 14

How was Grandmother just like Link?

What was Grandmother's advice to Link regarding respecting others?

What was Link's greatest understanding about himself?

What are the two parts of Link's personality that seem to conflict with each other?

What do you value more, feeling free or feeling like you belong?

How was Link like a shooting star?

How are parts of you like Link?

What shooting stars do you want to chase?

What have you learned about yourself by reading about Link?
What did you like about this story?
What parts would you change?

www.ingramcontent.com/pod-product-compliance
Lightning Source LLC
Chambersburg PA
CBHW062120020426
42335CB00013B/1038